DogLife 🐾 Lifelong Care for Your Dog™

LABRADOR
RETRIEVER

tfh

Linda Rehkopf

LABRADOR RETRIEVER

Project Team
Editor: Stephanie Fornino, Mary E. Grangeia, Heather Russell-Revesz
Copy Editor: Joann Woy
Indexer: Lucie Haskins
Design: Angela Stanford
Series Design: Mary Ann Kahn

T.F.H. Publications
President/CEO: Glen S. Axelrod
Executive Vice President: Mark E. Johnson
Publisher: Christopher T. Reggio
Production Manager: Kathy Bontz

T.F.H. Publications, Inc.
One TFH Plaza
Third and Union Avenues
Neptune City, NJ 07753

Printed and bound in China

10 11 12 13 14   1 3 5 7 9 8 6 4 2

Library of Congress Cataloging-in-Publication Data
Rehkopf, Linda.
  Labrador retriever / Linda Rehkopf.
     p. cm.
  Includes index.
  ISBN 978-0-7938-3608-6 (alk. paper)
  1. Labrador retriever. I. Title.
  SF429.L3R44 2010
  636.752'7--dc22
                                2010011365

This book has been published with the intent to provide accurate and authoritative information in regard to the subject matter within. While every reasonable precaution has been taken in preparation of this book, the author and publisher expressly disclaim responsibility for any errors, omissions, or adverse effects arising from the use or application of the information contained herein. The techniques and suggestions are used at the reader's discretion and are not to be considered a substitute for veterinary care.
If you suspect a medical problem consult your veterinarian.

Note: In the interest of concise writing, "he" is used when referring to puppies and dogs unless the text is specifically referring to females or males. "She" is used when referring to people. However, the information contained herein is equally applicable to both sexes.

The Leader In Responsible Animal Care for Over 50 Years!®
www.tfh.com

CONTENTS

INTRODUCTION

INTRODUCING THE LABRADOR RETRIEVER

The Labrador Retriever, arguably one of the most versatile breeds, delights owners who want a dog who will either sit at their feet or retrieve game. Although the Lab is a relatively newer breed than many, its rapid rise in popularity has made it a favorite dog around the world, whether as a family pet, a hunting companion, or a search-and-rescue dog.

THE DOMESTICATION OF THE DOG

The adaptability of the Labrador Retriever, whether he's a companion pet or a champion retriever, reflects the developing roles that dogs were expected to play as they became more important to humans. The study of dog domestication suggests that our pets evolved from Eurasian wolf populations in Asia, between 15,000 and 40,000 years ago.

The Wolf as Ancestor

Imagine this: Your ancestor, finished with his daily hunting, stoked a campfire. As he cooked his game and fed his family, bones and other inedible remnants were tossed outside of the camp area. If he looked closely—and he probably did —he would see the amber eyes of a Eurasian gray wolf staring through the darkness, intent on the trash heap. The trash—and then the humans—interested these wolves enough so that the animals began to follow the hunters. The hunters, in turn, became more interested in the wolves.

Over hundreds of years, wolves began to display submission to our ancestors, and as female wolves began to whelp in the presence of humans, and their pups became accustomed to humans from birth, humans began to tame them. As people selected and kept only those wolf pups who were friendly and nonaggressive toward humans, domestication began. Wolves not only followed the hunters, they settled down with our ancestors as they began to clear forests and farm small plots.

An analysis of the DNA of today's regional dogs shows that the greatest genetic diversity among dogs exists in southern China, which indicates a larger genetic pool of wolves in the initial domestication. The least amount of diversity exists in dogs in Europe. Researchers believe that as humans moved from Asia toward Europe, the tamed wolves or their descendents—the dog—followed man. As mating continued between the dogs, the genetic diversity decreased.

The Labrador Retriever is arguably one of the most versatile dogs among all breeds.

words, they became a staple of human diets if the relationship didn't work out.

African village dogs show genetic diversity similar to those studied in Asia, which means that wolf domestication could have occurred in Africa at the same time that the dog developed in Asia or shortly thereafter. Regardless of the exact location of domestication, it is clear that as humans began developing their agricultural skills and keeping livestock for sustenance, their trash heaps and their herds attracted wolf packs.

As a result of the domestication process, wolves became less afraid of humans. In return, humans began to use this domesticated wolf—this dog—as a helper in the fields, on the farms, and around their homes. Dogs who were mutually beneficial to them were kept, and those that weren't became another food source. The helpful dogs traveled with their humans throughout Asia, Africa, and into Europe. In Europe, dogs were trained as herders and guardians of flocks of sheep, goats, and chickens. Prior to transoceanic travel in the 1400s, domesticated dogs traversed the Bering Straight into the Americas and mingled with native gray wolf populations there.

Archeological research and limited genetic analysis also supports a theory of independent domestication of these native wolves in the New World. The oldest canine remains in the United States have been found in caves in Utah and are dated to about 10,000 years ago. This timeframe occurs later in the records than domestication in Asia but also suggests that native wolf populations were all subject to domestication as humans began to travel the globe.

The farther that dogs traveled, the more roles they took on to help their masters. Indigenous human populations—Native Americans— relied on dogs to pull sleds and retrieve game. By the early 1500s, dogs were helping fishermen in cold Canadian waters. Fishing

Where Domestication Occurred

The most recently published scientific studies place dog domestication in Asia, specifically south of the Yangtze River, in China, about 16,000 years ago. This timeline correlates with the period when human societies developed from strictly hunter-gatherers to more agricultural settlements. Rice farming became prevalent in the region. Researchers in Sweden and China estimate that dogs evolved from several hundred tamed wolves, apparently another important part of the culture. Wolves likely were tamed for their protein; in other became the major reason for colonization of the North Atlantic islands, especially in the frigid waters off Newfoundland.

EARLY DEVELOPMENT OF THE BREED

British fishing fleets sailed for these productive waters each spring, filled their nets during the summer, and sailed back to England as the waters began to ice over. Fleet workers were left in Newfoundland during the winter, and the dogs who remained were probably trained as hunting dogs. These forbears of the present-day Labrador Retriever helped their human caretakers survive the long, cold, icy winters. The dogs became valuable because of their abilities to work hard for long periods in a harsh climate.

The Lab as Fish Retriever

On the island of Newfoundland, a small black dog was referred to as the St. John's Water Dog or the Lesser Newfoundland (because he was smaller than the already-established breed of the Newfoundland). This dog could be fitted in a specialty harness and lowered from the deck of a fishing boat, to retrieve any fish that haphazardly flopped out of the nets. The St. John's Water Dog would also swim to grab the lines of errant fishing nets, and with the line firmly in his powerful jaws, swim back to the boat. The dog developed a thick, oily outer coat that repelled ice and cold water and a softer inner coat that helped keep him warm. He had webbing between his toes that enhanced his swimming capabilities and a tail described as otter-like, which helped the dog maintain speed and direction in the water. Although most of these dogs were black, occasionally a yellow or chocolate-colored puppy was whelped. Most of the nonblack dogs were culled, as early devotees believed

that only the black Labs were capable of the demanding work. Some gamekeepers, however, began to specialize in breeding the yellows and chocolates. Today, a Labrador of any coat color is a capable companion in the home or the field.

The Lab as Bird Retriever

In the early 1800s, two activities—ornithology (the study of birds) and wildfowling (the shooting of birds for sport)—converged at about the same time. Both scientists and

In Europe, dogs were trained as herders and guardians of flocks of sheep, goats, and chickens.

In England and Scotland, the Lab was used to retrieve game.

sportsmen needed a reliable retrieving dog, although for vastly different reasons.

Among the ornithologists, it was typical to shoot or trap birds that were being studied because the strong binoculars used today had yet to be developed. The scientists noted that anything missed became lost. This meant that birds lost after being shot, or birds that escaped perhaps injured from the traps, could not be examined for their plumage. Important scientific records in bird types and migration patterns had holes that needed to be plugged.

In England and Scotland, the sport of shooting became popular on the vast land holdings of the gentry. Advances in gun technology from flintlocks to shotguns meant that more birds could be shot for sport or for food. Shot game that landed in marshes,

ponds, or rivers could not be retrieved easily by the sportsmen. They needed a better system; they needed a dog who could retrieve game from water.

Wealthy British landowners who employed fishermen on the transatlantic schooners became interested in the medium-sized St. John's dog. These dogs typically were black with white chest blazes and white hair on their feet, and some had white guard hair on their muzzle. British and Scottish gamekeepers began to import the dogs and keep large kennels for the landowners. They named this dog the Labrador Retriever, partly because it was easier on the tongue than the "Lesser Newfoundland" and partly because the islands of Labrador and Newfoundland were so close geographically and politically.

A man named Colonel Hawker, who was a talented shooter and wildfowler, owned a schooner that traveled between Poole in England and Newfoundland. Comparing the larger Newfoundland dog with the Labrador dogs, he is quoted in 1830 as saying, "[The Labrador] is by far the best for any kind of shooting, he is generally black and no bigger than a pointer, very fine in legs, with short smooth hair and does not carry his tail so much curled as the other; is extremely quick running, swimming and fighting . . . chiefly used on the native coast by fishermen, their sense of smell is hardly to be credited; in finding wounded game there is not a living equal in the canine race." (From *"The Early Labradors," by Jo Coulson, in "The Labrador Retriever Club 1916–1991, A Celebration of 75 Years."*)

As this dog began to be exported to England, unfortunately the St. John's Water Dog became extinct. A tax on dogs had been imposed in the Canadian Maritimes, and thus puppies became expendable because of the cost. Female dogs, especially, were culled. Trade between Newfoundland and Great Britain ceased, and the dogs who remained in Newfoundland were no longer imported to Britain.

THE LABRADOR IN GREAT BRITAIN

Fortunately, however, for Labrador enthusiasts, two men had developed a serious interest in the versatile dog from Newfoundland. The Second Earl of Malmesbury needed dogs to pursue his passion for ornithology at his home in Hurn, near Christchurch in England. A widower with three young sons, the Earl also wanted a dog who would be a good companion during his family's lonely hours. His home was near the marshlands at Christchurch Harbour, which was famous for the bird migrations routes there. Also, the town was small, consisting only of a few fishermen's cottages. Between the isolation and the birds, Malmesbury contented himself with his imported dogs, both for pleasure and for the pursuit of science. He began a serious Labrador Retriever breeding program.

At about the same time, a Scot, the Fifth Duke of Buccleuch, had imported the dogs from Newfoundland and began to breed them for use as waterfowl retrievers on his vast estate. He also regularly took his dogs out on boats during pleasure cruises, and his dogs showed great affinity for their work in the water.

Through selective breeding with other retrieving dogs, perhaps Flat-Coated Retrievers and pointing breeds, these early breeders

The Labrador works well in the water, as well as on land.

established the dog who today is known as the Labrador Retriever. The Sixth Duke of Buccleuch and the Third Earl of Malmesbury met by chance at a sport shoot, and each was impressed with the other's dogs. Malmsbury gave some of his waterfowling Labradors to Buccleuch, who mated bitches of the original imported strain back to the Malsmbury dogs. The resulting pups were the foundation of today's multitalented Labrador Retrievers.

Writing in 1887, the Third Earl of Malmsbury told the Duke, "We always call mine Labrador dogs and I have kept the breed as pure as I could from the first I had from Poole. The real breed may be known by their having a close coat which turns the water off like oil and, above all, a tail like an otter." Malmsbury's dogs were also described as "small, compact and very active; their coats were short, thick and smooth with sometimes a brown tinge at certain seasons. The eyes of most were in colour, something like burnt sugar. Their heads, which were not big, were broad and the skull shapely and not long in muzzle. Their bright countenances denoted their sweet tempers and high courage."

Labrador Temperament

The Labrador "tempers," or more aptly, lack of a temper, led sportsmen to attempt the first retriever field trial in England in 1899. At the time, spaniel and pointing breed owners had enjoyed regular tests of their shooting ability and their dogs' prowess in flushing and finding game. But some of the shooters wanted a dog who could also retrieve through bad weather or icy water. According to reports from field trial writers of that era, the other retrieving breeds—notably Flat-Coats and Curly Coated Retrievers—were not steady on the line, and the dogs required a handler to hold them until they were released.

The Retriever Society

At the first recorded retriever trial in 1899, not one Labrador was among the ten entries. However, as a result of that trial, a Retriever Society was begun, a new club of sorts in the International Gundog League. A Labrador Retriever first ran in the Society's 1904 trial and was awarded a Certificate of Merit. This first Labrador field winner was Munden Single, owned by the Honorable A. Holland-Hibbert, later known as Lord Knutsford. Single had also won a CC from the Kennel Club (KC) in England, which is that country's show ring championship designation.

Knutsford made sure that the British press and public knew about Single's accomplishments in the show ring and in the field. The Labrador Retriever's temperament and game-finding abilities began to be noticed outside of strictly wealthy patronages. In 1907, when the Duchess of Hamilton ran her own dogs in a retriever

Early breeders in England established the dog who today is known as the Labrador Retriever.

By 1908 more Labs were entered in field trials than any other breed.

test, called a stake, and placed third, retriever trials became acceptable avenues for women hobbyists in Great Britain.

Field Trials

The Labrador Retriever was tapped more often in the field because he was a calm, methodical, eager-to-please hard worker. By 1908, more Labs were entered in field trials than any other breed. Once that domination began, Labrador Retrievers and their owners, handlers, and trainers never looked back. By 1913, the last year of field trials before the start of World War I, 247 dogs had been entered in 14 trials and included 50 Flat Coats, 13 Golden Retrievers, 1 Curly Coat, and 179 Labrador Retrievers.

The Labrador Retriever Club

Although the field trials ceased for a time during the war years, work to protect the development of the purebred Labrador did not end. In 1916, the Labrador Retriever Club was formed to protect the breed and to run its own field trials. Early on, most of the Labradors shown in the breed ring were also run in field trials, and the club encouraged breeders of those dual-purpose dogs. Special awards were given for show dogs who ran in field trials and for field dogs who excelled in the show ring.

Membership was given by invitation at first, and numbered 129 in its first year. Now, there are well more than 2,000 members from around the world. The club also wrote the first standard for the breed, which is a description of what the perfect Labrador Retriever should look like and how he should behave. From the start, the Lab was described as a sturdy dog with a double coat, an otter tail, and a sweet nature.

Responsible breeders aim to produce dogs who are fit for both the conformation ring and the field.

In 1912, the Kennel Club (KC) registered 281 Labrador Retrievers. In 2007, the most recent figures available, there were 45,079 Labradors registered. The breed has been the most popular in England since 1991.

THE LABRADOR IN THE UNITED STATES

Wealthy sportsmen in the United States began importing Labrador Retrievers in the early 1900s, mostly because they were impressed with this amenable breed that performed so well at organized shoots and field trials in Scotland and England. Before World War I, few retrievers of any kind had been registered with the American Kennel Club (AKC), and those low numbers continued even after the Labrador was recognized as a separate breed for AKC purposes.

The Labrador Retriever Club, Inc. (LRC)

By the 1930s, however, an American group began to organize much like their counterparts in England. Led by influential sportsmen and sportswomen Audrey J. Field, Franklin P. Lord, New York Governor W. Averell Harriman, Jay F. Carlisle, Robert Goelet, Dr. Samuel Milbanks, C.L. Lawrence, and T.M. Howell, these individuals helped form the first club devoted to their beloved Labradors. The Labrador Retriever Club, Inc. (LRC) was formed in New York State in 1931, and the club's first field trial was held by December of that year. The mission of the club was and still is to preserve the integrity of the Labrador Retriever standard and to hold national specialties that showcased the versatility of the dog in field work, the conformation ring, agility, obedience, tracking, and rally. Today, the LRC sponsors educational seminars for judges and owners, helps place rescued Labs in appropriate homes, and offers assistance to future owners with its many publications and puppy buyer guidelines. The LRC is the official parent club of the AKC in the United States, which means that it is responsible for maintaining the breed standard. Only the parent club can request changes to this written description of the Labrador Retriever, and few changes have been made since the AKC registered 84 Labs in 1933, when the breed was separated as distinct from other retrievers.

In 2008 and for the 18th consecutive year, the Labrador Retriever has been the most popular purebred dog in America. More than twice as many Labs were registered that year than any other breed, and there is no sign that those numbers will decrease. This versatile dog, whether a devoted family pet or highly trained guide dog for disabled owners, has proven his worthiness as top dog in the United States, England, and around the world.

In the United States, as in Great Britain, concern has grown that the Labradors in the conformation ring are unfit for the field and vice versa. Responsible breeders aim to produce dogs that can do both.

THE LABRADOR AROUND THE WORLD

The Labrador Retriever is a popular breed across the globe, too. International clubs that subscribe to the same breed standard are members of the Fédération Cynologique Internationale, or FCI (www.fci.be), which maintains records, trains judges, and hosts a world dog show every year. More than 80 countries belong to the FCI, an organization

that began in Eastern Europe. Some registries and parent breed clubs, notably the AKC and LRC, do not recognize the same written standard for the Lab, but reciprocal agreements among all of the various clubs expect that international judges will evaluate the dogs in their rings based on the host country's standard.

Regardless of the differences, one trend remains throughout the world: The Lab is a treasured and favorite from families to sportsmen. According to the Canadian Kennel Club (CKC), the Lab is the most popular dog in the world, based on registration statistics.

The Lab in Australia, New Zealand, and Africa

Clubs in other countries that boast sizeable numbers of Labs and knowledgeable breeders include the Australian National Kennel Club (www.ankc.org.au) and, in New Zealand, The Labrador Club Inc. (www.labradorclub.org.nz). The Kennel Club of Southern Africa, one of the oldest dog registry clubs in the world and one of the largest, allows individual owners to hold membership alongside delegates from affiliated specialty clubs.

The Lab in Canada

The CKC (www.ckc.ca), founded in 1887, has a long and rich history. Its 25,000 members worldwide include individuals, clubs, breeders, sportsmen and -women, Labrador Retriever breed clubs, and specialty field clubs. The Labrador Retriever Club of Canada (www.labradorretrieverclub.ca), organized in 1979, holds Lab specialties throughout Canada, with competitions in conformation, obedience, and hunting retrieving tests. The Lab tops the list in registration in the CKC, making it that country's most popular breed.

The Labrador in Newfoundland

We cannot forget the place where Labradors first were discovered and where breeders, owners, and trainers still love and work their Labs: the island of Newfoundland. In 1967, the Best in Match at The Newfoundland Kennel Club's first all-breed show went to Labrador Retriever Knaith Beatty, owned by well-known breeder Lady Jacqueline Barlow of Newfoundland. At the club's 2009 all-breed show, Onarock Kennels Labradors won both the puppy awards and a Sporting Dog Group First.

From Newfoundland's rocky shores to the snow and ice-covered waterways, Labrador Retrievers still perform the work they were bred to do: recover game and provide companionship.

INFLUENTIAL PEOPLE AND THEIR DOGS

As mentioned earlier, Lord Malmesbury's dogs excelled at work and play. Most English Labradors can be traced back to Malmesbury's dogs Tramp, Avon, and Ned. Tramp was said at the time to be the most correct Labrador in type, expression, and working ability, and his progeny continued for many decades to prove his distinct mark on the breed.

Avon was a direct ancestor of the famous Dual Ch. Banchory Bolo, owned by Lorna, Countess Howe, one of the early British Labrador breeders. In 1922, she was the first person in England to finish a dual champion with Bolo, which meant that the dog won both bench and field trial championships. No other dog at the time exerted the influence that Bolo did in the ring, the field, and at stud. In 1933 and 1934, her Dual Ch. Banchory Bob won Best in Show at Crufts. Over the years the Banchory Kennels developed 4 dual champions, 29 bench champions, and 7 field champions.

After World War II, the great estates in England diminished, and owner–handlers became more prevalent. Mary Roslin-Williams, who became a renowned international judge and author of numerous books about Labrador Retrievers, handled her Carry of Mansergh to a win. This bitch, traced back to Malmesbury's Tramp, became Roslin-Williams' foundation bitch for her Mansergh kennel. Ch. Midnight of Mansergh sired many field and show winners, exerting excellent influence on the breed in the post-war years in England and in America, where some of her puppies were sent. Mansergh descendants continue to excel in the field and show ring, proving that Labrador Retrievers should be dual-purpose dogs.

The Labrador Retriever is the most popular registered breed in the United States and Canada.

Labrador Retrievers still perform the work they were bred to do: recover game and provide companionship.

As the Lab gained popularity in England, Scotland, and the United States, influential breeders produced tremendous dogs. Marjorie Cairns of Glasgow, Scotland, owned Blaircourt Kennels and bred the outstanding dog Ch. Ruler of Blaircourt.

In England, Gwen Broadley started her Sandylands kennel in the 1930s with descendants of the famous Bolo. Sandylands dogs and bitches are in the pedigree of Spenrock Labradors in the United States, including Ch. Spenrock Banner WC, one of the most influential dogs in America, owned by Janet Churchill.

The list of memorable breeders, owners, and handlers and their dogs could fill a whole book. The important message from all of them, however, would be that the Labrador Retriever must be bred to perform as well in the field as he does in the show ring. Our beloved Labs should have the complete package: sound body, sound mind, strong work ethic, proper coat and bone, and a happy, willing nature.

In subsequent chapters, we'll talk about all those ingredients that make up the Labrador Retriever. Let's begin with the puppy.

PART I

PUPPYHOOD

CHAPTER 1

IS THE LABRADOR RETRIEVER RIGHT FOR YOU?

Labrador Retriever puppies are darn cute, with their soft fur, soulful eyes, and alert and playful natures. The adorable black, yellow, or chocolate-colored eight-week-old bundle of fun who sits in your lap and licks your nose won't change much in appearance through the puppy stage—other than size, of course. The pup grows rapidly—most Labs are physically mature from 9 months to 18 months old, but mentally, they retain their puppy brain for much longer. How well a Lab pup will get along with members of the family and with strangers depends on the time a new owner invests in the dog's physical and emotional maturity during the critical puppy stage.

BREED CHARACTERISTICS

The dog is easily recognizable around the world, but what makes a Labrador Retriever, well, a Lab? Is it the coat, the tail, the work ethic, or the temperament? All of these features make up this dog, who is ideal for families or for sportspeople, but possibly the most important feature is the Labrador Retriever's nature.

A Labrador Retriever is gentle and intelligent, traits that often can be seen just by looking into his almond-shaped, friendly eyes. Of course, to get that close to the dog's face is an invitation for the Labrador to kick-start his licker. Labrador Retrievers are sometimes referred to as their owner's personal ear swab because the dog's tongue will make contact with just about anybody's face, ears, and neck, given that opportunity. From the dog's wide grin to its thick, always wagging tail, the Labrador exudes friendliness, intelligence, and strength.

The American Kennel Club (AKC) standard for the breed refers to a Labrador Retriever's eyes as "expressing character, intelligence, and good temperament," and ranks temperament as one of the Lab's most important qualities, "as much a hallmark of the breed as the 'otter' tail." The Labrador's "gentle ways, intelligence, and adaptability make him an ideal dog," according to the standard.

To perform all of the different jobs he might be trained for, the Lab must always be easygoing and willing for fun and hard work. Aggression, fear, and shyness are serious faults in a Labrador, but even puppies who display those temperament issues can be trained for work or companionship.

Labrador Retrievers are sporting dogs, and they require much more exercise and

The Labrador Retriever is a gentle and intelligent dog.

interaction with the people in their lives than most first-time owners realize. The saying "A tired puppy makes for a happy owner" is especially true with Labs. Structured playtime, exercise, and time with his owner will keep a Lab happy and healthy.

PHYSICAL DESCRIPTION OF THE LABRADOR

In addition to his temperament, other qualities that make a Labrador Retriever the ideal dog are his size and substance. All of the parts of a Lab combine together to form the perfect package: a dog who is content lying in front of a hearth with his owners or in the field undertaking far more strenuous pursuits.

Size
An adult dog is medium-sized and strong. A male dog should be from 22.5 to 24.5 inches (57 to 62 cm) tall if you measure him from the floor to his shoulder; females (called bitches) are a bit shorter and will be from 21.5 to 23.5 inches (54.5 to 60 cm) tall. Dogs in working condition can range from 65 to 80 pounds (29.5 to 36.5 cm); bitches are 55 to 70 pounds (22.5 to 31.5 kg). Is a Lab not a Lab if he falls outside of this range? Absolutely not—many Labrador Retrievers are taller or shorter or weigh more or less than indicated in the standard. These measurements are guidelines for the perfect conformation dog.

Coat

The Labrador Retriever was bred to retrieve downed birds in hot or cold weather, for long hours at a time, and to be a calm companion around the house. The dense double coat a Labrador sports serves multiple duties: the hard, oily outer hair helps repel ice, rain, or snow; the down-like inner coat keeps the dog warm during cold weather and cool during hot weather. The coat might have a wave down the back, but it shouldn't have a distinct curl, nor should it be sparse, meaning it would be too thin to keep the dog warm.

Coat Colors

Labrador Retrievers have three coat colors: black, yellow, and chocolate. A litter will sometimes have all three colors of puppies, or all black puppies, or all yellows, or any combination. Regardless of the color, each dog will develop that dense, short, straight double coat.

Some black Labrador Retrievers will have a white splash on their chests or an occasional white hair on the pads, feet, or withers. These white splotches don't keep black Labs from being called black, and they certainly don't keep these dogs from being called Labrador Retrievers. Some breeders refer to white patches of hair around the black Lab's feet as "Bolo" blotches. (As mentioned in the Introduction, Bolo was one of the breed's early, most famous sires, one of the original dogs bred from those imported from Newfoundland to England.) A large white chest blaze or blotch is a fault in the conformation show ring.

Black Labradors should have black noses and eye rims. Any other pigmentation or a lack of pigment is a serious fault, and in the conformation ring, is a reason for disqualification.

The black, yellow, and chocolate Labradors can carry recessive coat color genes that lead to incorrect pigmentation or color. Rarely, a puppy will have brindle or tan markings. These color combinations are a disqualification in the show ring and are highly discouraged. Tan-pointed and brindle Labradors show evidence of recessive coat color genes, and possibly are throwbacks to the early development of the breed, when Labs were mated to other retrievers like Curly Coats or Chesapeake Bay Retrievers. Puppies with these incorrect coat colors go on to lead normal lives as pets, however. There is no evidence that tan-marked or brindle-colored

By the Numbers

Good breeders test their Labrador Retriever breeding stock for genetic diseases and other disorders common to the Lab. Genetic testing is available for five diseases: centronuclear myopathy (CNM), cystinuria, exercise-induced collapse (EIC), narcolepsy, and progressive retinal atrophy (PRA). Health registries issue clearances from four disorders common to Labrador Retrievers after required testing indicates healthy breeding stock. Hip and elbow dysplasia and heart health clearances are issued by the Orthopedic Foundation for Animals (OFA). The Canine Eye Registration Foundation (CERF) exam rules out cataracts and glaucoma.

Labrador Retrievers come in three coat colors: chocolate (top), black (bottom left), and yellow (bottom right).

Labrador Retrievers have behavioral or health issues, and the centuries-ago practice of culling those puppies from litters is no longer done by reputable breeders.

While there are anecdotal tales that black Labradors are the hardest and smartest workers, yellow Labradors are the gentlest, and chocolate Labradors are the goofiest, no scientific proof exists that correlates coat color with any marker of intelligence. A black Lab puppy can be just as silly as a chocolate-colored pup, and many yellow Labradors have multiple titles in hunt and obedience titles. Plenty of chocolate Labradors work as search-and-rescue dogs and as service dogs. Regardless of coat color, a Labrador Retriever should be able to do any job required of him.

Yellow Labs

Yellow Labrador Retrievers can range from a light cream color to a darker fox red, but all are referred to as yellows. A yellow Lab might be very light, almost white, on much of its body but have darker ears, about the color of well-baked biscuits. He might sport darker yellow hair just beyond his neck that gives the appearance of an "angel wing" pattern across the withers. His undercoat might be almost white or a creamy colored yellow. The nose, though, should be black, although it can fade to liver or even pink as the dog ages or during winter months. The yellow Lab's eye rims are black, just like the black Labrador.

Black Labs

Black Labrador Retrievers will have a black undercoat and topcoat. An occasional whisp of white hair is acceptable. Some dogs have a wave pattern along their back, but the coat should be short; curls are not preferred on a black Lab's coat. His nose is black, but may fade to a brownish-black as he ages.

Chocolate Labs

The chocolate Labrador Retriever coat can vary in shading from light to dark chocolate with a complementary undercoat in the same shade. Like black Labs, chocolate Labs can sport a white chest blaze, which may disqualify the dog from the show ring (but not from being a terrific pet).Their noses and eye rims should be the same shade as the coat, though. As with the black and yellow Labs, a chocolate Lab's nose might fade with age or during the winter months, and it can even sport pink splotches from time to time.

Yellow Labs can range from a light cream color to a darker fox red.

Body Type

Your Lab will grow quickly, and his overall structure helps the dog perform his duties. Labs are medium-sized dogs with a square look. In other words, the height of the dog from withers to ground is about the same as his length from withers to flank, or rump. The height from elbow to ground should be equal to the height from elbow to shoulder. This ratio gives the Labrador Retriever his square, well-balanced look. As he matures, his chest will deepen and should extend and taper down to about his elbows by maturity. The Lab doesn't have a wide chest and nor is it too narrow; rather, his chest will show evidence of strong lungs and all-over musculature. There is very little tuck up from the chest to the loin; rather, the belly has more of a straight-line appearance. Viewed from above, though, the dog should have an apparent "waistline" behind the ribcage.

Tail

An otter tail is as much a hallmark of the breed as any other physical trait and makes the Labrador instantly recognizable. Thick at the base and tapered at the end, the Lab's tail should come off level or slightly below the top of the back and extend down to the dog's hocks. The fur on the Labrador Retriever's tail wraps tightly around the bone and is free of any excess hair, or "feathers." The tail is powerful enough to help the Lab navigate through water or to clear a coffee table. Plenty of Labrador Retriever owners call their dogs "cocktail cleaners," which means that the dog's height, coupled with a tail that rarely stops wagging, can knock even heavy objects off a sofa-height table.

Bone Structure

The "substance" of the Labrador Retriever refers to his bone structure. The Labrador's bone shouldn't be so thick and heavy that he has trouble moving, nor be so light and weedy that he couldn't work all day. A heavy Lab, called "cloddy" and "lumbering" in the standard, is just as incorrect as a dog who has too-thin bones.

After all, athleticism is important. As he grows, a Labrador Retriever needs to have visible, strong muscles, or he cannot do the job he was bred to do, which is to hunt for long hours. Proper bone structure to support proper musculature will allow the Labrador to enjoy any game or activity for long hours without tiring. As the dog grows, muscles develop on the back legs that are sometimes referred to as a "second thigh." These powerful muscles, descending from the flank to just above the hock, help give the Labrador

Training Tidbit

A hands-on daily inspection of a Lab puppy allows his owner chances to monitor changes in the dog's health. Gentle handling that includes touching the pup's muzzle, feet, and tail, as well as inspecting his teeth and clipping nails, helps the dog learn confidence in strange situations, such as a visit to the veterinarian. Make these handling sessions a game, and pair a command with an action and then a small treat. "Show teeth" teaches a youngster that a quick examination of his mouth leads to either playtime, a bit of food, or sometimes both.

The Lab has a wide head in proportion to the rest of his body.

Retriever the power in his rear limbs to swim in strong currents, to help him run for hundreds of yards (m) after a downed bird, or to chase a toy for hours. Owners of those Labs who beg for "just one more tennis ball toss" witness this phenomenal strength and athleticism; their throwing arm will tire long before their dog tires.

Head

A Labrador Retriever has a wide head in proportion to the rest of his body. The top of the skull is rather flat; some Labs are taught to balance objects such as a dog biscuit or ball on the straight plane of the skull. The head structure again is designed for the job of tracking a shot game bird and then picking it up. The muzzle is not in a straight line from the top of the head to the end of the nose. This "stop," as it is called, from the brow down to the dog's foreface, gives him a good line of sight to his quarry. Also, the length of the dog's skull is about the same as the length of his face, contributing to the dog's square and balanced appearance.

Compared to some of the more wrinkly-looking dogs, the Labrador doesn't carry a lot of flesh on his head. His lips, or flews, can fling drool with the best of them (like Bloodhounds), but he doesn't have drooping, pendulous, excessive flesh. Instead, Labrador lips, to those who are lucky enough to be kissed by a Lab, frame a mouth that is gentle enough to pluck small stuffed toys from a pile or a bird from a creek without damaging feather or fluff.

Nose

Most dogs have excellent sniffers, and the wide, always-working Labrador Retriever nose at the end of that square muzzle contains all of the traits necessary to help the Lab detect drugs or explosives, find lost children, or know if a piece of cheese is hidden in his owner's pocket. Multiple whiskers on the Lab's muzzle help him do his job of finding stuff, whether that might be the dog's dinner or his owner's.

Teeth

A Labrador Retriever cannot do a good job of retrieving without a full set of teeth, and for that reason, missing molars are a serious fault in the show ring. Many dogs, however, can have less than full dentition and not ever miss a meal. The teeth are strong, closing in a scissors bite, which means that the top teeth will just cover the bottom teeth. Although a more level bite, in which top and bottom front

The Lab has kind eyes that show a friendly, eager-to-please dog.

teeth meet, is not a disqualification; that type of dentition is not as desirable as the scissors bite. Teeth that are undershot, overshot, or otherwise seriously misaligned are "serious faults" according to the standard. Again, form follows function, and if a Labrador Retriever's teeth make him look as if he needs braces, that dog wouldn't be able to retrieve game without damage to the bird.

Neck

Also important for retrieving purposes is the Labrador's neck. The term "reach of neck" refers to the length from the back of the head down to the dog's shoulders. There is only a moderate arch in the Lab's neck when viewed from the side, but there are visible strong muscles, which help the dog pick up game.

Eyes

Look into a Labrador Retriever's eyes and you will see a friendly, eager-to-please dog who is smart and alert to his surroundings. The eyes should be slightly almond-shaped, sit well apart on the face, and be medium-sized, neither bulging nor deeply set. These kind eyes are as much a true feature of the Lab as his otter tail and even temperament.

Black and yellow Labradors should have brown eyes, and chocolate Labrador's eyes will be either brown or a lighter hazel. Eyes that are black or yellow are not favored and can indicate a harsh expression on an otherwise beautiful head. Eyes that are round, set closely together, or are too small in proportion to the rest of the head are not typically found on a well-bred Labrador Retriever. The eye rims are black in yellow and blacks, and brown in chocolate Labradors. Eyes rims that have no color pigmentation are not typical, either, and a show dog can be disqualified from the ring if he does not have that "permanent eyeliner" look around his eyes.

Ears

The infamously soft Labrador Retriever ears are set close to the head and rather far back on the skull. Large, heavy ears are incorrect; after all, the Labrador shouldn't worry about dragging his ear tips along the ground when seeking downed fowl. The ear should be just long enough so that, if pulled forward and over the eye, the tip would barely reach the inside of the socket.

Expression

A Labrador Retriever's expression—alert eyes, ears brought forward, his large pink tongue slightly panting—is one of anticipation and intelligence. Between the nostrils that softly expand and contract, a gaze that always looks eager for his owner's interaction, and ears that can twirl or twitch seemingly independent of the other ear while the dog is listening for an invitation to play or work, a Labrador Retriever is a dog who is always ready: Ready to retrieve. Ready to eat. Ready to play.

Prospective owners should be willing and able to reciprocate.

LIVING WITH THE LABRADOR

The physical traits and temperament of the Labrador Retriever add up to a hard worker who is eager to please in all venues, a dog who will hold up to the rigors of hunting through sunny heat or icy cold, a dog who is easily trained for service work, a dog who excels in most canine sports, and a dog who will plop down by his

owner's feet and snore the night away.

Coat Shedding

Regardless of the color, coat shedding is common; some owners say that a Labrador Retriever sheds his under coat or outer guard hairs all but five minutes of the year. Bitches will typically shed heavily twice a year, just before they come into heat. Even spayed females will continue that pattern of "dropping coat" long after their ovaries have been removed. Owners should be armed with a strong vacuum cleaner, mops, and brooms. At the least, coordinating rugs and furniture color with the color of the pet Labrador is prudent.

Environment

A Labrador Retriever doesn't care where he lays his head at night—whether a city dog, country dog, or suburban dog—as long as he can breathe the same air as his owner. While this breed can be happy and healthy in any environment, there are some challenges that

Multi-Dog Tip

Labrador Retriever puppies are cute, and these dogs do well in a household with other pets. But owners are wise to only bring home one puppy rather than two siblings or even more from a litter. Can you handle the space, time, training, and playtime needs of one puppy, much less more? An owner committed to all of the needs of a growing Labrador Retriever is not likely to get frustrated if she's just dealing with one dog.

The Labrador Retriever needs regular exercise, from the time he's a puppy through his senior years.

prospective owners should consider. This breed needs rigorous exercise, enough room to stretch his legs, and daily training sessions and interaction with his owner. For those reasons, a Lab might be unsuitable for those who cannot devote the time, space, and energy for such an active dog.

Exercise

From puppyhood to his senior years, a Labrador Retriever needs exercise. Whether that means a long walk through city blocks (stopping frequently to be petted and to lick adoring fans) or fast, uninterrupted runs down country lanes, or daily obedience lessons in the backyard, punctuated by an occasional squirrel chase, the Labrador Retriever is an active dog. Without daily activity, a Labrador can get bored easily and quickly. And a bored Labrador can be a destructive Labrador.

Labrador Retrievers are sporting dogs, and they require much more exercise and interaction with the people in their lives than most first-time owners realize. The saying "A tired puppy makes for a happy owner" is especially true with Labs. Structured playtime, exercise, and time with his owner will keep a Lab happy and healthy.

The type of play and exercise is important also. To grow up into that friendly, goofy dog who everyone in the family will love, the Labrador Retriever needs to learn how to get along with each member of the family, with strangers, and with other animals, whether it's the family's pet cat or the neighbor's dog. Excursions to the bank or baseball fields or meet-and-greets at public dog parks are excellent ways to socialize the Labrador Retriever.

"Mouthiness"

The Lab puppy is typically curious, but his eyes and ears won't be fully operational for about 10 to 14 days. To compensate, a Lab newborn uses his mouth to explore the world at first. This "mouthy" quality is a Labrador pup's first expression of his future life as a retriever. In other words, he will have his mouth on anything he can grab. Inappropriate chewing and destruction of household and personal items will develop in a Lab if he isn't given

acceptable toys or taught better manners. This common behavior can be challenging to control in a young dog, and many owners discover that while their Lab is stealing their heart, he's is also stealing their eyeglasses and television remotes.

Companionability With People

Labs and children just seem to fit together, whether the dog is surrounded by students in a library reading room or curled around the youngest children on a family room sofa. Because a Labrador Retriever grows quickly, very young children can be knocked to the ground by a rambunctious puppy. Regardless of the breed, youngsters should never be without adult supervision around a dog, including Labradors. Although an adult Labrador Retriever should be reliable and calm around children, during his awkward and boisterous

Labs are generally easygoing with other animals in the same household, but any new dog needs to be gradually introduced.

Many Labradors swim daily, then dry themselves by shaking off and lying in the sun.

Companionability With Other Pets

Labrador Retrievers are generally easygoing with other animals in the same household, but a new dog needs to be gradually introduced to his new housemates. A puppy, depending on his personality, might chase resident cats or try to hang onto the earflaps of other dogs. He'll need to be taught that those behaviors are not acceptable.

A new puppy will soon learn the hierarchy of the established pets in your home, and if you don't help the youngster learn the rules, his new pack members will soon put him in his place. Cats could hiss, paw, scratch, or bite a too-inquisitive Labrador Retriever puppy. Other dogs might allow some puppy antics, such as play lunging, barking, and needle-like teeth on muzzles, paws, or ears, but may eventually roll a rambunctious newcomer onto his back, just as his dam would have corrected him when he displayed these nuisance behaviors with her.

Whether you are introducing a puppy or an older Labrador Retriever to your established "pack," keeping the newcomer in your lap or on a short leash or houseline until everyone has had a chance to "meet and greet" will ensure a peaceful transition. Other commonsense approaches can help with the introductions also.

The new dog should not be allowed to feed from the resident pet's food bowls, although a shared water bucket or bowl is usually okay. If all of the resident dogs are crate-trained, including the newcomer, each pack member should have his own den, a safe place for retreat and rest. Behavioral issues can be addressed easily if the new puppy has his own "time-out" place, such as a crate or a separate exercise pen.

Any newcomer, be it a Labrador Retriever puppy or an older dog, might try to establish a dominant position in the pack. This is what

puppyhood, the dog can unwittingly harm a child during play.

Most Labrador Retrievers "have never met a stranger," as the saying goes. So, don't expect your Lab to be a good guard dog. While most Labs will bark to announce visitors at the door, and an untrained Labrador might jump up on guests to show delight or excitement, strangers to the home won't be pounced on unless it's to lick their faces. Aggression, whether from fear or shyness, is atypical of the Labrador Retriever. Your Lab more likely will try and engage a stranger in play or sit and beg for a treat.

Being the social animal that he is, a Labrador Retriever craves time with his owner, which can be as involved as structured play or as simple as a daily grooming session.

usually leads to infighting among dogs in a home—a type of sibling rivalry. Owners can help all of the dogs avoid problem behaviors by establishing some simple rules: Never allow the young upstart puppy to go first through a doorway, place food bowls out for the established canines prior to feeding the new dog, and pay attention to the changing dynamics among the dogs. Transgressions can be spotted and stopped if owners are willing to put in the time required when adding a Labrador Retriever to a home where other animals already live.

Grooming Requirements

Grooming a Labrador Retriever is relatively easy because the dog has a "wash-and-wear" coat that seldom needs bathing. Many Labradors swim daily, then dry themselves by shaking off and lying in the sun—dirt and grime will not become embedded in their coats. Matting of the coat is almost unheard of in a Labrador. A weekly brushing with a good stiff-bristle brush is usually all that's needed to keep the Labrador Retriever's double coat in top condition. During a heavier shedding time, daily brushing will keep most of the Lab's coat in the trash rather than on furniture, floors, and rugs.

Indications that a Labrador Retriever might need a bath could range from flaking skin that arises in low-humidity areas to more serious allergies that cause itching, and in turn, incessant scratching. Country (and some suburban and urban) Labrador Retrievers might come in contact with the wrong end of a skunk. And Labradors love to roll in "stuff"—the stinkier, the better, it sometimes seems. If your Labrador Retriever needs a bath, the right shampoo is important. Oatmeal-based formulas can help dry or soothe allergy-induced skin conditions, and commercial

preparations are available for "skunk-stink" dog bathing. The most important point to remember when bathing a Labrador is that the protective oils in his coat and skin must not be stripped away by harsh shampoos. Also, a Labrador's coat should not be fluffy and soft, even after a bath. Air drying is preferable to force drying, whether using a home handheld hair dryer or a more powerful commercial forced-air dryer.

A weekly hands-on examination of your dog, when nails are trimmed, pads examined for cracks or punctures, and coat brushed, is

The Lab is renowned for his trainability and is often used in pet-assisted therapy programs.

The Lab is one of the most versatile and trainable breeds.

a good time to check for unusual lumps and bumps, which are typical as a dog gets older. This is also a good routine to establish to check your dog's teeth and gums for tartar buildup. Some owners brush their dog's teeth; others prefer to let their veterinarian staff take care of their Labrador's oral health. Labradors typically have strong, healthy teeth and gums, and professional cleaning might not be indicated until your dog ages.

Health Issues

Labrador Retrievers are strong, healthy dogs, but health issues may develop either during puppyhood or well into the Lab's senior years. Some are genetic-based disorders, some result from the Labrador's activities, and some are expected of most senior-status dogs. Obtaining a Labrador Retriever from a reputable breeder, one who provides health

and DNA checks on all breeding stock and who will guarantee the health status of puppies, is the most important step toward ensuring that your Labrador will be healthy and emotionally stable. Of course, no one can determine with any certainty that a particular dog will remain healthy all of his life.

In the Labrador Retriever breed, the most talked- and written-about issue is hip dysplasia (HD). But the Labrador is predisposed to a number of other conditions, as well, including elbow dysplasia, progressive retinal atrophy (PRA), centronuclear myopathy (CNM), cystinuria,

Want to Know More?

To learn more about health issues, see Chapter 8: Labrador Retriever Health and Wellness.

laryngeal paralysis, cranial cruciate ligament (CCL) injury, dropped tail, and hemangiosarcoma. These issues will be covered in greater detail in Chapter 8: Labrador Retriever Health and Wellness.

Trainability

This breed is simply renowned for its trainability. Labrador Retrievers learn quickly, retain their lessons, and can understand and perform upward of hundreds of commands. From the simplest *sit* or *down* to the more complex tasks of guiding a blind person through crowded urban areas, to even sniffing out cancerous cells in a laboratory beaker, the Labrador Retriever is indisputably one of the most versatile and trainable of dog breeds. He thrives on hard work, and will keep working for hours if required.

For this reason, Labrador Retrievers are often seen at airports, where they work as drug detection dogs. They are trained as service dogs for people with seizure disorders, diabetes, blindness or other low-vision disorders, and for wheelchair-bound children and adults with neuromuscular disorders. Labs can also be trained as tracking dogs, to find lost children or escaped criminals. Once fully mature emotionally, Labrador Retrievers are willing and loving participants in pet-assisted therapy programs. Various organizations around the United States certify animals as therapy dogs, and Labrador Retrievers can be seen volunteering with their owners in libraries as reading-assist dogs, in hospitals and hospices to provide comfort for patients, in elder-care centers to bring smiles to senior citizens, and in rehabilitation centers, where the dogs allow patients to brush and stroke their coats, whisper in their ears, and in turn, give gentle loving licks with their huge pink tongues.

More Labrador Retrievers compete in the AKC's canine obedience and rally sports than any other breed, and they and their owners win more titles—partly because there are just more Labs registered than any other breed, but also because they are so easily trained. Indeed, the AKC National Obedience Invitational winner in 2008 and 2009 was a black Labrador Retriever. The breed also dominates retrieving hunt tests and trials.

Training a Labrador Retriever can be easy or difficult, depending on the owner's experience with dogs in general and also on the personality of the individual dog, the type of training undertaken, and the time invested on a daily basis. The key is consistency on the owner's part. In return, a Labrador will work hard and long and be a devoted, happy companion for his owner.

The Labrador Retriever dominates retrieving hunt tests and trials.

CHAPTER 2

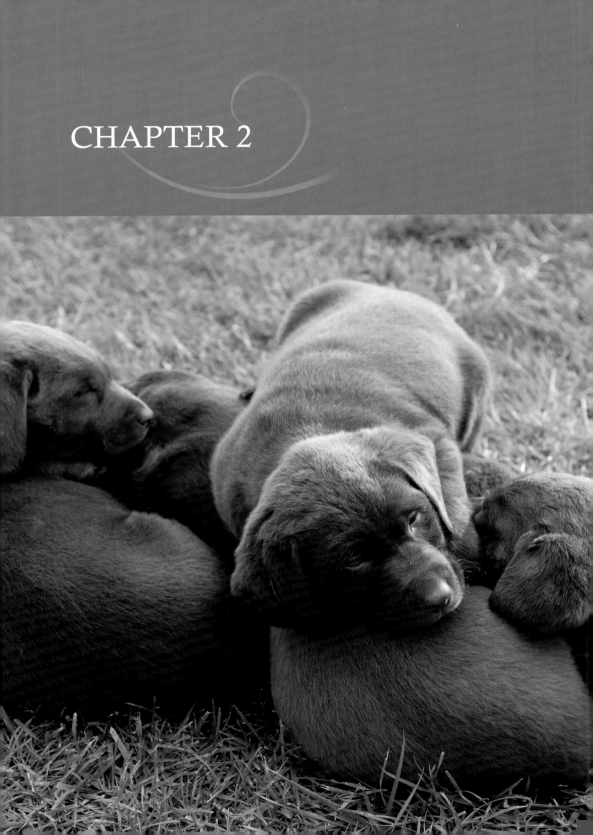

FINDING AND PREPPING FOR YOUR LABRADOR RETRIEVER PUPPY

Where you get your Labrador Retriever puppy is the most important thing to consider, vital for your dog's emotional and physical well-being over the course of his life. Whichever one of those adorable chocolate, black, or yellow puppies is selected for a new home and family, proper planning for his arrival is essential. Preparations can reduce the stress and frustrations that come with adding a puppy to the family, so take the time to find the right dog from the right breeder, buy supplies in advance, and steel yourself for the demands of this creatively curious breed, and your Labrador Retriever puppy will settle right into his new life and home.

WHY GET A PUPPY?

An eight-week-old Labrador Retriever puppy, unlike an adolescent or adult dog, comes with less baggage. Bad habits aren't ingrained. More than likely, the new owner will know the puppy's history, his vaccination record and preferred food, sleep and playtime schedule, and training history. A puppy might already be housetrained and crate-trained, whereas an adult dog might have lived half of his life in a shelter, with little human contact and no

place to call a private den. Although Labrador Retrievers are trainable throughout their lives, behaviors are more easily taught to a puppy. For example, if you want a dog who won't jump up on visitors, it's much easier to train a 15-pound (7-kg) puppy to sit and wait for petting than a 60-pound (27-kg) jumble of excited muscle.

THINGS TO CONSIDER

Puppies might be sold as "pet quality" or "show quality," and while there are important differences, potential owners need to know what they will require of their Labrador Retriever before selecting a puppy. Also important is the selection of a "field-bred" or "American-line" Labrador versus what is typically called an "English" or "British-line" pup. Although most breeders and members of Labrador Retriever clubs would rather there be no distinction, there are important differences.

Field-bred Labrador Retrievers come from kennels that specialize in dogs bred for demanding hunt tests and hard work in the field. These dogs might be lighter boned, measure taller by 1 inch (2.5 cm) or more, and could have hyperactive temperaments, depending on how the puppies were socialized. English-type Labradors are shorter and stockier and could be calmer. But a Lab is a Lab is a Lab. Just because a Labrador comes from hunting or retrieving stock does not mean that he can't perform other functions. And just because a dog is derived from mostly British breeding dogs and bitches doesn't mean that he shouldn't or couldn't hunt. All Labradors, no matter their history, still should be able to do their job, and they should work willingly, maintain calm temperaments, and be free of health issues.

WHERE TO GET YOUR PUPPY

Good breeders will put in long hours to breed the right dogs, and that is where any search for the right Labrador Retriever begins.

Show Quality Versus Pet Quality

"Show-quality" puppies are expected to develop into a Labrador Retriever who is representative of the breed standard, physically and temperamentally. These puppies usually won't be sold by a breeder to a first-time owner; after all, a breeder's reputation rides on how often and well her dogs are handled in the conformation ring. Show-quality dogs and bitches are expected to carry on the breeder's hopes and plans for her line of Labrador Retrievers. Many show-quality puppies don't even develop until later in their careers; some won't mature physically until the age of two or three. For that reason, breeders will hold back puppies who show potential, and many breeders will hold onto their prospective show puppies until they are three or four months old before they decide whether or not to sell.

"Pet-quality" Labrador Retrievers are perfectly acceptable puppies, with good health and temperaments. What makes them pets rather than show quality? Perhaps the young puppy

There is a difference between pet-quality and show-quality Labradors.

already has a disqualifying fault under the breed standard that would prohibit any conformation career. The puppy might have front feet that toe out rather than face perfectly forward (although toeing out sometimes self-corrects as a dog matures). The puppy might be lighter boned than a breeder would hope for in a conformation dog, or his eyes could be too light or dark, not the deep brown color preferred.

Breeders who show their dogs and bitches in conformation are well versed on all the specifics of the Labrador Retriever standard and usually know before they place any of their puppies which ones might measure up to those qualities.

Where Not to Purchase Your Puppy

Regardless of the puppy desired, searching for the right Labrador Retriever puppy—color, gender, expectations for future work—are all considerations that must be decided long before contacting breeders. How do you find that one special Lab, and how do you know if the breeder is reputable? There are accepted standards and rules for breeders, and any red flags should be a sign that you should walk away from the purchase.

Sources that acquire their puppies from puppy mills are never a good idea. Most of these puppies are mass produced in an assembly line environment. Living conditions for sires and dams are horrid, with many dogs residing in wire cages with barely enough room to stand up and turn around. Little

By the Numbers

At eight weeks of age, your Labrador Retriever puppy can begin potty training. The use of a crate will facilitate this training because most puppies don't want to soil their sleeping area and will whine if they have to urinate or defecate. Within a few days, your puppy will reliably let you know when he needs to leave his crate; after he has pottied in a designated area, playtime begins again.

Pet-quality Labrador Retrievers make great pets, as do show-quality dogs.

Purchase a Lab puppy from a reputable breeder, not over the Internet, sight unseen.

to no regard is given to health issues, and vaccinations, dewormings, or preventive medicines for an illness such as heartworm might or might not have been administered. Most assuredly, the accepted health screenings for hip and elbow dysplasia and eyes disorders have not been performed on the parents of these puppies. The puppies themselves could look healthy, but too many owners find out the heartbreaking, expensive truth when their dog gets home and develops an illness that should have been screened for in his sire and dam.

Similarly, the online, sight-unseen purchase of a Labrador Retriever puppy also is a bad idea. Ideally, the prospective owner will have researched a reputable breeder and personally seen the living conditions of all of the dogs in a kennel or home. Also, Internet scams

that tug at heart strings abound. Any person who requests money online in exchange for the promise of a puppy shipment could be after one thing: your money. Keep your wallet in your pocket and walk away from the computer.

Advertisements in newspapers and magazines are usually placed by so-called "backyard breeders." These sometimes well-meaning folks have Labrador Retriever puppies to sell because they thought it would be a good idea to breed their own dog or bitch because they want one puppy out of the breeding, or they want their children to "witness the miracle of a puppy birth." Usually no regard is given to the health of the dogs involved, and while "papers" or "AKC registration" might be offered, buyers should be aware that even dog registries have no power to guarantee the health of a puppy. The only way to be sure that a puppy is healthy is to buy from a Labrador Retriever breeder who has studied the breed, offers health guarantees, and is available for your questions and concerns long after the pup leaves the breeder's home.

How to Find a Good Breeder

Just as there is a wrong way to find a Labrador Retriever puppy, there's a right way.

How to Start Your Search

Start the search with local kennel clubs, visit conformation dog shows or obedience and agility trials, and talk with people who exhibit or compete with their Labrador Retrievers. Spend as much time asking questions about their dogs as you would take asking questions about any other major purchase you've made, such as a car or a refrigerator. Look at it this way: Your Labrador Retriever will be with you for 12 to 14 years, far longer than any time you might own a particular vehicle.

Research kennels online, too, as most breeders will have a website that features their winning dogs and bitches. The kennel website may also have a list of requirements for potential future owners and a prospective owner questionnaire. Again, if a breeder offers to sell a puppy online, sight unseen, and no questions are asked or answered, this is a red flag. Instead, look for a breeder who is affiliated with the Labrador Retriever Club, Inc. (LRC), a local kennel club, or a regional Labrador Retriever club. The American Kennel Club's (AKC) website includes a searchable database for contacts with all member or affiliated clubs (www.akc.org). Make a short list of breeders whose dogs you admire, then make contact with those breeders directly. Reputable breeders all have the best interest of the Labrador Retriever at the heart of their kennels, and most have standard practices.

None of them breed dogs to make money; that idea is simply laughable. Labrador Retriever breeders do what they do for the love of the breed. Some might also breed one or two other types of breeds, but none will breed "designer dogs" like a Labrador Retriever–Poodle cross. The breeder should participate in canine sports or conformation shows and possibly earn the AKC Canine Good Citizen certificate with her dogs, which indicates that she is serious about her dogs' temperaments and trainability.

Reputable breeders do not offer "silver" Labrador Retrievers. Most likely, these dogs have been cross-bred in the past with a Weimaraner to get the silver sheen, but this coat color is incorrect in a Labrador Retriever. Also, be wary of "all-white" Labradors, as these are simply lacking in all pigment, or are actually a very pale yellow and registered as yellow Labs.

Contact Potential Breeders

Once you've identified the breeders you want to contact, don't be shy! Write, e-mail, telephone, or talk to the breeder in person. Ask to visit, so that you can see where and how

My First Labrador

My first Labrador Retriever, Sam, was a gift from my family. They responded to several local newspaper advertisers, went to look at puppies, and picked out the "runt" from a litter of 11 black, fat, happy male pups. There was no contract, no health guarantee, and later, after I studied Sam's pedigree (which the breeder did provide), I could tell that my first Labrador was a field-bred dog rather than a show-line dog. Because these were local backyard breeders, they were available for questions, and to their credit, they knew a lot about raising a rambunctious puppy. They helped me get Sam's AKC registration papers transferred to my name so that I could compete with him in canine sports.

Eventually my "runt" grew into a 90-pound (41-kg), 26-inch-tall (66-cm) dog, so Sam was never a true representative of the breed standard. Although he was a big dog, he had the accompanying big heart, and Sam had the true, steady Labrador Retriever temperament and willingness to please. He never had serious health issues. We got lucky with our backyard-bred dog—but many Labrador Retriever puppy buyers don't.

Ask to visit your potential breeder so that you can see where and how the dogs actually live.

the dogs actually live. This will accomplish two important goals: The breeder can watch how a prospective owner interacts with her puppies and adult dogs, and the puppy buyer can check the conditions of the kennel. If the dogs are dirty—we're talking beyond normal daily rough-and-tumble playing in the mud type dirt that a good brush would remove—or seem unhealthy in any way, turn around and leave. Similarly, if the breeder thinks that a puppy buyer is aloof, afraid of the dogs, or just wants a dog for the kids with no parental involvement, the breeder should refuse to sell a puppy to that family.

Paperwork

A reputable breeder will have important paperwork on all of her dogs, and the prospective puppy buyers should inspect each document. These include health clearances on the sire and dam for hip and elbow dysplasia, and eye exam certifications. The breeder can also show you or tell you how to find the health certifications on past litters and also on the grandparents, aunts, uncles, and cousins of the puppy. Some breeders have heart exams performed on their breeding stock. A three- to five-generation puppy pedigree will be included in the sale, along with a contract that spells out any conditions for the sale.

For example, most breeders sell their Labrador Retriever puppies on what's called a "limited AKC registration." This means that the puppy, once grown and trained, can compete in AKC companion or performance events, but should not be bred and cannot compete in conformation shows. Future litters from a limited registration dog cannot be registered with the AKC. The limited registration listing helps a breeder maintain control over all of her stock, and it reduces the numbers of puppies from unwanted, unplanned breeding.

A Labrador Retriever puppy's paperwork will also have his vaccination and deworming history, a record of the first veterinarian examination, tips on puppy training and grooming, and the pup's registration record. The breeder will show buyers how to transfer the AKC registration and even how to pick a registered name for the puppy.

Answer the Breeder's Questions

Expect to answer just as many questions as you ask. A responsible breeder will want to know the living situation of a puppy who is sold: Is there a fenced yard? Are there other dogs and cats in the home, and if there are children, what are their ages? Where will the puppy spend his days and nights (in the yard or in the house?), and who will supervise the puppy while he acclimates to his new home? You might have to give references from your friends and your veterinarian, answer questions about prior dog experience, and talk about your future plans with this puppy in canine sports or hunting activities.

This type of interrogation is typical from a responsible breeder, who only has the best interest of the puppy and the breed foremost in her heart and head. The breeder knows which puppy from the litter will be a perfect match for a new family based not just on the family information but on the puppy's temperament. Each puppy in the litter has his own personality, and the breeder knows best how and where to place her pups.

Ask the Breeder Questions

Ask the breeder for references from past puppy buyers and from the breeder's veterinarian. Do a background check on the breeder as thoroughly as the one the breeder will perform on her buyers, and ask about health issues that may have cropped up either in her line or in siblings, cousins, or grandparents of the puppy you want.

The Breeder's Contract

The breeder's contract should detail not just what is expected of a puppy buyer but also what the buyer can expect from the breeder. The contract should have some

Expect the breeder to ask you a variety of questions so that she can be sure that you'll make a good parent for one of her puppies.

health guarantee so that if a serious condition develops as the puppy grows, the breeder will offer to take back the puppy and refund the purchase price or give a replacement puppy. Most contracts require that the puppy be spayed or neutered at an age-appropriate time; this could be months in the future or a couple of years, depending on the breeder.

Also, the breeder will want to have an ongoing relationship with the new owner. If serious health issues do appear in any puppy, the breeder will contact the owners of all the puppies in that litter to alert them. For example, if a puppy is diagnosed with hip dysplasia at ten months, a responsible breeder will inform the buyers of all the puppies in that litter so that all siblings can be screened and monitored for that condition.

Years ago, I had a young 11-month-old bitch in the conformation ring at a local dog show. As soon as we exited the ring with a blue ribbon from the puppy class, her breeder rushed over and said, "Don't show her again. There may be a problem with the litter." Her

Puppy Availability

Keep in mind that a breeder might not have a puppy available; most litters are planned well in advance, and all of the puppies could already be spoken for. If you are set on a particular kennel or want puppies from a particular dog or bitch, expect to put your name on a waiting list and give the breeder a "good faith" deposit for a future puppy. A reputable breeder would also happily refer you to another kennel if she doesn't have a litter on the ground or planned.

Want to Know More?

For more information on how to housetrain a puppy, see Chapter 4: Training Your Labrador Retriever Puppy.

mouth twisted and she burst into tears as she told me that a sibling of my bitch had been diagnosed with severe hip dysplasia and would undergo a double hip replacement. The next week, I took my perfectly healthy-appearing bitch for hip radiographs and received similarly devastating news. There was no apparent reason for the dysplasia, as both parents and all of the grandparents of my puppy had been checked for hip and elbow dysplasia. I know, however, that conversation with the breeder had been just about the most difficult thing she'd ever done during her lifetime with Labrador Retrievers. True to her word, she stayed involved with me and with that puppy for many months as we made treatment decisions.

In addition, a breeder will insist on "cradle-to-grave" responsibility for all of her puppies: If any of the puppies needs to be rehomed for any reason, the breeder will either take the puppy back or help find a more appropriate placement. No breeder wants her puppies to wind up in a shelter or to be moved around from one relative to another, with no input at all in the selection of a more suitable home.

PREPARING FOR YOUR PUPPY

So you've picked your breeder, she's helped you select the right Labrador Retriever puppy for you and your family, and you have decided on a date to bring him home. Before that date, which you've circled in red ink on the wall

A breeder will take the puppy back if you need to rehome the dog for any reason.

calendar, creeps up, think about the puppy's future needs and begin to prepare.

Puppy-Proof the Home

First, your home should be puppy-proofed to guard against accidents and to help the puppy adjust. Labrador Retriever puppies are incredibly curious and inventive in the ways of trouble. Get down on your hands and knees and go through the house, pretending you are a young pup, and see what comes into view. Plug electrical sockets with protectors that can be found in baby-supply stores. Move cords so that a roaming puppy can't get hold of one to bite; this will prevent electrical shock, and it will also prevent replacing appliances or lamps. Check the yard where the puppy will play and exercise, and plug all of the holes in the fence. Put cleaning supplies well out of puppy reach, and make sure that toxic chemicals like antifreeze have not been spilled in the garage and are in secure, tamper-resistant, original containers. In short, if anything seems dangerous for a small child or baby, it will be dangerous—and tempting—for a Labrador Retriever puppy.

Set Up a Schedule

Decide who in the family will be able to take the puppy on predetermined walks or supervised outside play. Make a schedule for the middle of the night also: until your Labrador Retriever is housetrained, he will need to go out to potty every few hours. Tempting as it might be to kick your partner at three in the morning when your puppy is crying or whining, and say "It's your turn," that's not really fair to the dog. Ideally, someone in the family will be home with the puppy for the first few days or couple of weeks to help with the transition. Also, decide which chores are appropriate for children—feeding, grooming, training, and playing. Children should never be the sole caregivers for a puppy or dog, however; adequate adult supervision prevents most accidents from happening, whether they are housetraining accidents or an unexpected play bite from an exuberant puppy.

Supplies

Labrador Retriever puppies don't need a lot of supplies, especially for the first few months. Purchase or borrow the essentials before your puppy comes home. Taking a trip to the pet store with an eight-week-old puppy in your arms is never a good idea. He will not be up to date on all of his vaccinations yet, and exposure to other dogs and their germs can lead to expensive, avoidable bills.

Bed

Your Lab puppy typically won't need a fancy dog bed in your house. This mouthy breed seems to think that a comfortable bed is made specifically for him to teethe on, and your big investment in a doggy bed might need to be replaced regularly. Until your puppy is older and more reliable, and until he isn't using everything in sight as a teething ring, you don't really need to give him a separate bed. Save your money for when he grows up

and doesn't need to be constantly monitored for inappropriate chewing. Most breeders and experienced Lab owners crate their puppies and young dogs at night so that housetraining accidents and destructive teething are prevented.

Collar

Because of the Lab's rapid growth, an adjustable collar that will grow with your puppy is a good investment. Still, you should plan to buy two or three collars as he grows. A rolled leather collar will prevent tearing, flattening, or matting of the hair around his neck; these, however, can be expensive, and you might want to wait until your Labrador Retriever puppy has reached full physical maturity before buying his "big boy" collar. If you can place two fingers between the collar and his neck, the collar is the right

Most likely, the breeder will recommend a specific food that your puppy is accustomed to eating.

size for him. Your puppy should not wear a collar in his crate if you decide to crate train him because it can snag on crate doors or ventilation windows.

Crate

Your puppy's training—housetraining and obedience lessons—will all progress much more quickly if your puppy has his own crate. Several options are available. Some are hard, molded plastic with plenty of wire "windows" and doors for ventilation; others are all wire and either fold up suitcase-style or not; still other crates are made of heavy-duty canvas, easy to move around the house and collapsible for ease of travel. However, because heavy-duty canvas and nylon crates can be destroyed by a Lab, supervision will be necessary if you choose to use this style crate.

The importance of a crate, which will be your puppy's "home away from home" and his private den to sleep, cannot be overemphasized. When his family is away, your puppy should be crated so that he doesn't get into trouble. A Labrador Retriever puppy's middle name could be "Trouble," and for that reason, your job as his owner is to keep him away from temptation.

Because a Labrador Retriever puppy grows so quickly, some crates now have wire inserts that allow them to be adjusted depending upon the puppy's size. Buy a crate that will be big enough for an adult Labrador to lie down, stand up, and turn around in comfortably; it may seem huge for your new little guy, but he'll need all that space as he grows.

Decide if you'll want a crate pad or mat for your puppy. Some of my dogs have appreciated the extra consideration, others have shredded crate pads, and still others have "rearranged their furniture" and tugged their mats to a far end of the crate so that they could sleep on the crate floor itself rather than on the comfortable cushion I provided. Most puppies, however, consider a crate pad as just another chew toy, and you might come home to find fluff strewn throughout your home. Many Labrador Retriever breeders advocate putting only newspaper in the new puppy's crate until that puppy is housetrained. If your puppy shreds or eats the newspaper, he is less likely to suffer any lasting or serious gastrointestinal upsets.

Training Tidbit

This is a breed that will definitely work for food. Start to train your puppy as soon as you bring him home. Use his kibble for a training lure; this will prevent unnecessary weight gain. Simple commands, such as learning to walk on a leash, are easy to teach to a food-motivated Labrador Retriever. At first, clip the leash to his collar and let him drag it around the house and yard. Only do this under constant supervision to prevent accidental injury or strangulation should the leash get tangled or caught on something. Encourage him to focus on the food in your hand and not the leash, and soon your puppy will eagerly follow you.

Food

Most likely the breeder will recommend a specific food that your puppy is accustomed to eating, and you'll already know your new puppy's feeding habits. The breeder might even give you a supply of food and tell you how to wean the puppy to a different brand of your choice. Your puppy might be used to eating "communally" with all of the other members of his litter, but you will need to purchase a new water bowl and food bowl or recycle ones that you already own, as long as the bowls are clean and sturdy.

Food and Water Bowls

Stainless steel food and water bowls will last the lifetime of your dog. They are dishwasher safe, and he won't be able to chew the bowls to bits, like he could with plastic bowls.

Grooming Supplies

Two grooming items are "must haves" for your Labrador Retriever: a sturdy brush and a nail clipper. Because your puppy is born with all the "clothes" he will ever need—a double coat as protection from the elements—fancy shirts or frilly jackets just look silly on a Labrador Retriever, although some Lab owners in harsh or rainy climates cover their dogs with "barn jackets" or rain gear to make grooming easier after an outing. If you invest in one of these items, keep in mind that your puppy will grow quickly, and most canine wear will be unusable within a short period of time.

Identification

Your puppy should come home with you possessing some type of identification. Many breeders implant microchips, which are tiny, rice-sized permanent identification with the owner's and/or breeder's name embedded on the chip. You should receive instructions on how to register your dog with the chip maker; plan to do that immediately. (Your vet can implant a microchip during your pup's first visit if he isn't already microchipped.) If your Labrador Retriever wanders and gets lost, he can be scanned with a special wand that most shelters and veterinarians already have on hand, and all of his contact information will be available.

Tattooing is another practical method of permanent identification. Typically, the dog's ear flap, inner thigh, or groin areas are the usual locations for a tattoo that can also tell a rescuer how to reach the dog's owner.

At the least, however, put an identification tag on your new puppy's collar. The tag should be stamped with your contact information, including a current telephone number. A word of caution about tags, however: Don't make your Labrador Retriever a target for a dog thief by putting your dog's name on the tag. My dogs wear several tags when we're out and about, including their rabies tag, the microchip company tag (which tells a rescuer which manufacturer's chip is implanted), and another tag that reads simply "Reward for Return" and has a telephone number. My dogs' names are not on their tags because I don't want someone sidling up to the fence and saying, "Rover, come with me" and having my always-willing-to-oblige dog responding to a stranger's command.

Leash

Your Labrador Retriever puppy might be used to walking on a leash, but most young puppies have to be taught that skill after they go to their new homes. This is another item you'll probably replace many times, so buy an inexpensive cloth leash at first, about 6 feet (2 m) in length. In lieu of a leash, you can use lengths of cotton clothesline to begin teaching your puppy that he will always be connected

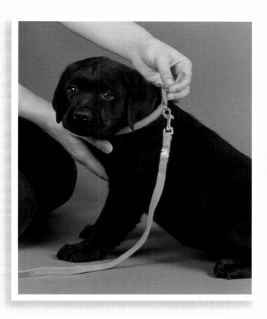

Your Lab will need a 6-foot (2-m) leash when you bring him home.

to you and also how to walk on leash without pulling and without attacking the leash.

Toys

Labrador Retriever puppies love their playtime, and toys are great items to have on hand when your puppy comes home. There are inappropriate toys, however, so be careful what you provide. Stuffed toys become disemboweled in fast order, and those with squeakers are especially enticing to a young Lab. If you buy a squeak toy, especially a plush one, try to remove the squeaker first, before your puppy does. If not, you might have an expensive veterinary bill when the squeaker ends up in your puppy's gut.

The best toys for a Labrador Retriever puppy are hard, chewable toys that are not easily destroyed. As he teethes, your puppy will want to mouth everything from the kitchen table legs to your hands and arms. Provide him with a more appropriate option, such as a Nylabone. Other good options are toys that will engage his brain, like hollow balls where his kibble is hidden. As the puppy rolls the ball, bits of food fall out. Labrador Retrievers are incredibly driven to find food, and your puppy can entertain himself for hours with a "magic" ball that dispenses his food.

Your puppy is born to retrieve, so toys that encourage this instinct will keep both of you busy for hours. Although tennis balls are popular choices, be careful that the felt covers don't wear down your dog's teeth. Other retrieving toys that can double as a tug toy—such as a rubber ball on a rope—will last longer and won't damage a young dog's teeth.

BRINGING PUPPY HOME

Today, most breeders and most airlines refuse to ship puppies long distance as baggage. If you've purchased your Labrador Retriever puppy from a kennel or breeder some distance away, plan to take a road trip. Long drives are easier on the puppy if he has a crate to curl up in and nap, but you'll need to make pit stops every two to three hours just to let him stretch his legs. He cannot hold his urine for much longer; remember, his bladder is about the size of a walnut. Don't feed your puppy before a road trip because you don't want a housetraining accident in your car. To prevent automobile accidents and injuries to you and your puppy, don't leave him unrestrained or in another family member's lap. He may whine or whimper in a crate, but you have just promised a breeder that you will provide security for this puppy—don't break that pledge just because your child wants to hold the puppy during the ride home.

If your trip is a short distance from your home, a sleeping puppy could be perfectly secure in a cardboard box or in the arms of another adult. Best judgment practices and common sense should guide you as you decide how to get your puppy from his breeder to his new home.

Bringing a puppy home is an exciting and confusing time, not just for a new owner and the children in the family, but it's equally disorienting for the puppy. The first day, especially, he might alternately explore his new surroundings (aren't you glad you puppy-proofed the house now?) and put his mouth on all items in his line of

The best toys for a Labrador Retriever puppy are hard and chewable and cannot be destroyed easily.

puppy to urinate and defecate on his schedule until he learns your own schedule. Anticipate that he will chew on anything and everything within reach, so keep shoes, socks, and valuables well out of his way. Give him more appropriate items that are his alone to chew on and destroy.

The first few days and weeks that your puppy lives with you can be difficult or they can be easy, depending on how well you have prepared to add this entertaining breed to your household. An adorable Labrador Retriever puppy won't stay that way for long, however, so get ready from the beginning to train him. He will be active every waking hour, and with his owner's help, can stay out of mischief. Consistency for the puppy can help ensure that you will raise an adult dog with good manners, a dog who will be healthy and happy for life, and a dog who will steal your heart rather than the keys to your car.

vision. Then he might display signs of distress when he cannot find his mother or siblings. He might fling himself at a toy, then collapse and sleep. He might chew the corner of a leather sofa but only pick at the food you place on the floor in his new bowl.

This is the time when huge amounts of understanding, along with cuddling, will reassure your puppy that he is safe, that he is loved, and that he is protected. To ease his transition, show him his crate and let him sleep there. Give him time to play with and bond with his principal caretaker. Expect your

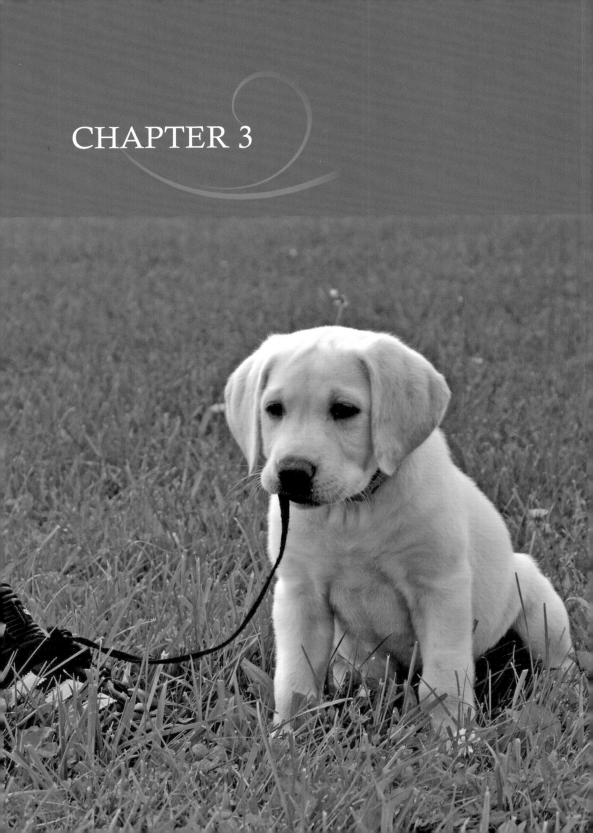

CHAPTER 3

CARE OF YOUR LABRADOR RETRIEVER PUPPY

The proper care and feeding of a Labrador Retriever during his puppy months ensures that he will become a strong and vital dog for many years. And while this breed is generally healthy and easy to care for, there will be operating instructions to follow from your puppy's breeder and your veterinarian. These range from the right food to a recommended vaccination schedule to grooming needs.

FEEDING A PUPPY

Your puppy will already have been weaned by the time she comes home with you. This means that she no longer suckles milk from her mother, with her plump little siblings in a long row alongside her. She has been started on a kibble that probably is softened with warm water and, at eight to ten weeks of age, she is ready to learn to eat without competition from all of those brothers and sisters. Most breeders have a favorite food for their dogs, and your puppy might come home with a few day's or week's supply of dry food. If not, ask your breeder what she recommends, and if there is no preference or if the recommended food is not available in your area, then you'll need to slowly switch your puppy over to a

food that you've pre-selected. Done over a period of seven to ten days, a food switch shouldn't upset your pup's gastrointestinal tract; sudden food changes can cause diarrhea even in hardy Labs.

Types of Foods

Puppy foods come in dry, canned, and frozen varieties. Typically, dry food, which can be bought in bulk, is less expensive than either canned or frozen foods. All dog food will meet or exceed basic nutritional needs for growing dogs, however. Dry kibble for puppies usually has a smaller size than the adult version of the same brand, and crunching on dry or slightly moistened food can help prevent plaque buildup on your puppy's teeth. Also, as your puppy loses his baby teeth over the next few months, dry food might help massage his aching gums.

A high-quality kibble that is nutritionally balanced should be adequate for most growing puppies. Take the time to read labels on pet foods, and choose one that is appropriate for the age and size of your Labrador Retriever. Look for a food that is labeled for "growth." Most bags of food will recommend specific amounts to be fed, depending on the puppy's weight at adulthood. Be careful not to overfeed, however, as most of these feeding charts suggest way more food than your puppy really needs. Particularly as he gets older, you'll need to monitor his weight because Labrador Retrievers gain weight easily.

Feeding Schedule

Puppies typically eat three or four times a day when very young; when your Labrador Retriever comes home, try to follow the same schedule for a few days before you switch him to more convenient feeding times. By 10 to 14 weeks of age, a puppy is ready to eat twice each day. If you are crate training your puppy, feeding him in his crate will help him associate his crate with good things, like his food. Teach him to go into his crate, and place his food bowl in there with the crate door remaining open.

Feed your puppy after the family has eaten breakfast and then at dinnertime. This will accomplish a couple of things: Your Labrador Retriever will come to understand that he is not the pack leader and only eats after the humans in the house have finished their meal, and it reinforces the notion that you are in charge, that everything he needs or wants will come from his owner's hand. This lays some important groundwork in his training.

Treats

Because a Labrador Retriever will try to convince his owner that he is always starving, you might be tempted to satiate that begging behavior with extra treats. While not harmful, treats should be given sparingly (such as offering a few pieces of kibble) to prevent stomach upsets, and only after the puppy has worked for his food. For example, pair his training with the offer of a treat. Ask him to sit and stay before you put down his food bowl

Dry kibble for puppies usually has a smaller size than the adult version of the same brand.

and before he receives a training treat. If you do feed treats to your puppy, try small bits of pared apple, cleaned baby carrots, pieces of low-fat string cheese, or turkey hotdog bits, microwaved and patted dry. Raw vegetables should always be cleaned and cut into puppy-sized bits. Some, like cauliflower, can cause gastrointestinal upset. Limit the amount of treats, and keep the empty calories to a minimum.

GROOMING

While your puppy is young, grooming sessions can help develop the important bond between you and your Labrador Retriever. He will learn that lying quietly for nail trims and ear inspections or standing patiently while you run your hands through his coat earns him a treat, a belly rub, and pleasant, quiet conversation. Moments stolen from busy days and nights, given just to your puppy, help lay the foundation for all of the lessons you will teach your Lab over the rest of his life. The mutual trust so necessary between owner and dog develops during this critical bonding time.

Brushing and Handling

Treats can help calm a squirming puppy when he needs to be groomed. As a wash-and-wear dog, Labrador Retrievers rarely need baths or extensive grooming. Rather, a good weekly brushing keeps the coat—both the topcoat and the undercoat—in healthy condition. Dead skin and shedding hair are more manageable with a weekly brush-out—and Labrador Retrievers are notorious shedders. Some owners decorate based on the color of their Lab, just to help mask the amount of hair in the environment. Shedding is easier to manage if the puppy is taught that brushing sessions mean that he'll get an extra treat.

Brushing a puppy regularly also helps teach him that human hands are not teething rings. For a puppy who insists on putting his mouth on anything within reach, place him into a stand and hold a treat close to his muzzle. The treat can even be a few bits of his regular kibble. As he reaches for the treat, rub your other hand over his body and check for lumps and bumps, stings, ticks, and rashes. This regular examination of your puppy will help him get used to handling by veterinarians and vet techs; also, you will more likely notice any irregularities as your puppy grows. In the future, should he need an emergency veterinary examination, regular puppy handling will help him remain calm no matter whose hands are checking him out.

To illustrate, I had a young dog who somehow managed to flip a raw meaty soup bone over and around her lower jaw, and it lodged firmly between her bottom canines and her jaw bone. Because she was accustomed to handling and because she was trained to be calm and steady during exams, once we arrived at our vet's office, she did not panic when surrounded by half a dozen vet techs and veterinarians. She stood perfectly still on the examination table while our vet used bolt cutters on the soup bone and afterward while all the technicians loved on her. No worse for

the experience, she bounded out the door and into the car and has never had a shaking fit of anxiety at future veterinarian visits.

Nail Trimming

Your Labrador Retriever puppy will also need regular nail trims. Tiny puppy nails are sharp and can catch and scratch anyone within reach, so you will need to teach your puppy to be still while you handle his feet. Begin slowly. When your puppy is exhausted from his long day of investigation, running, playing, eating, finding trouble, eating, pooping, peeing, eating some more, and pulling dirty laundry from the hamper, wait

Grooming sessions will keep your puppy healthy and happy.

until just before he falls asleep, take each paw, and lightly touch his toes. Again, if he objects, a treat or piece of kibble in front of his nose will take his mind off the fact that his toes are being touched. If his nails need to be trimmed, a human nail clipper is usually adequate for the first couple of weeks. After that, invest in a clipper or nail grinder specifically for canines, and learn how to use it.

Canine nails have a soft quick just beyond the obvious curve in the hard nail. This soft tissue is sensitive and will bleed if it's nicked. If the quick is cut during a nail clip, styptic powder will stop the bleeding. Usually the quick is easily seen on the nails of yellow Labrador Retrievers; on black or chocolate Labs, the quick might not be so readily apparent. Some owners leave nail trims up to vet techs or groomers, while others get the hang of trimming their dog's nails in short order.

The first time I "quicked" my black Lab, I lost my nerve and stopped trimming his nails. After that, our monthly trips to the groomer or the vet tech became a ritual we both enjoyed. I no longer suffered from nail trim anxiety, and he got to ride in the car, one of his favorite activities. Whichever method you choose for nail trims for your Lab puppy, the job is easier to perform if your puppy is used to having his feet examined.

While your puppy gets comfortable with a toe-by-toe exam, this is a good time to check his pads for cracks and for burrs, splinters, or cockles that may be embedded either in the pads or between them. Any deep crack that oozes or bleeds should be examined by your veterinarian, but simple burr removal can be done at home, and you'll likely be rewarded with appreciative licks and kisses from your puppy.

After your puppy gets a little older, invest in a pair of nail clippers.

Ear Care

Because Labrador Retriever puppies have a magnetic attraction to water, can sniff out the closest mud puddle or creek, and believe that any excuse to get wet is an opportunity for playtime, check your puppy regularly for signs of an ear infection. The ear flap—or "leather" as it is called—along with hair in the ear canal combine to protect the Labrador Retriever's ear but can also trap irritants and set up the right combination of moisture and inflammation for an infection. Sniff the puppy's ear canal; a yeasty or cheesy odor means that infection could be taking hold deep in the puppy's ear canal. Never pluck the excess hair from your puppy's ear, and don't try to treat an ear infection with over-the-counter medications. Your veterinarian can determine the best treatment if your puppy develops an ear infection and can also advise methods to prevent future ear problems.

Regular ear cleansing, at least monthly, will help your Labrador Retriever puppy to be able to hear the refrigerator door opening for years to come. Commercial preparations, usually a foaming cleaner and a rinse agent are available. You pour these cleansers into your puppy's ear, and the cleanser will dislodge irritants and dirt as it foams. Then, using a soft cotton ball, gently cleanse the ear leather. Squirt the rinse into the puppy ear canal, and then get out of the way. He'll shake his head and run in circles, with ear cleanser and rinse spraying around the room. It's best to do this outside, lest the house take on the scent of Labrador Retriever ear cologne.

HEALTH

There is one other person in your Labrador Retriever puppy's world who will be a critical partner in his healthy growth and development: your veterinarian. Because the Labrador Retriever is by nature a curious whirlwind of a puppy who may try to ingest even the most disgusting yard trash, and is a breed not known to exercise caution during work or play, the person you pick to treat your dog in times of health and illness should be someone you trust.

Selecting the Right Vet

Spend as much time selecting a veterinarian as you did in selecting a breeder. First-time dog owners can ask for references from friends and neighbors and get honest appraisals about their veterinarians. Ask similar questions about a prospective veterinarian as you did of the breeders, such as her experience treating Labrador Retrievers. While most dog wellness protocols and illness treatments are the same from breed to breed, the veterinarian who knows the special talents and needs

Your veterinarian is a critical partner in your Lab's healthy growth and development.

of a growing Labrador Retriever can help throughout your dog's life. Your vet can help with referrals to canine behaviorists for training challenges and retriever specialists if you decide to teach your dog to bring in downed birds, and she can help you manage your Labrador Retriever's weight over his lifetime. If your dog suffers an injury, such as a CCL rupture or a pinched spinal disc, your veterinarian has relationships with canine orthopedic surgeons, rehabilitation specialists, and massage, acupuncture, and chiropractic practitioners.

Fees

Ask your prospective veterinarian about her fees, and keep in mind that unplanned health costs can break the bank. Many vets, once they know their clients, are willing to accept special arrangements for payment plans. Others participate in low-to-no-interest credit plans. For catastrophic health emergencies, some veterinarians refer clients to university-based practitioners, where the costs might be lower. Also, some veterinarians know about breed-specific health care options; for instance, many rescues have funding available for their dogs and puppies who need extraordinary health care, and regional and national Labrador Retriever referral organizations exist for financial support if necessary.

Observe the Staff and Clinic

Talk to the technicians and office managers at your selected clinic. The techs, especially, may become your new best friends as your puppy settles in and you have questions about his care and feeding. Office managers will arrange visits to the practice, so take advantage of their hospitality. Ask the manager, the vet, and the techs how they handle emergencies during the day, and ask who covers the practice for after-hour emergencies. Is this a 24-hour clinic, or will they want you to go to another clinic or emergency care center after their office closes for the day? Find out whether they accept

Before you entrust your puppy to someone, interview the staff and observe the office amenities to make sure that they're what you're looking for.

e-mail questions or appointment requests, if they have separate "sick animal" waiting rooms or treatment areas so that your well puppy won't be exposed to other pathogens, and if they offer boarding and grooming. If the clinic also treats felines, are there separate dog and cat treatment and boarding rooms?

When you visit, is the clinic clean, and does the staff dress professionally? Are all of the doctors members of a professional veterinary association, and are the technicians certified? Do they take continuing education courses and stay current on canine treatment options? Will the veterinarian give you written instructions about your puppy's illness or help you find answers to your questions, either in her reference books at the clinic or from reputable online resources? Ask if she has online references that she considers superior to others. Are there puppy and adult dog care and training books that she recommends? Is she affiliated with a trainer in the area, or can she recommend someone who has experience with Labrador Retrievers? Does she sponsor canine welfare coalitions? If you have questions, how accessible is the office and professional staff?

The proactive owner who plans for unexpected visits along with well-puppy examinations, who asks for advice and carefully considers her options for her Labrador Retriever's continued health and wellness, and who isn't afraid to ask thoughtful questions will become a treasured client. That is the person who a veterinarian and her staff will bend over backward to help.

The First Vet Visit

Schedule your puppy's first veterinary visit within the first few days after he comes home. Most breeders insist on this, and it might even be a requirement of the contract you've

Vigorous jumping before your puppy's growth plates have closed can cause orthopedic problems later on.

signed. Even though your puppy is a healthy bundle of energy, his wellness visits at a young age accomplish three things: If he associates the veterinary office as a pleasant place, he is less likely to stress during an emergency visit; the veterinarian will perform a complete exam and make a baseline assessment of the puppy's health; and any hidden or unknown underlying health issues can be treated before they become a major problem.

The veterinarian will perform a physical examination, listen to your puppy's heart and lungs, check the range of motion of his joints, take baseline weight and height measurements, and check for internal or external parasites. His teeth will be examined for a level bite and for any missing baby teeth and for indications that adult canines and molars have begun to emerge.

Your veterinarian will discuss your puppy's food and give advice and suggestions if necessary. Because Labrador Retrievers grow so rapidly, a large-breed puppy food might be recommended to control growth spurts and minimize the development of hip or elbow dysplasia. If your puppy seems to be on the chunky side, the vet will suggest an alternative feeding schedule, reduced amounts of food, or increased exercise (as if your puppy needs an excuse to play). The type of exercise is important too. Vigorous jumping before your puppy's growth plates have closed can cause orthopedic problems later on, so the veterinarian might advise against high-stress activities.

Also important is a skin examination for evidence of fleas or for allergic inflammation. Labrador Retrievers—possibly because they are in all types of outdoor environments, including grass and pollen—can develop skin allergies. Constant itching and scratching can lead to development of a hot spot on your Labrador Retriever's skin, a painful ugly patch that oozes or bleeds. The veterinarian can help stop a hot spot before it gets infected or needs more aggressive therapy. Sometimes, though, an itch is just an itch, and a puppy's furious scratching is just his need to stop what he's doing and turn his attention to something else. But because fleas can be a vector for internal parasite transmission, if he has fleas or evidence of fleas, like the black detritus left by fleas or obvious flea bites on his skin, the vet will recommend a course of treatment to rid

not just the pup, but your house and yard of these pests.

Vaccinations

The breeder of your Labrador Retriever likely has already performed your puppy's first deworming and initial set of vaccinations. Many puppies are born with internal parasites, acquired from their dam during the whelping process. A puppy who has diarrhea unrelated to a food change, vomits, suffers weight loss or failure to gain weight, or who exhibits signs of dehydration or anemia could have parasites that must be treated. Parasites can be internal or external. Internal parasites include worms (tapeworms, hookworms, and roundworms); protozoa (e.g., giardia); and spore-forming coccidia. External parasites include fleas, ticks, and mites.

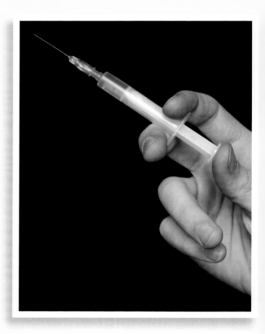

Your puppy will receive certain vaccinations at designated periods.

Your puppy's first exam should include a comprehensive stool exam for internal parasites. Arrive prepared with a fresh stool sample if possible—double-bag your puppy's most recent deposit and take it with you to the veterinarian office.

Puppies are also born with certain antibodies that they've received from their dam, which are special proteins that will protect them for a short time from certain bacteria and viruses. Because this protection wanes as the puppies are weaned, vaccinations are vital to the youngsters' continued health. If the breeder has already given your puppy his first set of shots, she also should give you a copy of the shot record: which vaccinations were administered, the age of the puppy, and the brand or maker of the vaccine.

Because Labrador Retrievers spend so much time out of doors, the vaccines recommended for this breed might differ from other breeds. Also, depending on the activities you engage in with your dog, he could be exposed to certain diseases that can be prevented or the symptoms lessened with proper vaccinations. Regardless of the activities and the area, all puppies will follow much the same protocol for vaccinations against distemper, parvovirus, and rabies. Your veterinarian might also recommend vaccines to protect against infections of bordetella, coronavirus, leptospirosis, tick-borne diseases, and parainfluenza.

Core Vaccines

Your puppy's first shot, a combination distemper and parvovirus vaccine, should be administered at around six weeks of age. This is followed by booster shots every two to four weeks until the puppy is about 20 weeks old. The first vaccine tells your pup's immune system that a foreign body has

Distemper is a highly contagious virus that infects dogs and puppies.

invaded, and a pathogen-specific response is mounted in defense. The booster shots increase the immune response so that the puppy is protected in case of future exposure to a disease. However, if you wait longer than two to four weeks between boosters, the puppy might not have adequate immune protection. In that case, discuss with your veterinarian the best way to proceed with these important inoculations.

Distemper: Distemper is a highly contagious virus that infects dogs and puppies by direct contact with an infected animal or by viral droplets in the air. Canine distemper also affects wildlife, so contact between domestic dogs and wild animals—foxes, skunks, wolves, coyotes, raccoons, and ferrets are the usual suspects—can cause the disease to spread.

Shelters and foster homes have been known locations where distemper spreads, so if your puppy has been housed, even briefly, at a shelter or foster home until your adoption, then pay particular attention to his health.

Infected dogs develop runny eyes and nose, a fever, coughing, vomiting, diarrhea, lethargy, seizures, and/or paralysis. Distemper is difficult to treat in young puppies because they lose nutrients and become dehydrated quickly from fluid loss; the disease will kill a young puppy or dog. Neurological symptoms might remain for the rest of a dog's life if he survives the infection. Because distemper is so serious, and because the signs so varied, only a veterinarian should make this diagnosis, which can be made based on clinical signs and laboratory tests.

No drug is available to kill the virus in a dog who is infected, but treatments do exist to help control the symptoms of dehydration, vomiting, and diarrhea. A puppy or dog with distemper should always be quarantined from other dogs in the household.

The distemper vaccine, however, is highly effective, and is considered a vital, "core" puppy shot. A series of vaccinations for distemper is necessary to narrow gaps in protection that occur between weaning and optimal protection. Even then, some puppies contract and succumb to distemper. To help your Labrador Retriever puppy avoid this deadly illness, don't take him to the dog park, puppy kindergarten classes, or to pet stores or grooming shops until he has received the go-ahead from his veterinarian.

Parvovirus: Parvovirus is another highly contagious canine viral disease that attacks the gastrointestinal system. "Parvo" causes fever, vomiting, and severe diarrhea that may be tinged with blood, or it could be grossly bloody. This virus is spread by direct

By the Numbers

The number of vaccines available and the number that your veterinarian recommends will vary widely depending on where you live and what activities you plan to engage in with your Labrador Retriever. Expect your puppy to get at least three core puppy shots: one for distemper, one for parvovirus, and one for rabies. If you plan to board your dog or take him to puppy kindergarten, your puppy should receive the vaccine for bordetella and other canine respiratory diseases. Most facilities will require these vaccines so that all of their clients' puppies continue to be disease-free.

contact between dogs or between a dog and contaminated stool, yards or other environments, and on people who have had contact with a diseased dog. The virus can live on kennel floors and other surfaces, in food and water bowls, collars, leashes, and on the hands and clothes of people who handle infected dogs. Parvovirus can survive for long periods and is resistant to heat, humidity, and cold temperatures. Because minute amounts of the virus can infect other dogs, parvovirus is easily transmitted on the hair and feet of ill dogs or from contact with infected cages, shoes, and other typically clean surfaces.

This illness causes rapid dehydration, and most deaths from parvovirus happen within two or three days after the onset of symptoms.

Often a diagnosis can be made based on the symptoms, and a fecal test can confirm what your veterinarian may already suspect. If your puppy contracts parvovirus, supportive treatments include fluid and electrolyte replacement and medicine to control diarrhea and vomiting. Despite aggressive treatment, unless a sick puppy's immune system can fight off the viral infection and any other secondary infections that often accompany parvovirus, the puppy can die.

As with distemper, a puppy ill with parvovirus should be kept away from other household dogs. Because the virus is so difficult to kill, isolation helps prevent the spread of infection. After diagnosis, infection-control measures of all of the areas of the home and kennel are necessary. Management includes disinfecting and cleaning the areas where infected puppies have been housed or treated.

Rabies: In most states, your puppy will be required to receive a rabies vaccine when he is about three months old. This is a matter of state and local law rather than a moneymaker for your canine health practitioner. Some veterinarians do not administer the rabies vaccine at the same time as other booster shots. Ask your office practice manager or the vet about her protocols, and request that she not give all of the shots at once if you have concerns about your puppy being overwhelmed with the simultaneous inoculations.

Rabies is one of the most preventable canine diseases—and the most deadly. The virus is spread by saliva from an infected mammal, either from a bite or scratch contaminated with the infected saliva. Rabies vaccination is mandated by most state and local health departments, and today's vaccines are typically effective for three years or more. Depending on location, vaccinating your Labrador

Retriever might be required every year or every three years, but the interval should not exceed three years.

The virus attacks the nervous system in dogs, travels along the nerves, and eventually reaches the brain. Symptoms can be fearfulness or aggression, excessive drooling, difficulty in swallowing, a "drunken" stagger, and finally, seizures and death. Because rabies is more often seen in wild mammals, those animals that are infected might exhibit behavior that is unusual for the species; for example, a rabid raccoon might be seen in the daytime rather than at night, when it usually forages. There is no effective treatment for rabies once the disease develops, so the best way to prevent

Once your Labrador puppy has his core vaccines, you can take him almost anywhere.

the spread of rabies is through vaccination. Because Labrador Retrievers frequent wild habitats during tracking, hunt, or field trial tests, and are more likely to come into contact with a rabid animal than other more sedentary breeds, a rabies vaccination is vital for protection from the disease.

By about three months of age, your puppy will receive his first rabies vaccination. There is no good reason not to vaccinate a Labrador puppy unless the veterinarian shows proof of prior vaccine reaction (which is rare). Because today's rabies vaccine has a longer period of protection, some jurisdictions allow blood titers as proof that a prior vaccine is still effective in an individual dog.

Optional Vaccines

Once your Labrador puppy has his three core vaccines for rabies, parvovirus, and distemper, you'll be able to safely take him to puppy kindergarten socialization classes, to pet stores, to the dog park, and on walks through public and private fields. Obedience classes, doggy day care facilities, and boarding and grooming stores welcome vaccinated puppies, but there are some other puppy shots that you may want to consider. Depending on location and diseases found in your area, it's wise to consult your veterinarian about vaccinations for bordetella, parainfluenza, coronaviruses and canine influenza, leptospirosis, and tick-borne diseases such as Lyme disease.

Bordetella: Along with various upper respiratory viruses, bordetella is commonly implicated in causing kennel cough. This very contagious disease is spread by direct contact with infected dogs or by aerosolization of the infectious agent. Most puppies and dogs with bordetella develop a dry, hacking cough—hence the "kennel cough" nickname. Other symptoms include a snotty nose, lethargy,

fever, lack of appetite, and pneumonia. Antibiotics are used to treat it, but mild cases can be treated solely with rest, good nutrition, and cough suppressants.

Most boarding kennels, obedience training facilities, and grooming shops require that their clients' dogs show proof of bordetella vaccination. Your vet is your best source of advice on vaccinating your Labrador puppy, which can either be done with a shot given twice, about three or four weeks apart, or by an intranasal vaccine squirted into the puppy's nostril. The intranasal bordetella vaccine may

Regular health care is going to be an important part of your Labrador's life.

Consult with your vet about optional vaccines that may be appropriate for your area.

be a combination viral–bacterial vaccine that protects a puppy from both the bacterial cause of kennel cough, and parainfluenza, another virus that causes bronchial illness in puppies.

Parainfluenza: The parainfluenza virus usually causes mild respiratory symptoms like a watery nasal discharge, unless the puppy has a secondary bacterial illness. These symptoms will last around six to ten days. The combination vaccine can be given in Labrador Retriever puppies as young as three weeks old, and the protection from parainfluenza and bordetella infection usually occurs within three to four days.

Coronavirus and Canine Gastrointestinal Coronavirus (CCV): Coronavirus gets its name from the physical appearance of the virus: under microscopic examination, the virus appears to have a halo, or corona, that surrounds it. Initially thought to give puppies

and dogs only a gastrointestinal disease, different coronaviruses have been discovered. In addition to the diarrhea common to one disorder, another coronavirus is now known to cause a canine respiratory condition.

Canine respiratory coronavirus is genetically related to a human coronavirus that causes the common cold. First discovered in dogs in 2003 in England, the virus has now been found in North America, where almost half of dogs tested have antibodies to the virus. This means that those dogs had been infected with the virus at some time during their lives.

Unless your Labrador Retriever puppy has been obtained from a puppy mill or pet shop, or has been housed with large numbers of other dogs, such as at a boarding kennel or training facility, or has been to a dog show, it's unlikely that he has been exposed to canine respiratory coronavirus.

Highly contagious, the virus is spread by aerosols of respiratory secretions, such as from canine coughing or sneezing. It is also spread by direct dog-to-dog contact, and the virus can contaminate kennel surfaces, bowls, collars, and leashes, and has been found on the clothes and hands of people who handle infected dogs.

The symptoms are usually mild and include some nasal discharge, a cough, and/or sneezing. Even without symptoms, an infected dog can shed the virus. Treatment for the disease is supportive, and includes adequate hydration, rest to prevent a secondary bacterial infection, and isolation to prevent the spread of the disease to other puppies and dogs.

A new vaccine helps prevent canine respiratory influenza, also known as "dog flu." This is another highly contagious viral illness that will spread like fire through a kennel, pet store, boarding or grooming facility, and veterinary practices. Dog flu is contracted just like human flu, through direct contact with an infected dog, through contact with contaminated items, or by contact with people who have the virus on their hands and clothes. Symptoms in an ill canine include a runny nose, fever, and sneezing. Canine influenza can become very serious, and infected puppies can develop secondary infections, pneumonia, and bleeding in the lungs. Treatment is supportive, with a good diet, rest, and adequate hydration all part of the prescription. Seriously ill puppies might need oxygen and antibiotics to treat secondary bacterial infections. Most dogs recover, but in puppies or dogs with weakened immune systems or who contract a severe form, the mortality rate can be up to 5 percent.

A vaccine is available for the canine coronavirus that causes a diarrheal illness in puppies and dogs. Canine gastrointestinal coronavirus (CCV) is the second leading cause of diarrhea in puppies after parvovirus, but CCV does not usually cause death. Labrador Retriever puppies who are less than three months old are susceptible, but the vaccine can be given at six weeks, with boosters at 8, 12, and 15 weeks of age.

The virus is contracted by contact with the feces of infected dogs, and because Labrador Retrievers will eat anything and everything, including and especially the grossest dog poop they can find on their daily exercise walks, puppies are vulnerable to CCV infection. The diarrhea associated with CCV is usually very mild unless a co-infection of parvovirus exists. Because there is no way to determine the cause of a puppy's diarrhea without stool testing, any diarrheal illness that a Labrador Retriever puppy develops needs to be evaluated by a veterinarian.

Training Tidbit

If you feed your puppy kibble, the food itself can become a valuable training aid. Labrador Retriever puppies will eat anything, and proper weight management is a lifelong goal. Rather than using high-calorie training treats, a few bits of kibble can be used in each training session as a reward for good behavior. Teach the puppy that when he is still and calm while you touch his toes, he'll get a bit of his favorite food. Soon you'll be able to trim his nails while he waits patiently for his treat.

Like other viruses, there is no specific treatment for CCV. If diarrhea is severe, water can be force fed or administered intravenously or subcutaneously. Keep infected puppies away from other dogs, and let the ill puppy rest until CCV has run its course, which usually takes just a few days. Commercial cleaning disinfectants are effective on the virus, and the puppy's bedding and living areas should be cleaned.

Leptospirosis: Depending on where you live, your Labrador Retriever puppy may need to receive the vaccine for leptospirosis. This bacterial disease has been seen more and more frequently in Labrador Retrievers, especially those dogs who perform hunt and field work. The bacterium spreads through the urine of infected wild animals, and Labs can come in contact with leptospirosis from contaminated water, soil, and urine. The bacteria can enter the dog's body through a cut or scratch in his skin, through mucous membranes at his eyes, nose, and mouth, or by drinking or swimming in contaminated water.

The Lyme vaccine will help protect your dog from this tick-borne disease.

The symptoms vary from nothing at all to fever, vomiting, abdominal pain, diarrhea, refusal to eat, severe weakness, stiffness, severe muscle pain, or inability to conceive. The younger the puppy, the more serious the symptoms, but the illness is treatable with antibiotics. Recovery is rapid if the disease is caught early, but organ damage can occur.

Leptospirosis is a disease that your puppy can give to you, so your veterinarian may suggest that anyone in the home who has had contact with an infected dog also be tested for the disease. Anyone with a weakened or impaired immune system should not take care of a dog diagnosed with leptospirosis. Any high-risk contact, such as cleaning up an infected puppy's urine, stool, and blood, carries a risk of human contamination. Common human symptoms of leptospirosis include headache, fever, and muscle aches.

The best way to keep your pet from getting leptospirosis is to inoculate him if you intend to take him into the field or let him swim in streams, rivers, ponds, or lakes that wildlife frequent. The vaccine, given in two shots about three weeks apart, does not provide 100 percent protection, however. Because rats and mice transmit the disease through their droppings, keep rodent populations under control, and always wash your hands after handling your puppy or his urine and stool.

Lyme Disease: You may wish to consider the Lyme vaccine for your Labrador Retriever, which will protect him from this tick-borne disease. The Lyme vaccine usually is given at 12 to 14 weeks, with a booster shot 2 to 4 weeks later.

Lyme disease is caused by a type of bacteria called a spirochete, which is carried by the common deer tick. Bites from the tick will transmit the bacteria, so for those Labrador Retrievers who romp in fields and woods where Lyme has been found, daily tick checks and removal are vital. The infected tick must be attached to the host puppy or dog for about one to three days before infection will occur.

The symptoms of Lyme disease may not show up in an infected dog for two to five months after the initial tick bite. The most common symptoms are a fever, lameness, swelling of joints and lymph nodes, lethargy, and loss of appetite. Because Labrador Retrievers rarely lose their appetites, any refusal to eat should be taken seriously, especially if that symptom is accompanied by others typical of Lyme disease. The illness can cause severe progressive kidney failure and death, although those side effects are rare. Other dogs have developed cardiac or nervous system diseases after an initial infection with the Lyme bacterium.

Blood tests can help diagnosis Lyme disease, but many dogs will have a false-positive or false-negative result. A "snap test" antibody titer can determine the presence of antibodies to either a prior Lyme vaccination or actual exposure to Lyme disease, and it can be run in most veterinary offices. The test cannot distinguish between exposure and illness, however. If the test is positive for exposure, further tests should be done to see if your dog

Want to Know More?

For detailed information on illnesses specific to Labrador Retrievers, see Chapter 8: Labrador Retriever Health and Wellness.

Sam the Faker

My first Labrador Retriever, Sam, pulled up lame one day and started limping and holding his front right paw up off the ground. Off to the vet we went, and Sam was diagnosed with panosteitis. Of course, because he was such a darling puppy, Sam got lots of TLC from the veterinarian and the technicians. After that, Sam realized that any time he limped, I would put him back in the car and drive off to the vet again. After a couple of those "false alarm" trips, we realized that Sam had learned to fake injuries just so that he could ride in the car.

actually has the illness.

Treatment for Lyme disease is antibiotic use, which must be given for at least 14 days and continue for upward of 30 days. Some dogs relapse after the initial round of drugs and may have to stay on antibiotics for many months; some never rid themselves of the infection and will develop severe arthritis. For those dogs, pain relievers can help with the arthritis.

PUPPY-SPECIFIC ILLNESSES

Thankfully, the Labrador Retriever is a strong, hardy dog. Puppies are resilient and usually bounce back from any of the diseases they may contract. The best way to prevent these communicable illnesses is to practice common sense: Keep unvaccinated puppies out of areas where dogs congregate, like parks and training buildings, pet stores, and public paths. Give your puppy plenty of exercise in his own yard, and feed him quality food, offer fresh water, and give him lots of rest in between his frenzied playtime.

Panosteitis

As a large-boned dog, another illness your Labrador Retriever puppy might ever have is panosteitis. Dogs who grow rapidly, like Labs, experience a type of "growing pain" commonly referred to as "pano." If your puppy suddenly starts to limp or pulls up lame on a front leg, and if the leg seems painful or tender to him, he could have developed panosteitis. He also might develop a slight fever, act lethargically, and go off his feed. A definitive diagnosis can only be made by radiograph, but if your vet has experience with large-breed dogs, then she can probably tell you if pano is the culprit.

Rest, exercise modification, and mild analgesics usually are all the treatments needed for panosteitis. The discomfort goes away as the dog matures and once all his long bones have finished their rapid growth.

SPAYING AND NEUTERING

Your Labrador Retriever is smart. He'll devise any and all methods to get attention, love, and extra treats. He will try to outfox you, and if you're not careful, he will steal everything you own—including your heart. Naturally, you'll want to give him whatever he wants. But one

Spaying or neutering a dog helps prevent the dog overpopulation problem.

thing you don't want to do is allow your dog to breed unless your breeder has specifically requested that your puppy be evaluated as a potential stud dog or brood bitch.

Your veterinarian will tell you the best time to neuter or spay your Labrador Retriever puppy, and while the timing of the surgery is controversial among some enthusiasts, the fact remains that the breed has become so popular that rescue organizations have trouble giving homes to all of the Labs who are already there. There is really no good reason not to spay or neuter your puppy. The best age at which to schedule the surgery should be determined by a conversation you have with your veterinarian, preferably at the puppy's first vet care visit.

Females

In female puppies, the surgery removes the uterus and both ovaries, and afterward, eliminates secretion of the hormones estrogen and progesterone. Thus, your puppy won't experience swelling of the vulva or estrus bleeding, physical changes that occur as a bitch comes into "heat." She won't be attractive to neighboring dogs, and you will be less likely to have stray dogs come looking for her.

Males

Neutering a male puppy is a surgery that removes the testes and epididymis, and the surgery eliminates secretion of the hormone testosterone. A neutered dog is less likely to develop objectionable mounting of people, table legs, or pillows pulled from the sofa. Some researchers believe that a neutered dog is less likely to roam the neighborhood looking for a girlfriend.

Risks and Benefits

There are documented risks and benefits to the spay/neuter surgeries. Several studies demonstrate that spayed females and neutered males live longer than do intact bitches and dogs. Spayed bitches have less incidence of mammary cancer, although if the surgery is done before a puppy is three months old, there may be an increase in urinary incontinence as a result of the surgery. Neutered male puppies won't develop testicular cancer and are unlikely to develop prostate trouble.

In Labrador Retriever puppies, spaying or neutering at a young age has been associated with a slight increase in the risk of a future cranial cruciate ligament (CCL) injury. There also is a minimal increase in the incidence of both hemangiosarcoma and osteosarcoma.

Multi-Dog Tip

If you have multiple dogs in the house, meal time can become a tangle of Labrador Retriever legs. To keep the dogs from developing resource guarding behaviors, in which they each growl or bark at the other dogs who all want a piece of what the other dog is eating, or to prevent outright theft of the young, vulnerable puppy's food, feed them in their crates or in separate rooms. In fact, if the puppy is fed in his crate from the beginning, he is likely to feel secure during the multi-dog mealtime melee. This has the added benefit of making him more comfortable in his crate all the time. He'll associate the crate with the pleasure of eating, rather than the displeasure of confinement.

Breeding is expensive and time consuming, so leave it to the experts.

Spayed or neutered dogs and bitches gain weight more easily, and the incidence of hypothyroidism, another disorder that is seen in the Labrador Retriever, increases.

When to Spay/Neuter

Most researchers suggest spaying after the puppy has reached six months of age but before her first heat cycle begins. Many canine sports enthusiasts and researchers embrace a philosophy of waiting to spay or neuter a bitch or dog until after physical maturity, when the growth plates have closed at the ends of long bones. There is some evidence that suggests that sports injuries are less likely to occur or will be less catastrophic if spay or neuter surgeries are delayed until physical maturation. This maturation in Labrador Retrievers takes place as young as nine or ten months of age or as old as two to three years.

Post-Op Care

Your Labrador Retriever puppy's spay or neuter surgery is a common operation, and your veterinarian has likely performed hundreds of these procedures. Following the operation, your puppy may come home with an Elizabethan collar around his neck, a plastic cone designed so that he doesn't chew at his sutures and rip them out. Similarly, you want to keep your female puppy from licking the suture line on her abdomen. The puppy might not want to eat much at first, or he might be ravenous. If you bring your puppy home the same day, your vet might want him to eat a bland diet such as boiled chicken pieces mashed up with white rice. Don't let your post-op patient jump on you, the children, or the furniture, but do give him plenty of time to sleep off the effects of the anesthesia. This might take up to 24 hours, but soon your puppy will be back to his or her old self.

Decide on the best time in your puppy's development to have the surgery done, commit to the decision, and know that this is the single most important thing you can do, not just for your puppy but for the Labrador Retriever breed as a whole.

CHAPTER 4

TRAINING YOUR LABRADOR RETRIEVER PUPPY

A Labrador Retriever puppy is like a sponge: He will soak up his lessons, he'll remember them for a while, but then it's as if all of your hard work—the behaviors and commands you have taught him and the gains you've made to keep him out of the garbage or off the sofa—oozed out of his brain like water seeping out of a dishcloth. Don't be discouraged; your puppy is just being a puppy. But the importance of training early and often cannot be overstated. An active, intelligent, and curious breed, a Labrador Retriever puppy will respond to consistent training meted out with affection and patience.

INTRODUCTION TO TRAINING

Remember, this cute little puppy with the huge, pleading eyes will grow up to be 60 to 80 pounds (27 to 36.5 kg) of muscle and cunning. If you don't want your adult Labrador Retriever to crowd you off of the sofa, never let him sit with you or on you while he's a puppy. When the youngster is allowed to sit on his owner's lap while she's on a comfortable couch, he'll learn that the couch is an acceptable place for him. If you don't want a grown dog begging at the dinner table, show him while he's a puppy a more acceptable place where he can sit and wait until you finish your meal. To prevent injuries to guests when a full-grown Labrador Retriever jumps up to greet them at the door, never allow your puppy to jump on people.

When the puppy learns the house rules and the house manners, he will be less likely to run away with the remote control in his mouth, or a loaf of bread, or your reading glasses, or, well—the list goes on. Thankfully, the Labrador Retriever puppy learns quickly, and because he is food- and play-motivated (which means he will work for food or for an extra opportunity to play with his owner), the training of a Labrador can go smoothly.

Positive Training

Never use force or punishment-based training methods. The biddable nature of the Labrador Retriever means that he is willing to learn. Positive teaching methods—whether using food with or without a clicker or enticing the puppy with a special toy—will also teach your Labrador that he can trust his owner and that training is fun.

Labrador Retrievers learn quickly, which means that training this breed usually goes smoothly.

TRAINING CLASSES

Training classes can help the first-time Labrador owner both teach her puppy basic obedience commands and give the puppy an additional outlet for socialization and play. Although an Internet search can identify dozens of canine trainers, put as much time into finding the right trainer as you did in finding the right puppy and the best veterinarian. Ask lots of questions, and listen carefully to the answers from your prospective trainer.

Ask Around

Your breeder and your veterinarian might have relationships with established trainers in your area. Ask friends and neighbors (well, perhaps ask only those who have obedient dogs!) where they took their puppies for training. Visit dog obedience schools, especially those that offer puppy-only classes. Audit a class without your puppy, and ask students and other puppy owners what they like or dislike about the facility. If you have specific expectations for your Labrador Retriever, such as competing in obedience, rally, agility, tracking, or conformation, look for a trainer who specializes in some of those canine sports.

Look for Experience With the Breed

A good trainer for your Labrador Retriever puppy will have some experience with the breed or at the least with other sporting dogs. Because these breeds are such high-energy dogs, creative and cunning, she'll be able to help you head off bad behaviors, like barking, digging, and jumping on guests. A good trainer will expect puppies to misbehave and will have time-tested suggestions to rechannel your Labrador's energy. A good trainer will help you identify your goals for a well-behaved dog and

Consistency

The key to puppy training is consistency. Take time every day to teach your puppy what you want him to know, use the same word for a command, don't give a command without being able to enforce compliance (in other words, don't tell your puppy to sit down when you're in another room and can't see what he's doing), and reward him each time he performs his lessons correctly. Training sessions should be short to match your puppy's attention span; about five minutes two or three times each day is adequate.

will help implement a training plan to meet that list of goals.

SOCIALIZATION

One of the most important goals for your puppy is proper socialization. A Labrador Retriever puppy is insanely curious and excited about his world, and the proper introduction to people, animals, and situations around him will help him learn how to behave in the most disquieting circumstance. The process of socialization will help him learn that the world is generally safe and that he can trust his owner. How and when he is socialized has already begun by the time he moves to his forever home, if the breeder began the process in the whelping box.

Through early handling of the neonate, exposing each puppy to different surfaces and textures, and encouraging play with his siblings, the breeder will have begun the socialization of each puppy in a litter. His formal socialization does not end when he leaves the comfortable surroundings of his first home, however. The impressionable Labrador Retriever will continue to learn how to handle himself throughout the first few months.

By the Numbers

To help socialize your Labrador Retriever puppy, introduce him to two places, two people, and two dogs during each outing. Don't overwhelm him with more stimuli than 2 x 2 x 2 because you don't want him to become too tired or fearful in strange settings or with a crowd of people handling him at once.

Introduce Your Puppy Slowly

Rather than overwhelm the young puppy, introduce him slowly to new places, new people, new animals, and new experiences. Each positive experience will help him grow into a confident adult dog. The journey should be fun for both the puppy and the owner and not a set of physically or emotionally draining tasks.

Take Him Out to Explore

Once the puppy is immunized, begin to take him outside of his home and yard to explore and make new friends. Plan to spend no more than an hour on each excursion; any longer and your puppy might be too tired, fall asleep, or become cranky and unable to learn to make a positive association during a novel experience. Try to keep introductions to no more than two locations and no more than five people each day.

Keep Your Puppy Safe

To ensure that your puppy isn't exposed to a canine illness, make sure that any new dogs your puppy meets are healthy. Similarly, if you know that a dog has been ill, don't take him to that dog's house or allow him to romp in the yard. Some viruses and parasites lie dormant in environments for long periods, and you don't want to expose your puppy while his immature immune system is still developing.

Observe Dog–Dog Situations Carefully

Not all older dogs are good with puppies, so before planning a doggy play date, or if you meet another dog on the street, ask that owner if her dog is tolerant of puppies. Don't try and force a reluctant dog to play because not all adult dogs appreciate an enthusiastic Labrador Retriever puppy. An over-the-top,

Teach your children how to behave around puppies.

excited Labrador Retriever puppy can stretch the patience of an older dog, so the owners must closely watch the interaction between the puppy and older dog. During your pup's very early life, prevent accidents and emotional traumas before they happen by carefully monitoring rough play. Where the dam would have intervened with her litter of puppies if one got too forceful or dominant, you as the owner now must be vigilant and protective.

Observe Dog–Child Situations Carefully

This vigilance extends to roughhousing between young puppies and young children. Don't allow a toddler to grab your puppy's tail and tug, and watch that older children know how to pick up and hold your puppy appropriately before you allow the pup to be handled. When new people want to crowd around and pet or hold the adorable Labrador Retriever puppy, make sure that he doesn't seem frightened by the attention, and be quick to take him back into your arms if he seems overwhelmed or squirms for freedom.

Don't Push Your Puppy

Don't push your puppy beyond what he is capable of handling, and watch that he always acts comfortably in a new situation. Some signs that you are going too fast in the socialization process include a puppy who tucks his tail under his belly, tries to hide behind you, drops his ears, or pulls his ears back against his skull. If you see your puppy acting fearfully when he is meeting somebody new or is introduced to new surroundings, try feeding treats to him during the introduction stage. Move closer to the new situation if the puppy seems willing, but always intervene and stop if he seems hesitant.

A confident puppy will wag his tail nonstop, expresses curiosity by cocking his head from side to side, and he might "play bow," a singular canine invitation to engage in play. His head will go down, his butt will go up, and his tail will tick-tock back and forth like a fast metronome.

Exposure to Sights and Sounds

Every place your puppy goes and every person he meets is an opportunity to socialize him, to teach him that excursions are fun and that other people are safe. Take him to a beach so that he can feel sand under his paws, and let him play at the water's edge. When you visit a sidewalk restaurant, have a small towel for your puppy to lie on while you sit at the table, and let him rest and chew on a small toy.

Walk to a local park and picnic, and take your puppy's kibble so that he can enjoy a meal in a different location. Introduce him to people who wear hats or have beards. Let him watch bicyclists and runners, but don't allow him to give chase. Visit drive-through windows at dry cleaners and fast-food restaurants and banks.

Sound exposure is also important in the socialization process. Labrador Retrievers are hunting and retrieving dogs, and they are expected to remain calm when a gun fires over their heads. During thunderstorms, don't coo and cuddle a fearful puppy. Instead, say in a light voice, "Oh, you silly puppy. Let's watch the storm." Sit by a window and let your puppy experience the sights and sounds of a thunderstorm. Recent research has suggested that dogs who are truly thunderphobic have increased amounts of cortisol, a stress hormone, in their bloodstream. The owner who doesn't react fearfully to a storm can raise a puppy who

Your puppy should be exposed to people and other dogs.

A well-trained Labrador is a joy to live with.

is less likely to be storm reactive, a puppy who won't have a biological stress reaction to lightning or pops of thunder.

CRATE TRAINING

In between these socialization outings, your puppy needs his own private place at home to crash and sleep, to get away from the sometimes confusing world of rules and new experiences, and to eat his meals in peace. His own crate can be your puppy's retreat space, but the crate will also be an important tool as he learns self-control over his bladder and bowels.

Types of Crates

A crate can be hard plastic, study wire, or a wooden, furniture-grade enclosure with adequate ventilation and with no sharp edges that could injure your dog. For a puppy, especially a Labrador Retriever who will need more room as he grows, get a crate that will be big enough for the adult-sized dog rather than the little puppy. Some crates come

with a divider that can be moved so that as the puppy grows, the space can be enlarged. Some puppies do well with a crate pad on the floor of the enclosure, and others will shred anything that is put into their crate.

Crate Location

Decide on a location for your puppy's crate. Some owners place the crate in a kitchen area so that when the puppy is crated, he is still in the middle of the household action. Others will put the crate in the family den or living room for much the same reason. Most owners of new puppies put the crate in the bedroom of the principle caretaker, only because it's more convenient, and a whimpering puppy can be heard more quickly in the middle of the night, taken out to potty, and put back into his crate to sleep again.

How to Crate Train

If you feed your Labrador Retriever puppy in his crate, he will associate the enclosure with something really yummy, and he is less likely to resist crating. Also, the puppy who travels in a crate in the car is less likely to be injured in an accident, and he won't be as stressed during hospitalizations for spay or neuter surgery or other illnesses if he is used to a crate at home.

Because the primary purpose of a crate is to housetrain a puppy, he will not need a soft and cuddly pad or bed until he begins to control his bowels and bladder in the crate. A healthy puppy will want to keep his surroundings clean and will not want to soil his own sleep and lounge area. To help the puppy learn his potty skills, develop a schedule and stick to the same routine.

HOUSETRAINING

Puppies pee and puppies poop, and they do this all the time. Managing your puppy's schedule should be the highest priority for a new owner because the fewer mistakes he makes in the house, the happier you will be. The more success you both have while he learns the appropriate potty location, the more freedom he will get. The more freedom he gets, the more he will interact with his world and his people. The more interaction he is allowed, the more social skills he will develop.

Children and Crate Training

Make sure that any children in the house know and understand that if the puppy is in his crate, even if the door is open, the puppy should be left alone. The crate is the puppy's private quarters, and if he crawls into the crate for some "leave me alone" time, the children should honor his needs.

How to Housetrain

This all sounds pretty simple, but at first, it really isn't. The process of housetraining your puppy requires commitment on your part. To begin, introduce your puppy to his new crate; entice him through the crate door with a high-value treat like low-fat string cheese or a bit of apple. Let him come and go into and out of the crate under supervision, then take him outside to his designated potty place. When he squats and eliminates, throw a party—tell him what a good boy he is, and use the words you want him to association with proper elimination behavior. "Good pee," "good poop," "what a smart puppy you are to potty there," said in a happy voice, all will convey to the puppy that he is a genius. Take this opportunity to play, but do not allow him to engage in any play until he has finished his potty duty.

After he has played, explored, retrieved a stick over and over, and when he is tired, put him back in the crate and shut the door. He may whine or pout or whimper or bark, but these little protestations can be ignored. Soon he'll probably sleep for a couple of hours. As soon as he wakes, he'll make a fuss and demand to be let out of the crate. Even if this is in the middle of the night, pick him up and carry him outside the house in your arms to avoid those "almost made it" moments. Place him down at his special spot, and as soon as he eliminates, again praise him for being such a good puppy.

Plan to take your puppy outside after every meal, after every nap, and right before you retire for the night. This will help your puppy learn self-control, and he knows that if he whines, you will attend to his needs. Housetraining is a partnership and goes much more smoothly when the rules are followed to the letter. A young Labrador Retriever should be housetrained after a couple of weeks of this regimen, but at around three to four months, your puppy can relapse.

The process of housetraining requires commitment on your part.

Dealing With Distractions

As your puppy gets older and more curious, when he is taken outside he will be more distracted by the interesting details of his world. He might need to attack the garden hose or chase a butterfly instead of following the potty rules. When this happens, don't let him take all day. Instead, give him the usual amount of time to potty, and if he does not take advantage of this opportunity, take him back to his crate. He'll quickly realize that a nonproductive outing has led to his reconfinement. Give him 20 to 30 minutes of crate time before you scoop him up and take him out again. If you have a particularly stubborn or distracted Labrador Retriever, this sequence might be repeated over the course of an hour or two before he realizes his error. He can be taken outside and praised with positive reinforcement for immediately tending to his job of outside elimination.

Dealing With Accidents

Each "accident" that happens inside the house or in your puppy's crate is almost always a failure on the part of the human in charge, either because of household distractions, not being attentive to a whimpering puppy, or expecting the puppy to contain himself in the crate for far too long. If your Lab does have an indoor mistake, never punish him. Calmly interrupt him in the act; if possible, carry him outside to his designated area, and use your potty words. If you're too late for this, admit the mistake is your own and ask your puppy for forgiveness. Tell him that you'll try to be more attentive, clean up the mess, and don't give your puppy so much freedom.

A fairly common mistake on the part of Labrador Retriever owners is to send the puppy out to potty and then play, either on his own or with the kids. The puppy tumbles back through the door, maybe in a tangle of children, and his potty duties just didn't get done. After all, play is always more important to a Labrador Retriever puppy, with or without his owner. Or, you might be tempted to stand at the door, a treat in your pocket for praise, and send the puppy out by himself. Unsupervised, you won't know if he did or did not eliminate, but he will understand that when he comes back in the door after a minute or two, he gets a treat and praise. This can set

the puppy up for failure and cause him to backslide in his housetraining.

BASIC OBEDIENCE COMMANDS

In addition to housetraining, there are several basic obedience commands that a Labrador Retriever puppy should learn. Some of them are used to manage objectionable behavior, and some will keep your puppy out of harm's way. All of them will help him grow up to be an obedient adult dog, one who will be welcomed and enjoyed by neighbors, friends, and family.

Come

Whether you want a dog who will go to the end of the driveway, pick up a newspaper, and bring it back to the front door, or whether your puppy escapes out the gate and decides to run and visit all the neighbors, the *come* command and the associated behavior can either keep your dog out of trouble or give him a job. Because the Labrador Retriever is so energetic, any task he performs will give him satisfaction and keep his mind engaged.

How to Teach *Come*

The *come* is one of the most important commands a Labrador Retriever learns, a foundation skill that the puppy will work on for many months, if not years.

1. To teach the *come* command, clip a light cloth leash or clothesline to your puppy's collar and let him drag it behind him.
2. Once he is used to dragging the leash behind him, pick up the end and just hold it, and follow him around the yard. Let your puppy become accustomed to your presence, and he'll begin to understand that the two of you are attached.
3. Next, begin to walk backwards and encourage him to come along. Entice

Your Lab puppy should learn several basic obedience commands.

him with treats you keep in your pockets. When your puppy whirls around and comes running, reward him with a jackpot treat, something especially yummy, and give him lots of praise. Remind him again that he is the smartest puppy in the world.

4. Begin to pair his behavior with the word "come," and reward him every single time that he responds appropriately. Even if he just looks at you, reward him. Use an upbeat tone, and show him what you want. Gently tug and back up. Make this a game, and your puppy will play along.

One word, said one time, is a good rule to follow once the puppy knows the command. Don't stand there and holler, "Rover, I said come, come, come, come!" All you will teach him is that he doesn't have to respond until you've said the command word multiple times. Also, never call your puppy to you and then yell at or discipline him when he obeys the *come* command; he'll just associate the command with a negative consequence. If he behaves badly and needs a time out, then go and get him, pick him up, and put him in his crate for a few minutes.

Down

The *down* command falls under management skills right now, rather than an obedience skill. The puppy who learns to down is less likely to get underfoot during busy times. This is a useful command to use during dinnertime: If the puppy is taught to down, he won't be sitting next to the table, his drool dropping and pooling on the kitchen floor. The puppy owner who teaches her dog to down on command will have more control when there's an apple pie on the counter that the puppy is eyeballing or when the puppy cannot contain his excitement when a visitor rings the doorbell.

How to Teach *Down*

Down is also one of the easiest commands to teach a young puppy.

1. With a yummy treat in your closed hand, hold it at the puppy's nose.

2. Once he notices the treat, slowly move that hand down toward the floor. The puppy will follow the hand that holds the treat.

3. Once his head follows your hand, stretch the treat along the floor. The puppy will follow until his body is flat on the ground.

4. Then open your hand and allow him to eat the treat. Tell him how smart he is, and repeat the process. Begin to pair the action with the word "down."

He may want to sit up and lunge toward the hand with the treat. Put your free hand on his shoulders to prevent him from sitting up, but don't push him into a *down*. You only want to restrain his tendency to sit up and jump forward to get the treat. Your puppy is figuring out how to get that tasty

Training Tidbit

When training a young puppy, use the "20 times 20" rule: Repeat the command 20 times a day for 20 days in a row before you expect the puppy to understand what you want. Break up the training plan into mini sessions: Ask your puppy to sit five times in a row; do that four times a day for 20 days, and by the end of that third week, your puppy will reliably know what he's supposed to do when you say the word "sit."

The *sit* command is an easy one for most dogs to learn.

goodie, so never punish him for putting on his thinking cap. Encourage every effort he makes, and once he goes into a *down*, praise him for being such a smart dog and give him the treat. Train this action for a couple of minutes several times each day. If your Labrador Retriever puppy loves a particular toy, use the toy as an enticement. Once he is in the proper *down* position, offer the toy, then release him from the *down* and play a game with him.

Sit

The *sit* command is used so frequently that your puppy might come to think that his name is "Sit" rather than "Spot." Like the *down*, the *sit* is easy to train, and this behavior will allow you to manage your puppy's other antics until he is old enough to have self-control in certain situations.

For example, when the puppy hears a knock at the door and runs to investigate, then jumps on the visitor, he is learning that it's okay to

jump up on anyone who comes to call. For now, his enthusiasm will be easier to manage if he is taught to sit when the door opens.

How to Teach *Sit*

1. Get down to the puppy's level, either sitting on the floor next to him or in a chair as the puppy stands next to you.
2. Hold a treat close to his nose and let his head follow the treat as you slowly move your hand up.
3. As his head moves up, his butt will lower until he is sitting. Immediately give him the treat, praise him for his intelligence, and repeat.

Make sure that you don't hold the treat so high that he jumps for it; instead, hold it just high enough so that he must stretch his neck. Begin to pair the command word with the action: As soon as his rump contacts the floor, tell him "Good *sit*" in a happy tone of voice, and give him the treat. Make this a game, and it will become one that even the youngest children in the family can play with the puppy. Because the Labrador Retriever puppy will work for any tidbit of food, he is a willing participant in the *sit* game.

Repetitions are important, so train this behavior several times each day for a few minutes during each training session. This is a command that you can reinforce during other activities too. Let your puppy follow you from room to room, and teach him that he can sit next to you whether you are watching television or folding the laundry. You are beginning to teach the puppy that when you tell him to sit, you expect him to follow your command no matter where you are and no matter what else might be happening in his vicinity.

When visitors arrive, tell your puppy to sit away from the door. (Keep a light line attached to his collar, because he will want to rush the door and give the company his personal Labrador Retriever greeting.) Remind the excited puppy that his job is to sit and wait with a gentle, "Oh, oh, I said sit." If the command is reinforced every time you want your puppy to stay away from the door, he is less likely to make a run for it when the door opens.

Leash Training

As soon as you bring your pup home, help him get used to a light line or leash before you ever try to walk him on lead.

Before You Leash Train

Clip a very light cloth leash to his collar and let him drag it behind him under your supervision. The puppy might attack the leash, he might pick up the end and carry it around in his mouth (very proud of himself), or he might try to chew on the end. If he mouths the leash, gently remove it from between his needle-sharp baby teeth, tell him "Give," and drop the leash.

Want to Know More?

For more intermediate obedience commands, see Chapter 9: Labrador Retriever Training.

The added benefit of keeping him on a light line is that you will have something to grab when he decides to run through the house with your cell phone or your wallet in his mouth. Stop him gently, say "Give," and take the item away. This will begin to teach your retriever that he must deliver to your hand anything that you ask him to fetch.

Once he is used to dragging the leash behind him—you'll know because he won't be so intent on maiming or killing that "thing"—pick up the end and just hold it and follow him around the yard. Let the puppy get accustomed to your presence, and he'll begin to understand that the two of you are attached. Don't insist that he go in the direction you want to walk; he's still too young for that. Stop the lesson after five or ten minutes, then see if he will follow you while he's still on leash. Walk backward, squeal, clap, and encourage him to come along. Entice him with the treats that you keep in your pockets. If he digs in his hocks and objects to walking with you, then he's probably still small enough to be picked up and carried. Pick him up, walk a few steps, and try again.

When he whirls around and comes running toward you, reward him with a jackpot treat, something especially yummy, and give him lots of praise. Remind him once again that he is the smartest puppy in the world for coming to you. Begin to pair this behavior with the word "come," and reward him every single time that he responds appropriately.

How to Leash Train

Once your puppy has received all his vaccinations, you'll want to take him out on the town and show off your adorable Labrador Retriever. You've seen other people walking their dogs in and out of town, and it's a lovely sight: The dog obediently walks next to his owner, the owner can stop and chat with passersby, and the trained dog stands quietly until the walk resumes. You think, "That is what I want to do with my puppy."

Well, hold on. Literally, hold on, sometimes for dear life, while you teach your young retriever how to walk politely on a loose leash. Prepare your shoulders and back and legs, because he will try to pull you over in his rush to investigate every shrub, dog, and squirrel. The first time you take your puppy outside your yard, his sniffer will engage in overdrive. His brain might hear you plead, "Wait, sit, no, down, this way, come on puppy," but what he really hears is "blah blah blah." Teaching a dog how to walk politely on his leash is a behavior you will train and then retrain every time you take him into a new situation.

You have spent several hours or days letting the puppy drag his light line or leash around the house and yard. He knows that he is tethered to you, and you've made sure that the connection is always positive by giving him a small treat, a toy, and happy verbal praise and loving pats whenever he runs off to the end of the line and immediately comes back. Now it's time to teach him that pulling, tugging, or biting the leash are not acceptable behaviors. He needs to learn that he should walk with you, not against and away from you, when you're holding the end of the lead.

Your puppy should wear a flat buckle collar while he's learning polite leash walking.

1. Attach the leash and say, "Let's go."

2. The instant your puppy pulls ahead, stop in your tracks and don't move.

3. He might receive a jerk when he gets to the end of the line, but as soon as he stops to look back and you feel slack in the line, give him your verbal marker, "Yes," or if you are clicker training, give him a click followed immediately by a treat. He'll bounce back to you to get his goodie.

4. Follow this procedure every time you have him out on the leash. Practice the "be a tree" principle: When the puppy pulls, stand still as a tree until he stops the unwanted behavior and returns to your side.

5. Every time he comes back for his reward, resume the walk, and every time he pulls, stop and wait him out.

Your objective is to convince your puppy that you are the most exciting person he will ever encounter on a walk and that he does not need to investigate every blade of grass or every passing dog. If another person or dog approaches, tell your puppy to sit. If he's too excited to sit and wait while someone passes, start walking in the opposite direction. The puppy will think you've invented an exciting new game, and he'll run with you to find the party. When he catches up, stop and reward him with a cookie.

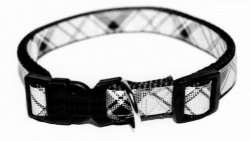

Your puppy should wear a flat buckle collar while he's learning polite leash walking.

Leash Problems

Even though you will begin to train your puppy to walk nicely by your side, Labrador Retrievers are notorious for their ability to forget their leash manners. However, consistency with the command and reinforcement of proper behavior are the keys to teaching your Lab puppy his leash walking duties. If these manners are neglected, the playful puppy will grow up to be an adult Labrador Retriever who is physically stronger than his owner, a dog who will be able to pull a child or an adult along the pavement and cause injuries, and a dog who all too frequently ends up in a shelter because he is deemed "unmanageable."

PUPPY KINDERGARTEN

A Labrador Retriever puppy's socialization, house manners, and obedience training can go more smoothly if his owner invests the time and patience necessary to train him. Puppy kindergarten classes are terrific resources for owners because Labrador Retrievers are incredibly social puppies. Any outlet for exploration and play, combined with simple lesson plans that are easy to follow between sessions, gives the Lab puppy a head start in his training. Before jumping into a class, however, investigate the facility.

Get Referrals

Referrals to puppy classes can be found at your veterinarian's office or from friends, family, and neighbors. Search the Internet for trainers nearby who use positive training methods. Steer clear of trainers who use force or punishment to teach puppies. Also, expect a good puppy kindergarten class to offer a good amount of simple play and socialization time for the puppy. Some formal lessons might be incorporated within the context of play.

Observe the Facility

Visit different facilities and audit a class before you enroll your puppy. Look for a class where the owners are smiling and watching their puppies run and tumble. The class might seem to be a confusing tangle of puppies of different sizes and temperaments, each puppy trailing a light line or shoelace attached to his collar.

Most puppy kindergarten class instructors insist that all of their students have proof of current inoculations. This ensures the continued health of all of the participants. Many instructors have incorporated the American Kennel Club's (AKC) S.T.A.R. Puppy Program into the curriculum. This stands for Socialization, Training, Activity, and Responsibility. While the puppy is learning his

Multi-Dog Tip

A puppy kindergarten class should have no more than eight or ten puppies enrolled. If there are too many puppies in a class, the instructor will have less time to help you with specific problems that you have in training. Aim for a class with about six puppies enrolled, and you and your Labrador Retriever puppy will have plenty of time and space in the class to practice training and to show off. He will be the most beautiful and trainable puppy in the class, so expect the other owners to have puppy envy when you return every week with a puppy who has learned his house manners, how to walk on a leash, and how to sit or come when called.

A puppy kindergarten class will give your Lab a chance to meet and play with other puppies.

expected behaviors, his owner learns what it means to be a responsible owner.

Whether a S.T.A.R. class or not, all of the lessons should be taught by experienced trainers who use positive motivation to teach the puppies how to be quiet and wait for their instructions. General puppy care, grooming, and first aid are topics for discussion with the owners, who should also be willing to show proof of veterinary care, a shot record, and permanent identification for the puppies, as well as a plan for daily exercise with the puppy. Ample class time is given to socialization, and the puppies should be allowed to interact with each other and with the other owners in the class.

Issues Addressed

In addition to socialization games, a puppy kindergarten class will address common issues like nuisance barking, jumping on people, and nipping. The class should include several minutes of loose-leash walking and ample opportunity to practice this with the puppy. The instructor should be able to utilize creative, calm methods to teach a puppy how to walk politely on lead.

The basic obedience commands—*come*, *down*, and *sit*—will be introduced, and during the typically six-week-long class, both puppy and owner will demonstrate the progress they have made from daily practice of these commands.

Age Restrictions

Most puppy kindergarten classes will be restricted to puppies six months of age or younger; older puppies and grown dogs need different lessons and a more structured setting than do young puppies.

PART II

ADULTHOOD

CHAPTER 5

FINDING YOUR LABRADOR RETRIEVER ADULT

The favorite puppy in the world, the Labrador Retriever, grows quickly; that snuggly black, yellow, or chocolate fur ball matures physically by about nine months of age. He may be at full height at that age, but he will add bulk—usually in the form of muscle—for another year or so. The adolescent Labrador Retriever is an awkward, gangly, strong dog with the mindset of a puppy, features that add to the allure of the breed. He needs an owner just as strong willed, someone who will enforce every rule and every obedience command. A full-grown Labrador Retriever usually doesn't settle down into emotional maturity until age three or older.

Because he goes through a distinct adolescence, his training, grooming, and nutritional needs change as the Labrador Retriever ages. That adorable puppy suddenly seems to have no use for his obedience training, and some young dogs regress in their housetraining. Male dogs begin to hike their leg and mark territory, delighting in their newfound skill and taking every opportunity to practice, sometimes in inappropriate locations. Bitches enter their first heat cycle if they haven't already been spayed and can become moody and bewildered. In short, the Labrador Retriever has entered the canine version of teenager angst.

Many first-time owners underestimate the challenges presented by adolescent and young adult Labrador Retrievers, which is the main reason why young adult Labs end up in rescue organizations, are surrendered to shelters, or are rehomed back to the breeder.

Some older Labradors end up in shelters or rescues because of economic reasons—owners have lost jobs and homes or have moved to a location that either doesn't allow pets or doesn't have the space necessary for a large, active dog. Some rescued dogs have been taken from overwhelmed shelters, neglectful or abusive homes, or are recovered from puppy mill operations. Dogs who are ill or injured are surrendered when owners cannot afford the cost of veterinary treatment. And puppies who were not properly trained become strong, out-

Want to Know More?

If you'd rather adopt or purchase a puppy, see Chapter 2: Finding and Prepping for Your Labrador Retriever Puppy.

A full-grown Labrador Retriever usually doesn't settle down into emotional maturity until age three or older.

of-control dogs whom owners either cannot or will not retrain.

WHERE TO GET YOUR LAB

Despite some of these challenges, adopting an adult Labrador Retriever is often the best option for some families. Local breeders sometimes have young adult or adult Labs for placement, either because the dog did not turn out to be a breeding prospect or because they sold a dog who was returned by the purchaser. Most adult Labs who need a new home, however, are adopted from shelters and breed rescue organizations.

Shelters

A shelter is a temporary home, typically run by a governmental agency but sometimes by local humane societies. Many shelters are excellent facilities with policies that support and benefit the dogs and cats in their care. Some have spacious tracts where dogs are free to run and play; most, however, house the animals in size-appropriate runs. Due to space considerations, dogs might not have their own kennel, and overcrowding is always a problem. With space and resources for food and veterinary care at a premium, many shelters have no choice but to euthanize. Statistics show that black dogs in shelters, including black Labrador Retrievers, are much harder to place with adoptive families. A perception exists that black dogs, especially larger black dogs, can be mean-spirited and hard to train. High numbers of black Labrador Retrievers are euthanized each year because of this misperception.

Shelter dogs might not receive the same level of veterinary and behavioral care, only because funds are limited and have to be allocated among all of the shelter animals. One rescue organization estimates that for every Labrador Retriever it places with its network of volunteers, another 30 will be euthanized. Those are horrible odds for any animal, but for the adult Labrador Retriever who just might need a different living situation or some basic veterinary care, the numbers are heartbreaking.

Most of Labs available in shelters will have had all required vaccinations, and spay or neuter surgery will have been performed. Most veterinary costs, which might be passed on to the new owner, are incurred to treat heartworm-positive dogs and for surgeries to repair injuries the dog might have suffered as a stray.

Breed Rescue Organizations

Breed rescue organizations for abandoned, ill, injured, or stray Labrador Retrievers operate around the country. Some of the groups are one- or two-person outfits; others have a large support staff and volunteers. All are operated on shoestring budgets and depend on donations from vendors, veterinarians, and volunteers to continue operations. Many breed rescuers will have relationships with nearby shelters, and when a Labrador Retriever or Lab mix is brought to the shelter, the breed rescue swoops in, scoops up the dog, and takes him to a volunteer foster home. If the dog needs veterinary care, that is arranged for, if possible. Rescue groups will not place dogs—even Labrador Retrievers—in new homes if the dog shows any aggression issues, whether dog-on-dog or dog-on-human. Adoptive families can be sure that temperament has been thoroughly tested.

THE BENEFITS OF AN ADULT LAB

Older Labrador Retrievers can be a much better choice for an individual or family that is set on the breed but that might not be ready for the constant attention that a puppy needs.

Housetrained

Labrador Retrievers who are adopted, either from a shelter or rescue association, are usually housetrained. A busy family that cannot commit to a regular schedule for a puppy's housetraining won't have to rush home and take care of a puppy's potty needs. An adopted adult Labrador might need some time—up to a couple of weeks—to learn his new routine, but once his potty schedule is established, he will not likely have any accidents in the house.

Teething and Chewing

Older dogs will mostly be past other puppy issues, like teething and chewing, although with the mouthy Labrador Retriever, inappropriate chewing can be a lifelong bad habit. These

By the Numbers

Labrador Retrievers are considered adults by the time they are 18 months old. Individual dogs, however, are usually physically mature at nine to ten months old. Mentally, though, this breed doesn't lose those lovable puppy qualities and settle down until age three or more. This is part of the charm of the Lab—he's a playful puppy until he's grown. It also is the main reason why Labrador Retrievers are surrendered to shelters. Consistent training and exhaustive exercise are two main activities that will keep your Lab where he belongs: by your side.

Statistics show that black dogs in shelters, including black Labrador Retrievers, are much harder to place with adoptive families.

behavioral issues, though, are easy to manage simply by giving the dog a toy made specifically for strong chewers, such as a durable Nylabone chew. A puppy might run through the house with underwear halfway down his throat or wrapped around his head, but the older dog will (when trained) politely pick up the dirty laundry and bring it to his owner.

Trainability

Older dogs are easier to train because they are able to focus more on their owners. Instead of a distracted and distractible puppy, an older dog is more willing to learn. That includes the ability to settle into an already established pack with other dogs in the home or into the family's schedule. And, once the older dog does acclimate into

his new routine (which does not take long with the lovable Labrador Retriever), the dog seems grateful for his second chance and reciprocates with love and affection toward his new owners.

Size

An older Labrador Retriever has already grown to his adult size, and his personality is obvious. Puppies often grow to be very different from initial assessments, but with an older dog, what you see is what you get. There are few surprises with the older dog. Because he is already grown, he's ready for more strenuous activities as well. Instead of waiting for growth plates to close or for muscle to bulk up for endurance on long hikes, the older dog can participate in canine sports and family vacations within the limits of any medical conditions he might have acquired or inherited.

Attention

The Lab adult also won't be as demanding as a puppy either. While the young Labrador Retriever will launch himself between his owner and the newspaper she was reading, the older dog is happier curled up next to her and content to breathe her air. He doesn't require the constant monitoring that a puppy would need. He won't root around in the garbage or scarf down a loaf of bread from the counter—well, most won't. But he will need to be monitored for bad habits, just as a puppy would be watched.

Evaluations

Those Labrador Retrievers who end up in shelters either because they were found wandering as a stray or because of owner surrender and then are "pulled" by a rescue organization are the lucky dogs. They will receive comprehensive health evaluations, undergo spay or neuter surgery, and are evaluated by trained foster volunteers. The evaluation includes temperament tests to decide the best type of home for the dog and whether he is good with children, cats, and other dogs. Volunteers can determine if the dog would be a good match for a young, active family or more suitable for a senior citizen. If the dog needs further obedience training or a housetraining refresher course, the volunteers will continue the dog's education in those areas.

Many rescue organizations will place their dogs in a foster home for this period during the evaluations so that the dog doesn't have to live in a kennel. Other rescue groups contract with established boarding or grooming kennels, and the rescued dogs continue to have daily contact with people and other animals. They are exercised and groomed on a regular basis; if the rescued dog has health issues, the organization funds the treatment, if possible.

Fostering

Some rescue organizations also allow a potential adoptive family to "try the dog on," so to speak. Days or weeks might go by before a family and its new dog are truly comfortable together. If the match doesn't work out for either the family or the dog, the rescue group will take the dog back into its foster system.

LIFE WITH YOUR NEW LAB

Potential adopters need to keep in mind some things about an older Labrador Retriever, and most rescues go over these in detail to ease the transition. First, a routine is important. So many older dogs have been stressed just because

Multi-Dog Tip

Most rescued Labrador Retrievers will adapt to the rest of the established dog pack if some simple rules are followed: Feed the new dog in a separate room to prevent food raids; walk the new dog on a leash, without the other pack members, so that he can get used to the surroundings; and expect the other dogs to engage in "snarking" pack behavior from time to time. Gnashing teeth, barking, and racing around the yard together are signs that the dogs are getting acquainted. Vigilance around all of the dogs can prevent most fights from breaking out, however, until all of them begin to adjust to the new member of the pack.

When your Lab is left alone, provide a secure dog-proofed area where he can spend his downtime.

Training Tidbit

A rescued Labrador Retriever might have already received some training, but many have not. Don't try to train a dog who has pent-up energy that he needs to release; instead, take him on a long walk or engage in a vigorous game of fetch to get him in the mindset to learn. Training will progress much more quickly once the rescued Lab is used to his new routine, so give him plenty of time to settle in before formal obedience training begins. Then use tasty, high-value treats like hot dogs and cheese as training lures.

they've lost their former family, and while a Lab is typically a laid-back dog when he's older, he will still exhibit signs of stress. These include panting, housebreaking accidents, pacing, and difficulty settling down on his bed or in a crate. He might not want to eat for a day or two, and he might cling to certain members of the family.

Potty on a Schedule

The dog's new schedule should include potty breaks at regular intervals. Don't just send the dog out into the yard; take him on a leash walk, without any other dogs in the household, and praise him for his potty skills. This one-on-one time will help forge the bond between the older Labrador and his new owner.

Feed on a Schedule

Feed your new dog at the same time and in the same location each day; for a grown Labrador Retriever, that should be twice, in the morning and evening. Don't free-feed because you will not be able to monitor your dog's food intake. He's more likely to have accidents in the house if he is allowed to eat any time he wants. Also, if there are other dogs in the household, they could help themselves to the new dog's food. If the dog is a picky eater, chalk it up to stress. Because Labrador Retrievers love their food, they rarely refuse a meal. Make sure that his food is high quality, and give each dog in the home his own bowl and a separate location for meals. This lessens the chance of food fights.

Exercise Your Lab

Give your rescued Labrador Retriever plenty of exercise. A young adult dog should have an hour of exercise a day, which will lessen any behavior issues. Remember, a tired dog is a happy dog, and a happy dog is more easily trained.

Give Him Lots of Time With You

Rather than adopt a dog, bring him home, and leave him alone during the day, try to give your rescued Labrador Retriever a lot of time with his new family. He will need reassurance that he has found his forever home, and your presence will help prevent the development of separation anxiety.

Provide a Crate and Dog-Proofed Area

When he is alone, at least until he's proven himself trustworthy, provide a secure crate or safe, dog-proofed area in the home where your rescued Lab can spend his downtime. Consider putting the crate in a quiet area, such as the bedroom. He might need an extra potty excursion at night, and older Labrador Retrievers may not have been housetrained using a crate. A soft "woof" in the middle of the night may be all the warning he can muster.

The older Labrador Retriever responds to love and kindness, a warm place to sleep, exercise, good food, and a lap where he can lay his head. Those who take in an adult Labrador, whether from a shelter or a rescue, are heroes to all who love this breed.

Rescue Groups

The Labrador Retriever Club, Inc., (LRC) maintains a list of more than 100 rescue groups in the United States and Canada. Each group has its own board of directors and policies for adoptive families, but many of the policies are standard across-the-board requirements. First, potential adopters are required to fill out an application, which might be one page long, or might be four pages long or more. The application is intended to find out as much about the individual or family as possible so that the best dog-human match can be made. Questions include address, contact information, occupation, type of living quarters, and if there is a fenced yard, as well as names of personal and professional references. If the potential adopter has other pets, the family's veterinarian might be questioned to find out if those animals receive regular, comprehensive veterinary care. In addition, most rescue organizations will send a volunteer to the house to check on the conditions and to see if a Labrador Retriever who is placed there will be secure, kept healthy and free from disease, and have plenty of opportunity for exercise.

CHAPTER 6

LABRADOR RETRIEVER GROOMING NEEDS

The Labrador Retriever's grooming needs don't change much from puppyhood through adulthood. His undercoat thickens and his soft, downy outer coat starts to harden and take on the oily properties that protect him in cold, icy water. Nails thicken and need monthly clipping, and the ears need to be checked for signs of infection on a weekly basis. The most important grooming and health need that often goes overlooked is the dog's dental health, but a regular schedule of dental care keeps the Labrador Retriever's teeth and gums in good condition to catch a ball or retrieve a bird.

WHY GROOMING IS IMPORTANT

Most dogs who are taught from puppyhood to stand for an examination and who don't object when their feet and teeth are examined come to enjoy weekly "hands-on" grooming by their owners. Routine is important to the Labrador Retriever, and his grooming sessions allow him one-on-one time with his owner, which adds to the incredible bond that develops between the two. The day of the week and the time of day are not as important as the methodical commitment to the dog's grooming. It's probably best to devote grooming to that time of day when your dog is tired out and able to settle, rather than during a hectic morning or when he has just exploded out of his crate. Grooming should not be stressful for either the dog or the owner.

Grooming is also a time for the owner to really become familiar with her dog. By putting hands on your dog on a regular basis, you can understand his bone structure, feel for lumps or bumps or ticks, and take action if something isn't quite right.

BRUSHING

Labrador Retrievers don't need fancy coat strippers or blades, nor do they need whiskers clipped or feathers scissored. The best brush for the Labrador is a good stiff-bristle brush or slicker brush, available at most pet supply stores. The dog's short coat is not likely to develop mats or tangles unless he has been neglected for a long time; if necessary, a short-toothed comb can be used to work out mats from the coat. Brushing improves circulation and stimulates his skin and helps remove dead hair, especially during his coat shed season, which might be year round.

Some owners like to use brushes with stripping blades, while other Labrador Retriever owners think that these brushes break the dog's hair rather than brushing out the old dead strands. I've found this type of brush useful during the heaviest shed period. When using a stripper, it's important to stroke in the direction the coat lies, not against the coat, in order to only pull out the already loose hair. Also, if you use this type of brush, never press it too close to the dog's skin, as a wiggling dog can suffer a cut from the very sharp blade.

Brushing will also loosen any dandruff on your dog. If his skin is particularly dry, the addition of fish oil to his diet will help. During the winter months when dry heat is forced into the house, your dog may develop dandruff. A humidifier run in all of the rooms the dog frequents—the bedroom, kitchen, and family rooms—might help add moisture to the air and lessen this type of dry skin.

How to Brush

To brush your Labrador Retriever, have him stand or sit next to you and start with the softer tool:

1. Gently brush his head, ears, and neck.
2. Stroke his tail and brush toward the tip.

With a stiffer brush or hand mitt:

1. Always stroke in the direction of the hair growth, never in the opposite direction.
2. Begin at his neck and withers, and brush toward his rump.
3. Groom each side using a back and down motion.
4. Don't forget the chin and belly, but be gentle on the ticklish areas.
5. Loosen the dirt and dead hair.
6. Follow with a pin brush or damp towel to remove dandruff and shedding hair.

If your dog wiggles, hold him firmly with one hand under his muzzle. Usually, if you can control his head, then his body will be still. For dogs unaccustomed to grooming, proceed slowly and offer him treats and praise for being so brave.

You might be surprised at the amount of dead hair you brush off your dog, but remember, the Labrador Retriever has a double coat. Both the undercoat and the outer hairs shed, and the best way to control the amount of hair in the carpet and on the furniture is by regular brushing sessions.

BATHING

Some owners try to control the shed by bathing their Labrador Retrievers, but bathing too often

Grooming is necessary for a healthy, happy Lab.

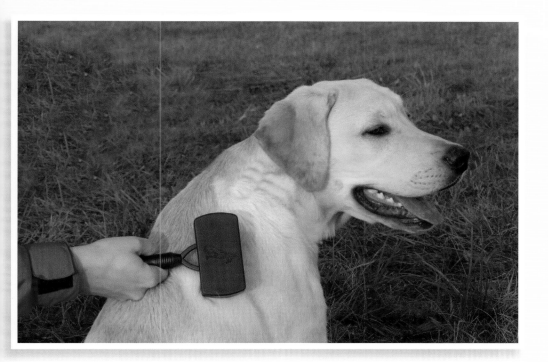

The best brush for the Labrador is a good stiff-bristle brush or slicker brush, available at most pet supply stores.

and with the wrong product can lead to skin irritations and cause the coat to become too soft. Because the Labrador's coat is designed to protect him during cold weather and to repel water during field work and keep his skin dry, if the oils are stripped out by too many baths with a harsh shampoo, his coat won't be functional.

A Labrador Retriever rarely needs bathing if he is brushed regularly and dirt, dead skin, and shedding hair is removed. He should be hosed off or bathed if he has swum in saltwater or in water that might be contaminated with parasites or pesticides; if he's romped, rolled, and wallowed in mud that can't be removed with a brush; if he's been crate confined for too long

By the Numbers

If a dog's oral health is neglected, then by age three he can have a dangerous buildup of plaque and tartar on his teeth and gum line. Because bacteria flourish in a dirty mouth, twice-weekly brushing is the best defense against offensive organisms and can prevent germs from infecting the dog's mouth, heart, liver, and other organs.

and has soiled himself; and if he has a skin condition, such as a contact or environmental allergy, that is best treated by more-frequent bathing.

The best shampoo for a Lab will be a gentle one designed only for use on dogs, and it's best to use a shampoo formulated without harsh chemicals and that will rinse easily. Bubbles in the Labrador's bath only makes for a soapy dog, and it will be harder to rinse his coat completely. An oatmeal-based shampoo is good for the dog with itchy skin; your veterinarian also can make recommendations for different products if your dog has skin problems.

Decide where you will bathe your dog; if you have a tub or shower enclosure with a handheld attachment, the job will go more quickly. Don't bathe a dog in frigid weather in the backyard using the outside hose; warm water will keep your dog from shivering. If he's that dirty, and you can't bathe him indoors, take him to a professional groomer. Inside, place a nonskid mat on the tub or shower floor. Then gather lots of towels and a helper, if you can find a volunteer.

How to Bathe

To bathe your Labrador Retriever:

1. Put dry cotton balls in your Lab's ears to prevent water from entering the canal and leading to an infection.
2. If he resists, keep his collar on him and control his head with one hand, holding the bottom of the collar under his neck.
3. Wet your Lab's coat thoroughly with warm water, starting at his head.
4. Start to lather the soap in around his neck first, then work your way back to his tail. Use your hands to lather the soap in all over his body.
5. To wash his face, use either your hands or a washcloth with a small amount of soap or shampoo and water, and gently work the suds along his muzzle. Keep the suds out of his eyes.
6. Begin to rinse, working from nose to tail, until the water runs clean off the dog and no shampoo residue remains in his coat. Rinse time should last twice the time it took to shampoo the dog.
7. The dog will start to shake himself as soon as the spigot is turned off; try to keep him from jumping out of the tub until he's a bit dry.
8. Vigorously rub him with absorbent towels, especially his head and neck and any other areas where he has folds in his skin.
9. Don't forget to dry his feet because as soon as you let him go, he will run through the house, one end to the other, back and

Training Tidbit

Don't expect your dog to like having his toenails clipped if his feet haven't been handled since puppyhood. Train a reluctant dog slowly: Every time you touch a toe, give him a treat. Break away from the footwork to play a game, or teach him to give a "paws-up" after his pedicure. Finish on a high note, rather than a struggle, cuddle with your dog, and praise him for being such a good boy. Short, daily toe touches, when combined with treats and praise, result in much less stress on his part.

The Labrador Retriever's beautiful eyes are excellent indicators of his overall health.

forth, again and again. You don't want him to slip on a smooth surface because his feet are still wet!

10. Remove the cotton balls from his ears if he hasn't already shaken them loose, and gently dry his ear flaps (but never stick swabs into your dog's ear canals!).

EAR CARE

Once your dog is clean and dry, take the time to check his ears for signs of inflammation or infection. If he and his canine companions perform the Labrador greeting by kissing and licking each other's ears, or if he swims regularly, the moisture can breed germs. Ear infections are a normal part of Labrador Retriever life, and most owners will know how to stop an infection before it takes hold.

If the dog shakes his head when he barks, that can indicate an ear infection or inflammation. Also, if he pulls away when you stroke his ears, or if his ear flap is obviously red, he may be suffering from an ear infection. Gritty, dark-looking material on the ear flap could be mites, but those can only be seen under a microscope. If you suspect ear mites, contact your veterinarian for treatment. A yeasty or pungent smell from the dog's ear canal also can indicate infection or inflammation.

How to Care for the Ears

To keep your Labrador Retriever's ears healthy, take simple steps to cleanse them. Over-the-counter ear cleansers work well, but don't use anything that is alcohol-based because it could irritate the ear. A messy job, it might be best to do this outside. To clean your dog's ears:

1. Hold his head at an angle so that the ear you want to clean is cocked upward.
2. Squirt a small amount of gentle, self-foaming cleanser into the ear canal; a little bit goes a long way, and the more you use, the longer it will take for the ear to dry.
3. Massage the base of the ear, which will help the cleanser travel farther down into the canal.
4. Follow with a liquid drying agent, and again, massage the base of the ear.
5. A cotton ball moistened with the cleanser can be used to gently wipe dirt off the ear flap. Never stick a swab or probe into the dog's ear; because the canal angles, you wouldn't be able to reach far enough with a swab, and the risk is too great that it could break off.
6. Your dog will naturally shake his head, and any cleanser or drying agent will fly out of his ears, so back up and duck!
7. Praise your Lab for being so brave.

EYE CARE

Those big, sad, pleading Labrador Retriever eyes are excellent indicators of his overall health, and an eye examination should be a routine part of grooming. Because working Labrador Retrievers rely so heavily on their excellent vision to mark and find game, watch a dumbbell thrown in the obedience ring, distinguish jumps in the agility ring, and watch for every crumb dropped in the kitchen, preservation of the Lab's eyesight is especially important.

Sporting dogs, including Labrador Retrievers, who work in heavy cover or even household pets who hang their head out the car window during a Sunday drive are especially prone to foreign objects in the eyes. Any dog who paws at his face or who has obvious redness and irritation should be checked for seeds, thorns, dust, or sand under the eyelids.

"Eye muck" or a slight discharge from the inside corner of the eye, isn't necessarily alarming and is easily wiped away with a tissue, a soft, dry cloth, or a moist towel. If the discharge is "goopy," green, yellow, or foul-smelling, or hardens into a thick crust, or if the tissue inside the lids is red and inflamed, take your dog to his veterinarian right away. Eye infections are easily treated, but if the infection is not recognized or treated properly, a dog can go blind.

Some Labrador Retrievers develop corneal abrasions because the lashes on their lower lids turn upward and inward, a condition called entropion. Dogs who have continually red and inflamed lower lids may be suffering from this. A simple "nip-tuck" surgery can be performed that will cure the problem. Other dogs exhibit signs of ectropion, a condition in which the lower eyelid rolls out from the eye, exposing the red membrane beneath the

Eye "Muck"

One of my dogs seems to always have a bit of muck at the inside corner of one or both eyes, and her eye health is absolutely fine. This type of dirt has more to do with her fondness for mud puddles than anything else because she'll dive in head first. If, however, the discharge turns to a more watery consistency, I've learned that she is probably developing an ear infection. At the first sign of the eye discharge, I clean her ears, and by doing so we've avoided some trips to the veterinarian.

lid. This condition is more obvious in breeds like the Bloodhound and some spaniels but is also seen in a hunting dog who has worked all day or in a Labrador Retriever puppy exhausted after a long day of play. If ectropion is severe and leads to continual eye infections or corneal abrasions, a corrective surgery that tightens the eyelid will help preserve the dog's vision health.

How to Care for the Eyes

1. Eye care for the Labrador Retriever is pretty simple and should be a regular part of the weekly grooming.
2. Use a soft cloth moistened with warm water to gently loosen and remove any dried discharge or crust on the lids.
3. For mild eye inflammation, flush the eye for ten minutes with cool water, a sterile saline eyewash, or with artificial tears.
4. Foreign body removal and infections must be treated immediately by a veterinarian.

NAIL CARE

The most difficult part of the Labrador Retriever's weekly grooming probably will be the nail trim, but this is a necessary task. Smooth and short nails are less likely to cause injury to the dog or to his playmates. Also, if your dog participates in canine sports that require jumping, nails that are too long will hinder his ability to plant his paw for take-offs and landings, leading to foot and forelimb injuries. The field-working Labrador Retriever with toenails that are not properly trimmed can have a toe ripped when the nail snags on branches or brush. Inside the house, carpets and floors are more likely to be damaged by a Labrador Retriever's long, untrimmed nails.

Too-long nails can cause the foot to splay and become deformed. Also, if the nails are not trimmed regularly, the vein within the toenail

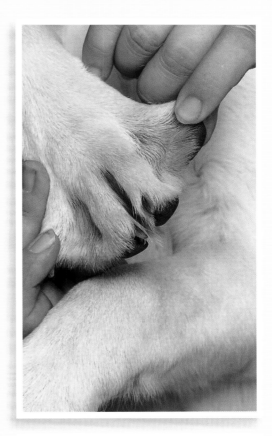

Inspect your dog's paws regularly.

will grow longer and make any nail trim more difficult and painful for the dog. This vein and the very tip of it, called the quick, are difficult to see in dark-nailed dogs such as the black Labrador Retriever. Even some yellow Labradors have one or two black nails, so care is needed when clipping nails to avoid the quick, which is very sensitive because of nerve endings around that area. If the quick is nicked, the vein will bleed, and the dog will experience pain. Keep styptic powder on hand to stop any bleeding; this comes in a powder or a pen, and each works equally well to staunch blood flow from a quick that has been nicked.

Most dogs object at first to having their nails trimmed, so the best way to proceed is to go slowly. Get your dog used to having his toes touched, and every time he is quiet and calm, give him praise and a treat, if necessary. Turn this into a game, and begin to ask for a "high five" paw-to-hand touch. It might take several days or even weeks to get a skittish dog accustomed to having every toe touched on one paw, then on all of his paws, before you can even introduce a nail trimmer or a grinder. Some dogs never become comfortable with nail grooming and need to be restrained during their trim. Some owners are never comfortable trimming their dog's toenails and decide to leave that job up to a groomer or veterinary technician.

Once the dog is comfortable and calm while his toes and paws are touched or held, it's time to introduce him to the pedicure procedure.

Nail clippers come in two different styles: the guillotine clipper, which has a single-sided sharp blade, and a crusher-clipper style, which clips the nail from two sides. To clip the dog's toenail:

1. Firmly hold the dog's paw.
2. Gently squeeze at the base of the toe so that the nail extends.
3. Clip just the tip, being careful to avoid the quick.
4. If your dog jumps or reacts fearfully, reassure him with a treat and soft praise.
5. Even if he objects, do not let him win this game. You don't have to trim every nail, but at least do two or three before you stop; always finish after at least one successful trim so that he will learn that the nail trim is not so stressful after all. He will be less likely to panic prior to each trim if he does not get the upper hand—or paw.
6. If the quick is nicked, apply gentle pressure to stop the bleeding, and if necessary, use styptic powder.
7. When the job is done for the day, give your dog lots of joyful praise and tell him how brave he has been.

A nail grinder will enable you to smooth your dog's nails and round them off at the edges, rather than leave a straight cut that can sometimes snag even after a proper trim. Getting a dog accustomed to the grinder might take longer, but grinding the nails rather than clipping them will allow you to slowly take nail off, and the quick can recede more rapidly. For the dog who has particularly long nails that have been neglected, a grinder can be a more humane process, and just a moment of grinding every day will remove longer nails quickly without damage to the quick.

Just like getting your dog used to having his toes touched, he will need to become acclimated to the sound and then the feel of the grinder. At first, touch the toes with the grinder off, and when your dog is comfortable,

Multi-Dog Tip

Grooming all of your dogs in a multiple-canine household might take more time, but it's important to give each dog his due. Designate an hour per dog per week and establish a routine: teeth, ears, eyes, coat, and toes. Once you get better at each task, the grooming will go smoothly and the rest of each dog's hour can be spent in one-on-one cuddle time, a special walk, game, or other activity. This promotes and strengthens the bond between each individual dog and owner.

Dental care is one of the easiest chores to perform.

turn on the grinder—away from him—so that he can hear the sound. Depending on his temperament and sensitivity to the sound, you may need to be generous with treats while he becomes accustomed to the smell, sight, and sound of the grinder. Go slowly, and never try to grind a squirming or fearful dog. Once your Lab is familiar with the sound, and after he knows that each time the grinder is turned on, he will get a treat, you are ready to proceed.

1. Hold your dog's paw and support the nail to help reduce vibration to the dog's foot.
2. Lightly touch the grinder to one nail without applying pressure, and then give the dog a treat and lots of praise.
3. Work up slowly to touching each nail on a paw, then all of the nails on all paws, and be generous with praise and/or treats.

4. Next, hold the grinder band against the nail for just a couple or three seconds. Don't apply pressure to the nail; rather, allow the grinder to do its job.
5. Try to grind in a swift, level motion on the underside of the nail.
6. Repeat every seven to ten days, which will cause the quick to recede and allow more hard nail to be removed with each session.
7. After every pedicure, be generous with praise and/or treats, and your dog will come to look forward to and even enjoy his special time with you.

DENTAL CARE

Good canine oral hygiene is the most neglected aspect of grooming any dog, but it's also one of the easiest chores to perform. A Labrador

Retriever needs all of his teeth, and he needs them to be healthy to do his job. Oral health goes far beyond just what can be seen in the dog's mouth and on his teeth, however.

A dog's mouth harbors bacteria. Think about all the items your Labrador Retriever put in his mouth, or all of the streams he drinks from, or all of the places on his body he licks. Yuck! If your Lab grabs rocks or sticks and runs through the yard, or if he has a habit of rearranging the furniture in his habitat, the potential for injury to his teeth and gums increases. Some studies suggest that up to 80 percent of all dogs have some dental disease by the age of three. A proactive program of brushing, along with a yearly exam by a veterinarian, can prevent most plaque buildup and gum disease.

The bacteria that create canine gum disease don't stay in his mouth, either. These germs hitch a ride in the bloodstream and travel through the dog's body, where they spread infection to the heart, liver, kidneys, lungs, and other organs.

Dogs can easily be trained to allow a twice-weekly brush with a canine dental paste, but they also enjoy this if it turns into a game. I've taught all of my Labrador Retrievers to "show teeth" at a young age, during their puppyhood. Just as they grew used to having their feet touched, I gently pull their gums back and inspect their bite, their gums, and look for any evidence of abscess, injury, or tartar buildup.

How to Care for the Teeth

1. To keep your canine's canines sparkling clean, examine your Labrador Retriever's mouth, and brush his teeth, starting with the baby teeth.
2. Gently pull back the lips and check for any discoloration on each tooth.
3. Examine the back teeth also for plaque or tartar buildup.

Want to Know More?

For information on grooming a puppy, see Chapter 3: Care of Your Labrador Retriever Puppy.

4. If your dog's mouth has a foul smell, he may have an infection that needs to be treated by the veterinarian.
5. At first, place a rubber finger brush on a fingertip and let the dog get used to the feel of this in his mouth and on his teeth.
6. Introduce your dog to the smell and taste of canine toothpaste by placing a small dollop on your fingertip; never use human toothpaste, which can irritate the dog's stomach when he swallows the paste. The taste and smell should entice the dog to lick it off your finger. Experiment with different flavors if your dog is picky.
7. Put a small amount on a canine toothbrush or on a finger brush and massage his gums and teeth. He'll lick it as you go, but he's just helping to get the paste on all of his teeth.
8. Brush daily if possible, but at the very least brush your dog's teeth two or three times each week.

If your Lab begins to paw at his muzzle, if his eating or drinking habits change, or if you notice any redness, irritations, or lumps in his mouth during your informal oral examination, then take him to the veterinarian. My yellow Labrador Retriever, Gracie, developed a painful lump along her gum line. Rather than displaying her usual Labrador exuberance at the thought and sight of food, she began to eat gingerly. The veterinarian examination revealed a mass, and we immediately scheduled surgery, fearing the worst. Instead of an oral cancer, however, Gracie had a splinter that had embedded itself between her teeth and gum and formed an abscess. Within a few hours of surgery, she was back to retrieving dirty socks from the hamper and eating her kibble with Labrador gusto.

Many veterinarians advocate a full dental cleaning for adult dogs, which is a simple procedure. The drawback, if any, is the use of anesthesia in order to properly scale and clean the dog's teeth. If the dog's oral health is so bad that his overall health is compromised, a full cleaning may be necessary to save his life.

PROFESSIONAL GROOMERS

Because of hectic lives, busy schedules, and other activities, some owners don't have the time or the patience to groom their Labs on a regular basis. Others don't have adequate space for a Labrador bath, or are afraid to clip nails because of the risk of cutting the quick. Professional groomers are experienced in all aspects of a dog's grooming needs and can be the best option for many Lab owners.

Some groomers have a "by appointment only" policy, and others accept drop-ins. Some groomers will accept a dog in the morning and let him stay at the shop all day, while others might insist that the dog be picked up as soon as he is dry, to free up crate space for other clients. Almost all groomers will require a copy of your dog's vaccination records and most likely will require the dog have a bordetella inoculation. Be sure that you know your groomer's policies so that there are no surprises.

To find a groomer, ask friends, family, neighbors, business associates, and your veterinarian for referrals. Some vets maintain affiliations with local groomers; others might have a groomer in the same building as the veterinary clinic. Be sure, however, that ill dogs and dogs to be groomed have separate entrances and crates so that disease transmission is kept to a minimum.

Grooming your dog is not only the most proactive measure you can take to keep him healthy and happy—the Labrador Retriever owner who grooms her own dog will help to forge a bond that will last throughout the dog's life. Grooming time will come to be the most welcome hour in the week, a time of gentle strokes and puppy kisses, when playful paws, shining coat, and sparkling teeth help to make your dog whole in body and mind.

CHAPTER 7

LABRADOR RETRIEVER NUTRITIONAL NEEDS

L abs will eat anything. They don't care if their food comes out of a bag, a box, the freezer, the refrigerator, a pouch, or a can. Dry, moist, semi-moist, damp, softened, or hard, they will eat it. Just because the Labrador Retriever is not considered a picky eater (although individual dogs may be), and just because his palate is not refined, does not mean that his nutrition isn't important.

WHY GOOD NUTRITION IS SO IMPORTANT

Pet owners are justifiably scared because of pet food recalls during the past few years. The dangers of some recalled food have taught us all one thing, which is to be more careful about what we feed our dogs. But how does a dog owner decide between the bags, the cans, the raw, homemade, and the organic diets? Labrador Retriever owners must weigh their options and separate marketing hype from good nutrition, then decide on a type of food and diet that will help their dog's growth and development. Consider the following questions, and use them as tools in your decision-making process: Does your Lab thrive on his current diet? Is he physically and emotionally healthy? Does his coat shine,

and are his eyes bright? Is he free of disease? Is his weight proper for his height and bone structure? If you can answer "yes" to all these questions, you're probably doing all the right things for your dog.

THE BUILDING BLOCKS OF NUTRITION

To weigh the dog diet options, to separate marketing hype from good nutrition and decide on the best diet for the Labrador Retriever, arm yourself with knowledge about what goes into a dog food. For a breed as active as the Lab, the diet will differ depending on his level of activity, his age, and the types of activities in which he engages, which range from sofa warmer to strenuous hunt tests and field trials. Regardless of his activity level, however, all good canine nutrition should meet basic needs for the dog, and will include specific "building blocks" that are formulated for a dog's optimum health and performance.

Carbohydrates

Carbohydrates are power. Broken down, they are carbon, hydrogen, and oxygen molecules, but they give a dog energy. Those bursts off the line in pursuit of a downed bird, the muscles that stretch to dive off a dock, and the chase after a squirrel in the backyard are all powered by carbohydrates.

Sugars, starches, and cellulose or fiber are examples of carbohydrates, which are digested in the small intestine and turned into glucose. Glucose powers almost all cells in the body. The problem with carbohydrates usually comes from feeding too much because excess carbohydrates are converted to fat.

In dog food, most carbohydrates are supplied by grains, including wheat, corn, and rice. The amount of carbs in dog food can be more than 50 percent in dry food, typically from processed corn, oats, rice, barley, wheat, or sorghum. Processing these grains improves not just palatability but also digestibility, making more of the glucose available to a dog.

Common sources of carbohydrates from dietary fiber in dog food include soybean hulls, beet pulp, pea fiber, and wheat, rice, and oat bran. Fiber typically is not as easily digested in a dog's intestine but is still necessary for proper intestinal function.

Just because the Labrador Retriever is not considered a picky eater does not mean that his nutrition isn't important.

Fat

Fat is a more concentrated form of energy because most of it has been converted from carbohydrates. Most dietary fat is made up of fatty acid chains, or triglycerides. Fat is also classified by its physical state: Saturated fat usually is solid at room temperature, and unsaturated fat is usually liquid.

An important component of a complete diet, fat is also a source of essential fatty acids, which promote clear skin, proper coat, and a well-functioning immune system. Essential fatty acids cannot be synthesized by a dog and must be supplied through dietary means. These include omega-6 and omega-3 fatty acids.

Omega-6 acids are found in vegetable oils and in animal fat. They help regulate blood flow to the body, aid clotting after an injury, are important for normal pet reproduction, support the immune system, and help with skin and coat maintenance. Omega-6 fatty acids have been deemed an essential component of dog nutrition, but the omega-3 fatty acids are not considered essential. Current research, however, suggests that some health conditions might benefit from omega-3s.

Fat digestion is complex in a canine, but most dogs typically digest up to 95 percent of the fat in their diets, so very little goes to waste.

Protein

Protein is also an essential nutrient that supports most of the dog's bodily functions. Muscle growth in a growing Labrador Retriever is supplied and supported by his dietary protein intake, as is tissue repair after an injury. His immune functions that suppress or overcome infections and the hormones necessary for reproduction are supplied in part from protein. Enzyme production, even the amount of oxygen that his blood supply transports to his brain, is regulated and enhanced by the proteins in his diet.

Proteins, in their simplest sense, are the basic building blocks for cells. They occur in all animal and vegetable matter and are essential to the dog's diet. A protein is a chain or group of amino acids, and depending on how the amino acids are connected, that determines the specific nature and job of the protein. As an analogy, look at different dog breeds and their function: A Labrador Retriever is built to be a hardworking sporting dog, whereas a toy breed, such as a Pomeranian, has an entirely different

The right amount of fats in the diet contributes to a healthy skin and coat.

job altogether. The same can be said about proteins: Form dictates function.

Dietary protein is digested in the dog's stomach and small intestine and then forms amino acids, which in turn travel to those area of the dog's body where they are needed. Because this need is constant, amino acids aren't stored in the body like fat; rather, they have to be provided all the time. Could this explain why the always-hungry Labrador Retriever is, well, always hungry? No, sorry. Your Lab just wants you to think that he is constantly starved for food. Without the right kind of protein in the right combination, though, he could be starved of essential amino acids. A diet low in protein could lead to health issues, such as decreased immune function, decreased milk production in lactating bitches, weight loss, poor growth, a dull coat, and depressed appetite. Diets that contain more protein than is needed

By the Numbers

The adult Labrador Retriever should be fed twice daily, in the morning and again at night. Depending on his activity, he might need a food high in protein and fat, or he might need a weight-control diet prescribed by his veterinarian. Overfeeding is a huge problem with Labradors, so be sure to follow the advice of your vet on what and how much to feed your dog.

Typically, in a high-end food, the protein will be listed first or second on the package label, and the label will also identify the source of the protein, either plant or animal.

for the dog and his lifestyle or activities can cause weight gain.

Most protein in dog food comes from a combination of animal and plant sources, because no one source can supply the right amount of amino acids. This is why a dog food label can be so confusing. Different proteins provide different amino acids. To make things even more confounding, dog food protein levels are also measured by the level of protein and the protein bioavailability, or how much of that protein is actually used by the dog. So, the amount of protein available to the dog from his food depends on how well he is able to digest that food source.

In most dog food, the protein is supplied by meat or meat by-products. Typically, in a high-end food, the protein will be listed first or second on the package label, and the label will also identify the source of the protein, either plant or animal.

Minerals

Compared to the carbs, fats, and protein, minerals are pretty simple collections of molecules that do their job and get out of there, like a Labrador Retriever in sneak-attack-for-that-sandwich mode. Minerals have to be coordinated with each other, nutritionally balanced, and they have to be available to the dog. In other words, they have to be able to seep out of the dog's gut and go off to their place of work in the dog's body.

Minerals help form bone and cartilage, maintain the correct fluid balance, help transport oxygen in the dog's blood, help enzymes, assist normal muscle and nerve function, and help make hormones. With so many different functions, minerals are kind of like our relationship to our Labs; they are hardworking, coordinated, and interconnected with each other. If one mineral is having an "off day" or the supplementation is not correct, all of the other minerals throw up their molecular strands and say, "Enough already!"

Macro minerals, which are needed in greater amounts by the dog, include calcium, phosphorus, sodium, chloride, potassium, and magnesium. Micro minerals, added in trace amounts to dog food, are iron, zinc, copper, manganese, selenium, and iodine. If the balance of any mineral is out of whack, the dog might exhibit symptoms such as weight gain and poor coat (iodine) or increased incidence of infection (zinc). Any suspected mineral deficiency should be evaluated and treated by your veterinarian.

Vitamins

The discovery of the importance of vitamins to humans and animals in the early 20th century had a profound impact on animal (and human) nutrition. Compared to the other essential nutrients, vitamins are only needed in small amounts, but they impact the work of all the other nutrients in nourishing the dog.

The fat-soluble vitamins A, D, E, and K cannot be utilized by the dog unless he has adequate amounts of dietary fat. Likewise, the water-soluble vitamins B and C can only work if the dog has adequate water. Vitamin A is implicated in normal vision, growth, immune system function, and reproduction. It's also an antioxidant, which means that it has certain cancer-fighting properties; it typically is

Training Tidbit

A good, low-fat alternative when you want to reward your dog during a training session is fresh green beans (washed and cut into pieces) or rice cakes. Any training treat should be easy for you to handle, not make a gooey mess in your pocket or training bag, and be easy for the dog to chew quickly so that the lesson can continue.

added to dog food from a plant source such as carrots. Vitamin D helps regulate calcium and helps the dog to grow strong bones. Vitamin E is another antioxidant, but it also has a role in reproduction. Safflower, wheat germ, and soybean oil are usual sources of vitamin E. Vitamin K, which helps the blood to clot after an injury, comes from green, leafy plants and vegetables. The water-soluble B-complex vitamins are critical for the metabolism of protein, carbohydrates, and fat, which results in energy for the dog. Vitamin C, which is necessary for humans and some other mammals, does not need to be added to dog food because dogs make their own vitamin C.

Water

All of these nutrients cannot work properly if they don't have water in which to do their jobs. Water, provided from the dog's bowl, mixed in the feed, or generated from certain metabolic processes in his body, helps regulate his body temperature, lubricates his joints and tissues, and gives the blood cells a medium in which to swoosh through the dog's body. Water is so important that any deviation will have adverse

Water helps regulate his body temperature, lubricates his joints and tissues, and gives the blood cells a medium in which to swoosh through the dog's body.

TYPES OF DIETS

So, with all of these essential nutrients so necessary for the Labrador Retriever's growth and development, how does the owner know what to feed her dog? The choices range from dry to raw, but the best type for each dog is different. The best food to feed your dog is *whatever works for the both of you, the owner and the dog.* If you feed your dog a high-quality kibble and he's healthy, that's okay. The choice of the individual owner should not be a guilt-provoking decision. If the dog has allergies, if the dog is failing to thrive, or if the dog is obese, there is a food for that dog. If the dog works the field or runs around an agility ring, there is a food for that dog. If the dog brings his owner's slippers and newspaper to her in the evening and then lies down at her feet, there is a food for that dog. The choices can be confusing and overwhelming, but remember, there are choices for your dog today, unlike for dogs of a century ago.

Commercial Food

Commercial food is already packaged, processed, and nutrient-complete. The advantage in feeding a commercial food is that it's easy for the owner. Pull the tab on a bag, slice open a pouch, or slide a can opener across the top, and the food is ready to be eaten by the dog. For most dogs, commercially prepared food will be adequate. Depending on the dog's activity levels, protein, fat, and carbohydrate content can fall into a range that will fit the dog's needs. An active Labrador Retriever might need a dry kibble with upward of 28 percent protein, while a slightly overweight Labrador Retriever might need a food with a low fat content. The labels on commercial foods will detail their nutritional content, so read them with your specific dog's needs in mind. Also, if

effects on the dog.

A dog's water requirement is determined mostly by his activity level and the amount of food he consumes each day. If he eats more, he will drink more. If he eats canned rather than dry food, he will drink less because canned food typically contains about 75 percent water. If the dog works hard and often in the field, he will drink more water; pregnant or lactating bitches and puppies also consume more water than most dogs.

Dogs lose water content when they pee, obviously. But water loss occurs through respiration, in feces, through the skin, out the nose, and from all that Labrador Retriever drool when he sits waiting for his meal.

you have questions, consult your veterinarian or a canine nutritionist.

Dry Food

Dry food comes in a bag and is processed and hardened into a shape that is easy for the dog to consume and convenient for the owner to store and dispense. Dry food stays fresher longer, which also adds to the convenience. Because Labrador Retrievers eat a lot, a 40-pound (18-kg) bag of food might be more economical for the owner in the long run. Dry food may have additives that make it more palatable and to restore the nutrients that were

Multi-Dog Tip

If you have Labrador Retrievers at different life stages, with different nutritional needs, you might need to prepare home-cooked meals for one but not another. The learning curve can be steep, but it gets easier the more experienced you get. Using recipes from your vet or a canine nutritionist, meals for a week can be prepared at once and portions individually frozen. Thaw what the dog needs each day. If each dog eats commercially prepared kibble, then buy individual containers (I have 40-pound [18-kg] plastic bins) where each dog's food is stored. Label each bin with the dog's name and the amount of kibble he is fed at each meal. This method makes it easy on dog sitters or neighbors who might be asked to feed your dog if you are away from home.

destroyed by the high-heat manufacturing process, in which the meat or vegetable matter used to make the food is extruded out, like a wet shirt going through a wringer. The label on dry food might be pretty long and read like an alphabet soup because of all of the minerals, vitamins, carbohydrates, protein, and fat sources used in production.

The ingredients on the label are listed by weight in descending order, and higher quality foods will have meat as the main protein source. If the protein is grain-based, that diet is not ideal because dogs don't necessarily digest grains as well as meats. Some Labs have been known to develop grain allergies, too, and a grain-based diet may be more expensive in the long run because of resultant veterinary bills. Grocery-store bagged food generally is less expensive because it has cheaper ingredients, and the food tends to contain more grain. More expensive dry food usually contains more meat protein. Of course, some of that expense might be to sustain a lot of marketing and provide a pretty bag, but when it comes to dog food, you usually get what you pay for.

If the label defines its protein source, that's even better. For example, look for a label that specifically reads "chicken or chicken meal," "lamb or lamb meal," rather than the generic term "meat." If the food has only two ingredients as the protein sources, say lamb and rice, and rice is listed first, that's okay. Other additions, such as blueberries and certain vegetables, add nutrients. Overall, the fewer ingredients there are, the less wiggle room there is, and the less likely the dog will develop a food allergy or be subject to extra chemicals that he doesn't need.

Semi-Moist

Semi-moist food generally offers higher palatability (your dog is thinking, "Oh, a hamburger, yeah, yeah, yeah!"), the food is smaller and easier to store, and it's convenient because you just rip open the container and plop the food into the dog's bowl. Semi-moist food contains water, so the dog won't drink as much out of his water bowl. That means less water trails through the house for those Labrador Retrievers who tend to go swimming or bob their noses in their bowl and blow bubbles, just to make sure the water is actually there. Semi-moist food might be convenient for the owner but might not be nutritionally complete for a large, active dog. Because these foods have shorter shelf lives, they contain large amounts of preservatives; they also contain extra sugars for palatability, which can cause weight gain in a less active dog

Canned food is especially appetizing to most dogs.

Canned

Canned food is no doubt convenient and palatable, but it contains upward of 75 percent water rather than food. For a Labrador Retriever owner, this might not be the best option. Once a can is opened, unused food cannot be stored—even in the refrigerator—for more than three days. Bacterial growth on the food happens almost as soon as the can is opened, so if your Labrador Retriever is unusual and doesn't scarf it down immediately, you could be inviting trouble in the form of a gastrointestinal bug.

Noncommercial Food

Noncommercial foods are like doggy gourmet meals—they might be prepared for a specific dog on a daily basis, or they are ordered from companies that specialize in canine nutrition. These dog foods have to be carefully managed and must contain the proper kinds and ratios of nutrients, vitamins, and minerals added. Most noncommercial dog diets are called home-cooked, raw, or special diets. Pet food recalls have caused many dog owners to reconsider what they feed their pets. As a result, dog owners have begun to switch from commercial to noncommercial foods. These special diets are much more time consuming to prepare, they cost more, and without advice from a specialist in canine nutrition, a dog could become deficient in one nutrient or have an excess of another nutrient, which will throw his whole system into disarray.

Many advocates of noncommercial dog food compare the canine diet with what a wolf eats in the wild. Personally, my opinion on this is that once we domesticated the dog and he began to eat what we eat rather than what his ancestors ate in the wild, we changed our dogs. My dogs bear no more resemblance to a wolf than I do to a Hollywood starlet. My dogs

Preparing a home-cooked diet gives you control over the ingredients.

depend on me for their food and their welfare, not what they might be able to scavenge in the forest. That said, if any of my dogs needed a special diet for optimal function, to treat a specific disease condition, or to manage his weight, I would not hesitate to prepare noncommercial food (and I have done this with one dog). This is an intensely personal decision, one highly charged with emotion, and the whole issue of commercial versus noncommercial food sparks debate like almost no other canine welfare conversation.

Home-Cooked

Preparing a home-cooked diet gives the dog owner total control over what goes into her dog's food. Recipes can be found in books and on the Internet and include a variety of meats, grains, and vegetables. Some home-cooking advocates begin slowly by adding fresh meat and vegetables to their dog's daily kibble. Others go "all-in" and prepare all of the dog's meals for a week, freeze what isn't immediately needed, and thaw and serve as the week goes along. Adding fresh food to a nutritionally balanced commercial food can upset the total nutrient content the dog receives, so there are some foods to avoid or be careful with if you add them to a kibble. Also, a dog who isn't healthy, especially one who has immune dysfunction, should not be fed a home-cooked (or raw) diet without involvement from a canine nutritionist or veterinarian.

A typical, easy-to-make home-cooked food for a Labrador Retriever will include lean, chopped, or ground meat, vegetable oil, calcium and vitamin supplements, bone meal, and some veggies. These ingredients can be combined and fed either cooked, raw, or frozen and thawed before mealtime. A canine nutritionist or veterinarian should be consulted before a dog is fed a home-cooked diet. If the dog has specific health concerns, never change his diet without talking with your vet. Also, don't just throw some meat and rice into a stockpot; it's much better to stick with proven recipes. What you cook and which supplements are used depend on the weight of your dog and his activity level. For example, you might need to add kelp or iodine salt in addition to specific multivitamins or minerals.

Raw

The raw diet, which includes the Biologically Appropriate Raw Diet (BARF), is just what it sounds like: all raw meat and vegetables. Most raw diets do not include grains but do include raw, meaty bones and some veggies. While not terribly difficult to prepare, a raw diet must be supplemented with vitamins and minerals. A raw diet typically is more expensive because

The Whole-Prey Diet

A variation of the raw diet is a "whole-animal" or "whole-prey" diet. Said to be nutritionally complete, it's really not a good idea for the squeamish owner. This diet means that you feed the dog a whole rabbit, chicken, or quail, which are the three most typical prey animals fed to a dog. Usually, you toss the dog his prey (already killed, by the way, but still fresh and not previously frozen); he will take the dead animal off to a corner of the yard and chomp away until his meal is finished.

you're buying fresh foods, not prepared foods.

Keep in mind that some raw fish can cause a vitamin deficiency, which will cause your dog to exhibit loss of appetite, weakness, or seizures. Raw liver fed daily and in large quantities can cause vitamin A toxicity. Small, soft, cooked bones like pork chop or chicken bones can and do splinter and lodge in the dog's mouth, throat, or stomach. If you're concerned about feeding bones to your dog, there are options. If the dog is a gulper (like many Labrador Retrievers), or if you can't reach into the dog's bowl and control his rate of consumption, don't feed him whole bones. Instead, have them ground up.

There can be harm involved in feeding any type of raw diet, but this depends on both the dog and the owner. For any immune-compromised Labrador Retriever or his owner (including any family members), a raw diet carries specific risks of disease contamination, including bacterial and parasitic infection. For this reason, the Food and Drug Administration (FDA) and the Centers for Disease Control and Prevention (CDC) carry warnings on their websites and literature about canine raw diets and immune-compromised dog owners.

Precautions when feeding a raw diet are pretty much commonsense considerations. If you buy raw meat that has not been inspected, and that meat is contaminated with parasites, both dog and owner can become infected. Purchase meat from a reputable butcher or grocery store. Also, don't buy the meat and then leave it in your car while you run errands for another four hours.

Table Scraps

What about table scraps? Well, that depends on what you're eating. It's okay to slip your Labrador Retriever broccoli occasionally, but never feed him onions, garlic, or cauliflower;

onions and garlic are toxic to a dog, and cauliflower and other plants in the cabbage family can cause flatulence in a dog. If all you eat is pepperoni pizza, the crust will not be nutritionally good for your Lab. If you save a sliver of steak and slip it to your dog when you are finished eating, he's going to love you forever. And he'll continue to expect steak, which leads to begging behaviors.

Special Diets

Some Labrador Retrievers need special diets, which include prescription formulas available only from your veterinarian. Some dogs may need a grain-free food because of food allergies, which typically show up as an insanely itching and scratching dog and the development of hot spots. Dogs in renal failure and dogs with gastrointestinal upsets need special diets to either prevent fluid buildup in their tissues or to prevent fluid loss. Talk to your veterinarian about special diets.

Two types of special diets get a lot of media hype these days: organic and holistic. Organic diets, by law, must be made from animal and plant materials that have never been exposed to any pesticides or chemicals. The animals must not have been given antibiotics or hormones. The plants cannot have been sprayed with anything other than water. In addition, the

Some Labrador Retrievers will need supplements, especially as they age.

Want to Know More?

To learn the *heel* command, see Chapter 9: Labrador Retriever Training.

feed given to animal-source protein must be totally organic: no additives, no hormones, and no pesticides. Organic diets will be more expensive, no doubt. For the allergic dog, however, organic diets can help him overcome his allergies and relieve suffering.

The term "holistic" is a buzzword with good marketing behind it, but it does not accurately describe dog food. Holistic is a way of looking at the whole dog, his lifestyle, his nutritional, emotional, physical, exercise, and veterinary needs. If you see the word "holistic" to describe a dog food, it's a seductive ploy. Unless you are raising your Labrador Retriever in a totally holistic way, using alternative medicine and alternative lifestyle choices, then a holistic-branded food is not going to be better or worse than almost any other dog food choice that you make.

SUPPLEMENTS

Some Labrador Retrievers are going to need supplements, especially as they age.

Glucosamine and Chondroitin

The most popular, and with very good science to support its use, is a combination glucosamine and chondroitin sulfate product. These supplements have been proven in humans to promote healthy joints, and the same holds true for our dogs. Joint disease is such a problem in Labrador Retrievers that many veterinarians recommend these supplements, either individually or in a combination, to prevent disorders or to treat the Lab who already suffers. Hip and elbow dysplasias are caused by the wearing away of cartilage, and glucosamine and chondroitin sulfates are thought to prevent cartilage deterioration and to help those dogs who already suffer the pains in their aging joints.

Prebiotics

Prebiotics are supplements to help a dog's intestines work better. These "good bacteria" supplements help to prevent the overgrowth of dangerous bacteria in a dog's large intestine. The good bacteria present in prebiotic supplements produce energy for intestinal cells and aid in the production of nutrients for the dog.

TREATS

Labrador Retrievers love their treats, whether given for just lying there and looking good or as a reward during an obedience lesson. Some treats now claim to provide a power boost or calm a dog; others offer protection for a dog's heart, immune system, or joints. Again, a good knowledge about what is in a treat can help decide what is best for your Lab. Many treats already duplicate the nutrients your dog is getting, and most contain too much fat, which add unnecessary calories to your Lab's diet.

Healthy treats include fresh foods like baby carrots and sliced apples. Quick energy boosts come from carbs and fat, but be sure not to feed too much. High-quality protein treats made from fresh eggs, milk, fish, and meats are good as long as the dog is fed a balanced diet.

Some commercially prepared treats contain kelp, which can be troublesome to dogs with thyroid disease because it adds iodine salt to the dog's diet. A dog with thyroid disease does not need the extra salt, so be careful if your Lab has a thyroid condition.

For highly active Labrador Retrievers, such as those in competition training or working in the field, rewards should be lean, like bites of cooked chicken breast. Tidbits of string cheese or slivers of lean turkey hotdogs are okay in moderation. For weight-conscious dogs (like my Gracie, and we don't use the word "F-A-T" since she lost all her extra weight), jackpot treats include rice cakes and lean steak, chicken, or liver. Story, my young'un, can use the extra energy and calories from a raw meaty bone, usually a soup or marrow bone from the grocery store. (Again, never feed bones that are likely to sliver, like cooked chicken bones.)

Because Labs work for food, any food, keep your dog's individual needs in mind before you start to toss treats at him or place his food bowl down. Make him work for a treat—either perform a "high-five," sit before he eats his meal, or walk an obedience pattern in *heel* position. Your adult Labrador Retriever should be fed twice daily, in the morning after you eat your breakfast and in the evening, after you eat your dinner. This teaches the all-important lessons that you are the leader of the pack, and he must learn to wait.

OBESITY

Obesity is a big problem in all dogs, and Labrador Retrievers seem to pack on the pounds overnight. They are food hounds and natural beggars. Don't fall for your dog's gimmicks or "Oh, I'm starving" tactics, and don't overfeed him. If his feed bag states a 60-pound (27-kg) dog needs four cups of dry kibble a day, you can probably cut that number in half and give him one cup twice daily.

Most veterinarians and canine nutritionists, physical therapists, and veterinary specialists in obesity issues will say that a dog is obese if you cannot easily feel his ribs or cannot see a "waistline" when the dog is viewed from above. This is true in most cases; however, we have to remember the Labrador Retriever standard:

There is no "tuck-up" underneath this dog. Also, the Lab has to have some subcutaneous fat to protect him from icy cold water. With a Lab, you should be able to feel the dog's ribs underneath that gorgeous, shiny double coat and beneath those strong muscles that keep him running all day. The best way to tell if your Labrador Retriever is fat is to weigh him on a weekly basis. Also, if he develops joint disease, he may be carrying too much weight.

Whether you feed your Labrador Retriever a prepared diet or you do all the cooking for him, he will love you and come back for more. And more. And even more. Guidance from your breeder, your veterinarian, and your dog will help you navigate the ever-trickier waters of canine nutrition.

Labs are natural beggars and can pack on the pounds easily.

CHAPTER 8

LABRADOR RETRIEVER HEALTH AND WELLNESS

The Labrador Retriever is a hardy dog and has few health issues, but your dog will still need an annual wellness examination, at which time your veterinarian will perform a comprehensive health checkup. She'll be looking for any evidence of external or internal parasites, allergies, heart or lung disorders, and joint issues. The adult Labrador Retriever who is well cared for and exercised regularly will rarely have serious disorders, but that doesn't mean that he will never have to be treated for a health problem.

ANNUAL EXAM

At his annual exam, the veterinarian will listen to your Lab's heart and lungs, palpate his abdomen, and check his eyes and ears. She should also gently extend the dog's rear legs to check for knee inflammation, swelling, or pain, any of which could indicate the need to test for cranial cruciate ligament (CCL) tears or ruptures. A hip laxity test should also be done. The vet will gently rotate each leg to see how far the upper leg will turn outward, a sign that the hip might not be tight enough in its socket. This preliminary test could determine the need for more extensive testing for hip dysplasia.

Blood will be drawn to check for blood-borne parasites like heartworms; even if the dog has been on heartworm preventive, the medication has been known to fail, albeit rarely. Because of this, most veterinarians will require an annual blood test before dispensing more heartworm preventive. Your vet is the best source of information on the need for testing.

VACCINATIONS

Vaccinations for rabies, distemper, parvovirus, and other illnesses commonly seen in your area are usually given during your pet's annual health exam. Titers are sometimes acceptable rather than the revaccination; however, a titer only indicates the dog has proper levels of antibodies to the illness being tested *at the time the titer is drawn*. A titer cannot determine how long a dog will continue to have acceptable levels of antibodies. Most recent studies, however, have proven that many of the canine vaccinations maintain acceptable levels of protection for three to five years. Discuss this with your veterinarian and decide together which vaccinations your Labrador Retriever needs. Because Labs are in fields, forests, rivers, creeks, and meadows, your dog may need vaccinations more often to protect him from exposure to illnesses that less-active dogs may never experience.

A veterinarian technician will check your dog's stool for the presence of internal parasites, such as worms. If you bring in a fresh stool sample, it will make the dog's exam easier; if not, a probe will be inserted into the dog's rectum to gather stool for testing. Most dogs tolerate this, although they squirm. In addition to the stool test, a rectal thermometer is used to check the dog's temperature.

PARASITES

Parasites run the gamut from internal to external. Some hide out and the dog won't experience symptoms. Usually, however, the conscientious Labrador Retriever owner will know that something is not quite right with her dog if he's infested with worms or fleas.

Internal Parasites

Most internal parasites are worms or single-celled organisms that live in the dog's intestines. Worms most commonly seen in canines are heartworms, hookworms, roundworms, tapeworms, and whipworms. Each parasite, however, can cause serious disease and distress in the Labrador Retriever.

Heartworms

Heartworms are spread by infected mosquitoes, and these preventable, although serious and possibly fatal, parasites infect a variety of animals. Canines, felines, and many wild animals can carry a heartworm infection. This parasite can only be transmitted from one animal to another via a mosquito bite.

Want to Know More?

If you're wondering how to find the perfect vet for your newly adopted adult dog, see Chapter 3: Care of Your Labrador Retriever Puppy.

When a mosquito bites an infected animal, heartworm microfilariae (baby heartworms) enter the insect's system and grow into larvae. When the mosquito bites its next victim, the microfilariae are transmitted to the animal, where they mature into adult heartworms over about six months. The adult worms continue to mate, so the dog will have not just adult worms that grow inside his body, but he'll also have larvae in various stages of development.

Heartworms can attain lengths of 14 inches (35.5 cm) and damage the dog's blood vessels, reduce the heart's pumping ability, and cause severe heart and lung disease. Some dogs don't exhibit symptoms of heartworm infection until the infestation is severe. The dog will cough, become lethargic, lose his appetite, or have difficulty breathing. If your Labrador Retriever becomes tired after even mild exercise, he needs to be tested for heartworm disease. Diagnosis can be made by blood tests, but the dog may need chest radiographs and an echocardiogram to confirm the diagnosis, evaluate the severity of the disease, and determine a treatment plan.

The goal in treatment is to kill the adult worms and microfilariae in as safe a manner as possible. Remember, your dog has adult worms amassing in his heart and lungs. The US Food and Drug Administration (FDA)-approved method of treatment is a powerful drug that kills the worms, but as they die, there is a serious risk of complications to the dog. He will need to be crated and kept calm and quiet for several weeks or months as the worms die. Other medications may be prescribed to reduce his inflammatory response while the worms die and are broken down in the dog's lungs. Very serious cases of heartworm disease have been treated surgically, but surgery is high risk and is reserved for the worst cases.

Because heartworm disease is almost 100 percent preventable and is found in every US state and in many other countries, keep your Labrador Retriever on a heartworm preventive. The medicine does not kill adult heartworms and won't eliminate the infection if your dog already carries heartworms. If you have adopted your adult Lab from a shelter or rescue group, your veterinarian will test him for adult heartworms before beginning any preventive medication. She will probably retest your dog in about six months in case he was in the early, larval, undetectable stage of an infection when it was initially tested.

Many of the heartworm preventive medications given to dogs also help protect or prevent infection from hookworms, roundworms, and whipworms. Some of the heartworm medicines also help protect a dog from external parasites, like fleas and ticks.

Hookworms

Hookworms are one of the most common internal parasites found in dogs. Your Labrador Retriever can become infected when hookworm larvae penetrate his skin or the lining of his mouth. An infected bitch can pass the parasite on to her puppies during lactation. Hookworms are dangerous because they actually bite into the dog's intestinal lining, where they hang on and suck the dog's blood. Untreated, hookworms cause life-threatening

A dog with internal parasites will show signs of lethargy, weight loss, or irregular bowel movements.

Puppies and seniors can be severely affected by internal parasites.

blood loss, weakness, and malnutrition. Puppies especially are at high risk of infection, and they can develop severe disease. Because hookworms are zoonotic, which means that humans can also be infected, treatment and good hygiene practices are vital to prevent the spread of this parasite.

Hookworms are not visible to the naked eye, so your veterinarian will diagnose this parasite from the dog's stool sample. Treatment is usually with medicine like pyrantel pamoate, and the dose is given two or three times over about three weeks. Dewormers come in liquid and pill form, and your vet will recommend which medicine and in which form will be best for your Lab. During treatment, the dog's feces should be immediately double-bagged and discarded. Family members should wash

their hands after petting the dog or cleaning up the dog's waste; don't go barefoot in the yard where your dog has defecated. Good hygiene will prevent hookworms from infecting the family.

Roundworms

Roundworms are the most common intestinal parasites found in dogs. Dogs become infected by eating soil that contains roundworm eggs, licking contaminated fur or paws, or by drinking contaminated water. In addition, a bitch can pass the larvae on to her puppies either before birth or afterward during lactation. Puppies are most vulnerable to roundworm infection.

The parasite lives in the small intestine and steals nutrients from the dog's food.

This causes malnutrition and intestinal symptoms like diarrhea; as the roundworm larvae move through the young dog, he can develop pneumonia. Your veterinarian will have to examine the dog's stool to diagnose roundworms, unless the parasite has grown so big and long that you can see the evidence—they look like long strings of spaghetti in the stool. Even after treatment, your dog can become reinfected from his outside environment. Because his feces are contaminated, make sure that you pick up his stool after every bowel movement and double-bag the droppings. Keep children out of the area, and practice good hygiene to prevent roundworm infection in family members.

Tapeworms

Tapeworm infection is usually accompanied by a flea infestation because flea larvae eat tapeworm eggs in the environment. Tapeworms develop inside a flea, and when a dog bites at and swallows the flea on his skin, the tapeworm goes to work inside the dog.

These worms, rarely a problem for people, get their name because of their appearance. They are thin, flat, and look like segmented tape strips. A tapeworm infection is usually diagnosed when the worm segments are excreted by the dog. White tapeworm egg sacs that may look like grains of rice can be seen under the pet's tail, around his anus, or in his stool. A dog who scoots his bottom along the carpet might have a tapeworm infection, although that's unlikely if he's had adequate flea preventive.

Tapeworms live in the small intestine of the dog and consume nutrients, which can lead to malnutrition and anemia. Unless the flea problem is treated at the same time as the tapeworm infection, a dog will continue to be reinfected.

Whipworms

Whipworms also get their name from their shape: They look like tiny whips, but are not noticeable to the naked eye. Microscopic examination of stool can diagnose whipworm. A dog becomes infected by licking contaminated soil, fur, or paws, or drinking contaminated water. These worms can cause diarrhea and anemia in a dog because they suck blood out of the host's intestines. Usually, however, only young puppies or immune-compromised dogs have severe illness. Whipworm larvae don't tend to infect humans, but good hygiene is recommended for any person living with an infected dog.

External Parasites

External parasites, such as fleas, ticks, and mites, can cause serious disease in dogs if left unchecked. Preventive treatments can help mitigate your dog's distress and discomfort, but the best way to keep him free of external parasites is through weekly grooming sessions. A proactive owner can successfully alleviate—or even prevent—many of the health problems associated with these pests.

Fleas

Dogs are probably tormented more by fleas than by any other parasite. These seed-sized black specks that look like miniature jumping beans with legs cling to tall and short grass and live along dirt roads and city streets. Depending on the area and climate, fleas may be a year-round problem, or they may only be a seasonal nuisance. Once a flea finds a home on a dog, though, it scurries around, makes itself comfortable, feeds, then lays up to 50 eggs at a time, all within 24 hours after it moves in. Then the egg larvae fall off the dog into your carpet, on your furniture, or into the soil around your home. The larvae spin themselves a cozy cocoon and can remain dormant for weeks before they emerge as adults, ready to begin a new assault. The flea life cycle can last from 12 days to 6 months, depending on the climate. In areas with high heat and humidity, fleas may never go dormant.

Once a dog is infested with fleas, he may become noticeably uncomfortable. His skin may have a few red spots from the bites, or he could develop hot spots, a serious open sore and skin infection. You might notice the black flea droppings on your dog's coat, but on black and chocolate Labrador Retrievers, owners might never see this "flea dirt." A flea comb raked through the dog's undercoat, close to the skin, may bring up a flea or two, or the droppings. The droppings, if moistened, will turn a dirty reddish brown, reflecting the bloodsucking nature of the parasite.

Some dogs may develop a flea bite allergy, which is an allergic reaction to flea saliva; one or two bites can send these dogs into a severe itching frenzy. Also, if a flea is ingested by the dog, the dog can become infected with tapeworms, which live and develop inside the flea.

If a flea infestation develops, you will need to treat the dog and his environment. Your veterinarian can recommend a good flea control plan, which will include an appropriate flea preventive to give the dog. The house and the dog's bed will need to be vacuumed almost daily, and the vacuum cleaner should be emptied and cleaned outside the house. Wash bed linens and sofa covers too. In the yard, some insecticides are adequate for flea control, but ask your vet which products are safe to use around your dog.

During "flea season" in your area, try to avoid walking your dog through vacant lots and tall grass. Keep him on his preventive treatment all year if you live in an area where fleas never really die off during the winter.

Mites

Mites are external parasites that are tinier than fleas and more difficult to see without a microscope. There are several kinds of mites, but those most likely to infect a dog are ear mites, sarcoptic mange mites, and demodectic mange mites.

Ear mites are common in young dogs and live pretty much in and around the ears. Dogs are infested by close contact with an already-infested pet or his bedding. Ear mites cause intense itching of the ear canal, and the dog might constantly shake his head or scratch his ears. He could develop bloody sores from scratching. A black or brown discharge from the ear canal is a symptom of ear mite

By the Numbers

One flea deposits hundreds of eggs on a dog, and if the population explosion isn't contained, your Lab might be a walking flea hotel. Many monthly heartworm preventives also kill fleas, but these medicines only work after the flea has bitten your dog. If you live in an area where fleas are a big problem, talk to your vet about other flea-control measures. Once a flea infestation takes hold, the dog, his bedding, and the house and yard will all have to be treated to get the problem under control.

infestation. Your veterinarian will swab the ear canal and examine the discharge under a microscope. Treatment includes thorough ear cleaning accompanied by medication.

Sarcoptic mange mites are also known as scabies. This mange can affect dogs of all ages, and the mites are highly contagious to other dogs. Sarcoptic mange mites are usually transmitted by close contact with an infested animal or his bedding, or through grooming tools. These mites burrow through the top layer of a dog's skin and cause itching. Other signs are hair loss, a skin rash, and crusting of the skin. Infections can develop along with the irritation from the scratching. People who are in close contact with an infested dog can also develop sarcoptic mange. This parasite can only be diagnosed by microscopic examination of a skin scraping. Dogs who are diagnosed with sarcoptic mange mites will have to be treated with medication both to kill the mites and to soothe the dog's irritated or infected skin. The dog's bedding and environment also will need to be cleaned.

Demodectic mange mites are also microscopic, but they are not as highly contagious either to other animals or to people. A nursing bitch might pass these mites on to her puppies. Most dogs who contract demodectic mange are young dogs, and the infestation appears as patches of scaly skin and redness on the face, legs, and trunk of the dog. If the dog contracts demodectic mange, he should be evaluated for other health conditions, as he may have a compromised immune system. A more severe form of demodectic mange can lead to widespread hair loss, and thick, scaly, red skin patches. Your veterinarian will have to diagnose demodectic mange mites by microscopic examination of skin scrapings. If the dog is young and the mange not severe, treatment with localized

Check your Lab for fleas and ticks after he's been playing outside.

medication usually is curative. The more serious illness, however, is much harder to treat; typically, only the symptoms are managed, and the dog may never be cured of demodectic mange.

Ringworm

Ringworm sounds like a worm, but it's really a fungal infection. Ringworm gets its name from the typical presentation, which can look like a red raised circle on the skin of pets or people. The infection can cause circular patches of hair loss on the skin of an infected dog. Ringworm is highly contagious and can cause intense itching and scratching at the site of infection. The fungus is spread by direct contact with an infected dog, his bedding, or anything else that has come in contact with the dog, such as his toys. The fungus also survives in the soil. Many dogs can recover from ringworm without treatment, but it's best to use a topical antifungal directly on lesions. Household members should practice good hygiene, including hand washing, to prevent the spread of this zoonotic disease.

Ticks

Tick-borne diseases have increased in the United States, and there is almost no area where ticks aren't found. Labrador Retrievers have an increased risk of a tick disease, especially those dogs allowed to roam free and those in the field. Ticks live in woods, brush, shrubs, and undergrowth, depending on the species.

After any excursion, the Labrador Retriever should be given a hands-on tick check. Ticks are most often found around the dog's neck, in his ears, in the folds of skin between his legs and body, and between the toes. Give your dog a full-body check, and feel and look for any tick that might be scurrying or already attached. Remove ticks by using tweezers, and grip the tick as close to the dog's skin as possible. Pull the tick free with a gentle, steady motion. If the head of the tick is still buried in the dog's skin, it might become a site for infection, so take your dog to his vet.

Lyme disease is the most common tick-borne illness, and it's caused by a bacteria found in the common deer tick, among others. Endemic to the northeastern United States, Lyme disease has been diagnosed in people and pets across the country. The tick must be attached to the host for 48 hours before transmittal of the bacteria occurs. Even then, only 10 percent of dogs who are exposed to the bacteria will actually contract Lyme disease. The onset of clinical illness takes from two to five months after the tick bite; the most common symptoms are fever, lameness, joint swelling, swollen lymph nodes, lethargy, and a loss of appetite. Rarely, dogs develop kidney disease, heart problems, or nervous system disorders. Dogs do not develop a "bull's-eye" rash or circular redness around the bite, which is a symptom seen in humans with the illness.

Treatment includes antibiotic use, sometimes for months. Dogs who develop severe arthritis from Lyme disease can be given pain relievers. Lyme vaccines are available, and Labrador Retriever owners and handlers should talk with their veterinarians if their dogs would benefit from inoculation. Also, an annual blood test for the presence of Lyme antibodies can detect the disease in asymptomatic dogs, so discuss this option with your vet at your dog's annual exam.

BREED-SPECIFIC HEALTH ISSUES

While Labrador Retrievers are hardy and hard-charging dogs, the breed does suffer its share of inherited or acquired health issues. Some can be treated easily, and others will require major surgeries and protracted rehabilitations. Labrador Retrievers who have been acquired from quality breeders are usually free of most heritable disorders, such as progressive retinal atrophy. Other diseases, like canine cancer, are impossible to predict and difficult to cure. If your Lab develops a serious health issue, he'll probably continue to be a happy dog despite the treatments he must endure.

Centronuclear Myopathy (CNM)

Centronuclear myopathy (CNM) is a heritable disease of the Labrador Retriever; a genetic

Labs with elbow dysplasia should not be exercised hard or for long periods.

mutation is responsible for the condition. The muscles of the affected dog do not develop properly, puppies have missing tendon reflexes, and the affected dogs fail to gain weight. By about five months of age, the CNM dog will begin to stumble and fall. He will have difficulty swallowing because his esophageal muscles are compromised, and food aspiration leads to pneumonia. The symptoms remain for the dog's life: there is no cure, and there is no medical treatment for CNM. A DNA test can confirm that a dog has CNM and can identify carriers of the genetic mutation.

Lifestyle modifications can help the Labrador Retriever with CNM and include feeding a soft gruel rather than hard kibble. Raised water bowls can lessen water aspiration into the lungs.

Elbow Dysplasia

Elbow dysplasia is a polygenic joint disease that affects Labrador Retrievers. Like hip dysplasia, dogs with ED develop very painful arthritis in affected elbows. The ED dog will begin to limp or refuse to bear weight on the limb. Pain and anti-inflammatory medications can be given to the ED-affected dog, but more and more Labrador Retriever owners are opting for surgical intervention for their affected dogs.

The Labrador Retriever with ED should not be exercised hard or for long periods, and that could be a problem because Labs are stoic and love to play. Swimming, short walks, and a healthy diet that keeps your Lab on the skinny side are all good treatments for the dog with ED.

Exercise-Induced Collapse (EIC)

Exercise-induced collapse is a genetic disease in Labrador Retrievers. It is inherited in a recessive manner, which means that two copies of the mutant gene are required for the dog to be affected. Recent advances in genetic testing have honed in on the gene responsible for EIC.

The dog affected with EIC typically is very athletic and works hard in the field. During or after a long training or work session, he will suddenly collapse, often dramatically. His gait will begin to rock, then the rear limbs collapse. Some dogs appear suddenly uncoordinated, lose their balance, and fall over. His muscles will become flaccid, he might begin to hyperventilate, and his temperature could increase. Some dogs have died of drowning when they collapsed during water work. Some dogs require life-saving measures to be taken, but others just need to rest, then seem to "shake it off" in Labrador Retriever fashion after 5 to 25 minutes.

Most affected dogs come from field-trial Labrador Retriever lines, and the distribution of illness crosses both genders and all three colors. The affected dogs have been described as extremely fit, muscular, and highly excitable, with intense personalities. The precise physiological basis of EIC is not yet known, but pedigree analysis, along with clinical and laboratory data, can determine those dogs who might be affected.

The best treatment for EIC is a vigilant owner. Stop exercising your dog at any sign of wobbliness or weakness, and don't allow him to become overexcited, like panting and drooling at the sight of his dumbbell sitting on the table. Some dogs have been treated with low doses of phenobarbital, a medication used for seizure disorders. Others have been treated with special medications for enzyme deficiencies. To date, there is no standard medical treatment other than rest and supportive veterinary measures if the attack is severe.

Any dog who suffers one EIC event should never be worked hard again, and activities that cause high excitement, like repetitive retrieves, should be halted. He can, however, go on to enjoy a long life as a pet and even participate in routine exercise. Light jogging, swimming, and easy hikes are not likely to induce an episode of EIC.

Although fairly healthy, Labrador Retrievers, like other breeds, are not completely free from hereditary health issues and genetic diseases.

Hip Dysplasia

By the time a Labrador Retriever has reached adulthood, he can be tested for hip dysplasia (HD). Because HD is polygenic, and there is no definitive genetic test for this painful orthopedic disorder, testing can only measure the level of disease already present or predict whether the dog will develop HD later in life. Several testing methods exist, including radiograph imaging and physical manipulation of the joints, which measure the laxity within the hip.

Hip dysplasia results from an improper fit between the ball of the femur and the socket of the hip. The dog experiences pain when he moves, sits, or is at rest if the disease is severe. Significant arthritis develops as the dog ages. The symptoms can also vary from dog to dog: some might be less tolerant of physical activity, others will limp, still others begin to sit "sloppy," and favor one hip over the other. Some dysplastic dogs exhibit stiffness and are reluctant to get up and move around or climb stairs. The most commonly inherited orthopedic disease in all dogs, HD is a major concern for Labrador Retrievers, whether the dog is a working retriever or a pet. Selective breeding practices can weed out some of the risk, but because the disease can skip a generation, there are no guarantees that a dog will not develop HD or the associated arthritis later in his life.

To diagnose HD, the veterinarian will palpate the hips and rotate the legs, checking for pain or stiffness in the joint. With the dog sedated (usually), the vet can X-ray the hips to check for proper leg and socket alignment. Radiographs are definitive at the time of the test, but they do not guarantee that the dog won't develop hip dysplasia in the future. The Orthopedic Foundation for Animals (OFA) maintains a registry of X-rays, and specialists rate the dog's hips as excellent, good, fair, or poor. The OFA registry is only comprehensive for those dogs whose radiographs are submitted, however. Many dog owners decide not to submit their dog's X-rays for OFA evaluation if they know that the dog will receive a poor rating or if the radiographs indicate a dog with severe disease.

The PennHIP evaluation for hip dysplasia can be performed by a veterinary specialist when a Labrador Retriever is still a puppy. The evaluation of the puppy includes X-rays of the young dog's joints in neutral and compression views to measure laxity. The measurements rank the puppy relative to other Labrador Retrievers, and offers a "percent likelihood" that the puppy will develop HD in the future. Age, rate of growth, and the degree of laxity in the young dog's hip all are figured into a formula that is up to 90 percent predictive of future disease. Some breeders use the PennHIP evaluation to decide future mating or to eliminate dogs and bitches from their breeding stock. An "open" registry, breeders who have PennHIP evaluations performed on their dogs must agree that the results are included in the database. More comprehensive descriptions of the OFA and PennHIP methods to determine HD or degenerative joint disease can be found on the respective websites of these organizations: www.offa.org and www.research. vet.upenn.edu.

There is no cure for HD, but effective treatments exist. Weight maintenance is critical; an overweight Labrador Retriever is much more likely to develop arthritis in his hips, even if he only has mild HD. Medications to relieve inflammation and pain are effective, and the most severe cases can be treated with hip replacement surgery. This is an expensive surgery, however, and the rehabilitation is extensive.

Progressive Retinal Atrophy (PRA)

Progressive retinal atrophy is the leading cause of blindness in the adult Labrador Retriever, but fortunately, a genetic marker test exists that can identify those dogs who are clear of the disease, as well those who are carriers of the gene, but are clear of PRA themselves. All breeding dogs and bitches should be tested for the PRA gene.

The symptoms of PRA include a loss of night vision, then a progressive loss of vision during daylight hours. The dog will have difficulty marking thrown or shot objects like birds, and then he will be unable to see stationary objects. Because a dog is able to adapt to gradual loss of vision, his owner might not even be aware that her dog is blind until the dog has lost all use of his eyes. Once the dog is blind, he can still lead an active life, albeit with lifestyle modifications.

Labrador Retrievers who are tested annually by a veterinary ophthalmologist and shown to be free of heritable eye disease can be registered by the Canine Eye Registration Foundation (CERF). Dogs are usually tested by one year of age, then annually at least through their breeding years.

GENERIC HEALTH ISSUES

Some health problems that individual Labs can develop are not breed-specific. These issues can be minor nuisances or they can be life-threatening. Your veterinarian is the best source of information when it comes to treatment, whether at the local clinic or from a canine health specialist.

Allergies

Labrador Retrievers are a pretty healthy breed. They do, however, suffer their share of allergies, either from food or environmental contact with allergens. Any allergy can cause the dog to scratch; lick his paws, tail, or anus excessively; break out in a rash; or develop a painful hot spot, which is a nasty inflammation on the skin characterized by loss of hair and oozing.

Exposure to grass, dead leaf matter, dirt, mud, and other environmental agents causes some contact allergies. The dog with contact allergies can be helped by keeping him away from the suspected allergen, although with Labrador Retrievers, the specific trigger might be difficult to identify. Sometimes treatment after exposure is the only way to keep a Labrador Retriever comfortable. Anti-inflammatory medications, antibiotics to control secondary infection after excessive scratching, and use of a collar cone (either Elizabethan or soft) to keep the dog from biting infected skin are the usual methods to treat allergies.

A food allergy can only be confirmed by a diet of exclusion. Some dogs are allergic to certain meat proteins, others to grains in the diet. A veterinarian can help develop an elimination

Training Tidbit

Teach your dog to be still for an unforeseen emergency veterinary exam. As part of his socialization and training, have as many strangers—or friends he does not know—as possible approach your dog slowly. Whisper quiet *stay* commands to him, and, as the stranger lightly touches your dog's head and back, give him a treat. Let him nibble on a piece of cheese during the "exam," and reward him for being still with a rousing game of fetch afterward.

Knowing how to recognize potential health problems and how to handle them is important to your dog's overall well-being.

diet to identify the specific allergen. Dogs with food allergies can go on to have long and happy lives, provided they are not given any food that contains that allergen. Some dogs develop food allergies early in life; others may be much older adults before something in their food starts to cause them grief. Still other dogs will be allergic to one food early in life, and then develop a new allergy to their food as they grow into adulthood.

Treatment for both contact and food allergies includes anti-itch shampoos and antihistamines to help control itching and scratching.

Cancer

Canine cancers are heartbreaking illnesses that often are discovered too far along before detection, with few treatments to offer the dog other than palliative care to improve his quality of life. Labrador Retrievers are not immune to cancer, and the two most studied in this breed are hemangiosarcoma and osteosarcoma.

Hemangiosarcoma

Hemangiosarcoma is a malignant tumor of blood vessels, and while it can affect all dogs, the disease is reported most often in Golden and Labrador Retrievers and in German Shepherd Dogs. The higher incidence suggests a genetic risk factor, which is a research topic at several canine cancer research veterinary hospitals.

This aggressive, highly malignant soft-tissue cancer affects the spleen and heart (visceral form) or can begin in the skin (dermal) and under the skin (hypodermal form). Hemangiosarcoma forms its own blood vessel network, which makes it difficult to detect. As it spreads, tumors form throughout the dog's body, which are almost beyond therapy by the time this cancer is detected.

Dermal hemangiosarcoma appears as a dark or purple skin lesion, and treatment is surgical excision if the lesion is small. Hypodermal tumors are soft or firm masses just beneath the skin, which can also be removed if the tumor hasn't already spread to other organs. For more advanced cases, chemotherapy has been prescribed, but the prognosis is still grim.

Visceral hemangiosarcoma symptoms include lethargy, loss of appetite, weight loss, difficulty breathing, pallor or other symptoms of blood loss, such as pale gums and accumulation of fluid in the dog's abdomen. Often, the dog will exhibit no warning signs until severe clinical symptoms appear, and death can occur six to eight weeks after diagnosis. Although chemotherapy and radiation therapy have been used, hemangiosarcoma continues to be called a silent killer. Supportive palliative care measures can keep the dog comfortable if treatment options fail.

Osteosarcoma

Osteosarcoma is a type of highly aggressive bone tumor that usually attacks a dog's limbs. Symptoms include lameness, a firm swelling on a bone, loss of appetite, weight loss, reluctance to exercise, and irritability and even aggression because of pain. The diagnosis can only be made by radiograph, blood work, and a biopsy of the tumor. The biopsy might be incisional for diagnostic purposes, or the tumor might be excised in its entirety.

Depending on the tumor type and whether the cancer has metastasized, treatment for osteosarcoma might include amputation of the affected limb. Because osteosarcoma spreads to other areas, chemotherapy also might be recommended; while these treatments won't cure osteosarcoma, they could prolong the dog's life and improve his quality of life. Pain relief measures, including powerful medications, are also indicated in cases of osteosarcoma.

Benign Growths

Not every lump and bump and swelling will be malignant, and Labrador Retrievers have their share of these benign growths, especially at the dog gets older. Skin tags and bumps just under the skin, called fatty tissue lipomas,

A weekly hands-on grooming session is a good way to monitor any changes in your Lab's body that may indicate a health problem.

either will be watched carefully for signs of change or the veterinarian will aspirate a few cells for microscopic evaluation. The area of the lump might be shaved, and the dog will receive a numbing anesthetic prior to the biopsy. Depending on the location, a lipoma or skin tag can interfere with a dog's correct movement or be subjected to irritation by his collar or hanging identification tags. Some may be unsightly.

My black Lab, Sam, had eight or nine lipomas removed at once because there were so many, and we had concerns that the lumps were malignant. They were not, and he left the vet's office with a "shave and a haircut" and a few stitches. My yellow Lab, Gracie, developed a larger swelling in her front right armpit; since she was a competition obedience dog at the time, the swelling began to interfere with her natural gait. The lump, when it was removed, was almost golf ball-sized, but it too proved benign. The surgery itself didn't interfere with her work ethic, and a week later Gracie finished her AKC Companion Dog title.

Because the Labrador Retriever is so stoic, even when very ill, owners must monitor their dogs for slight changes in demeanor and appearance. If caught early, some cancers are treatable, and nonmalignant neoplasms can be removed if they are bothersome to the dog or his owner. Again, a weekly hands-on grooming session is a good way to monitor your Lab's health.

ALTERNATIVE THERAPIES

Acupuncture, chiropractic, herbal therapy, homeopathy, and physical rehabilitation medicine have all become accepted standards of care in human medicine, but what about for dogs? These complementary practices now share the veterinary stage, and canine health has benefited from options that previously had not been available under strictly Western medical practices. Many Labrador Retriever owners take advantage of alternative therapies either to prevent illness or disease, to complement the effectiveness of traditional veterinary care, or to help their dogs when conventional veterinary medicine fails or is ineffectual.

Acupuncture

Acupuncture, which literally means "to pierce with a needle," is not quite that simple. More accurately, acupuncture involves the use of tiny needles placed in specific points on the dog's body to create a response that leads to a cure or a lessening of symptoms. The treatment is very effective for painful conditions like arthritis in a Labrador Retriever's dysplastic hips or to treat the pain of a ruptured CCL. Acupuncture can improve the quality of life in canine cancer patients, and is used to help control seizures in the epileptic dog.

Initially, the dog usually has acupuncture treatments several times a week until improvement in his condition peaks and levels out. Some dogs respond quickly to acupuncture and others may never respond, but a lot depends on the owner's level of comfort with the procedure and with the technique of the veterinary acupuncturist. Dogs rarely feel pain during the procedure, and because acupuncture has been shown to raise endorphin levels, many dogs appear to enjoy the sessions. The biggest risk to a canine acupuncture patient occurs when the dog fidgets and the needles fall out, which just means that the treatment won't be helpful. Most dogs tolerate the procedure, and improvement in his ailment should be evident by about the eighth treatment. If not, his condition will probably not be helped by acupuncture.

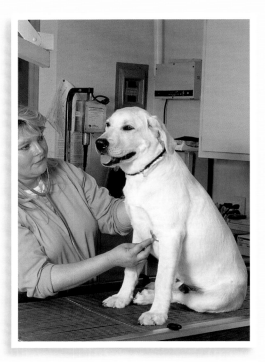

Alternative therapies are often used to compliment traditional medicine.

Chiropractic

Chiropractic care, long used as an alternative therapy in human health care to diagnose, treat, and prevent mechanical disorders of the spine and their effects on the body, is used in the same manner on canine patients. Chiropractors manipulate and adjust the vertebrae in the spine to relieve nerve and cord pressure, which then allows the body to recuperate from disease and injury.

Dogs with back pain are helped by chiropractic therapy, and those prone to spinal problems might have a reduction in incidence of disease or injury. Canine chiropractors treat illnesses as varied as lameness, some cases of incontinence, and lick granulomas. The American Veterinary Chiropractic Association (AVCA) trains and certifies animal chiropractors who practice in the United States.

Because Labrador Retrievers are such versatile athletes, all that jumping, retrieving, dock diving, running, and "welcome home, Mom" body slams can cause spinal problems over time. Excess weight puts incredible stress on the dog's back and causes spine disorders. A Labrador Retriever's "sloppy puppy sit" (both of his rear legs shifted to the same side), especially if he exhibits this as an adult, is an indication that something is not quite right in his spine.

At a chiropractic exam, the chiropractor will put her hands on the dog, and feel each spinal joint for subluxation, which is chiropractic-speak for an abnormally functioning joint. She checks the skin for any areas of warmth or coolness, and tests the mobility in the dog's joints. With very firm thrusts to specific locations, the chiropractor adjusts the misalignment of vertebrae. Unlike the human spine, a dog's vertebrae don't audibly "pop" when alignment is complete. Some dogs might be sore for a day or two following an adjustment because the adjustment is made to an area of his body that is already inflamed. A dog undergoing chiropractic care does not have to be confined, but he will do better if strenuous activity is limited for the first day or even longer, so that his body will continue to heal.

Herbal Therapy

Herbal therapy is the practice of concocting specific parts of specific plants to be given as a supplement to help heal the body, both human and canine. The use of herbs can help a dog fight infections, ease pain, help organs function properly, and improve hormone balance. Herbs have been shown to help a dog get rid of toxins in his body and enhance his resistance to stress. Herbs don't replace traditional pharmacology, but together with traditional medications, herbal therapy works in concert to help relieve illness and enhance canine well-being.

Plants have been used by people all over the world for centuries to fight disease and to maintain health. Herbal therapists claim that herbs cause fewer side effects than a chemical pharmaceutical used to treat the same condition. Modern pharmacology grew out of the study of herbs and other plants to treat disease, and herbalists continue to use the raw plant material to treat disease. Because herbal therapy can be delivered in any form—powder, pill, lotion, and liquid—a dog who is a picky eater might thumb his muzzle at a powder on his kibble, but he might lap up a tea added to his water bucket.

One criticism of herbal therapy is that the herb quality can be inconsistent. Variables such as the quality of the soil, the water availability, sunlight, and even pesticide runoff can affect the conditions of herb growth and potency. Because herbs are considered a supplement, manufacturers are not necessarily regulated or monitored, so all products are not equal from one manufacturer to the other.

Herbal remedies generally are canine-safe, but they can have side effects like nausea or vomiting. Some pets are allergic to certain herbs and will itch or swell. Other herbs are extremely toxic to dogs and shouldn't be administered. Those include tea tree oil, pennyroyal, hops, comfrey, and garlic. Dogs with thyroid disease should never be given kelp because the added iodine exacerbates thyroid conditions. Herbs and some drugs can interact, which can cause disastrous effects in dogs.

Before you begin herbal therapy to treat any condition in your dog, talk with your veterinarian. While only a few vets have extensive knowledge of herbal medicine, many have taken courses in veterinary herbalism. The Veterinary Botanical Medical Association (VBMA) maintains a list of veterinary herbalists at their website, www.vbma.org.

Homeopathy

Homeopathy is probably the least understood of all holistic health practices. Literally, the term means that "like cures

The use of herbs can help a dog fight infections, ease pain, help organs function properly, and improve hormone balance.

like," or that the symptoms or illness that any substance causes can also be cured by that same substance. Homeopathic remedies are inexpensive and available at health food stores, but prescribing homeopathic remedies for a dog is very complicated and should not be undertaken by a dog owner who does not have training in homeopathy. Veterinary homeopaths are certified by the Academy of Veterinary Homeopathy (AVH), which maintains a list of credentialed vets at their website, www.theavh.org. Owners interested in finding a veterinary homeopath can get referrals and information on the site.

Multi-Dog Tip

Most dogs who suffer bite wounds are bitten by other dogs, and a lot of those bites occur during fights between dogs in the same household. Some bites arise from territorial disputes or guarding of resources such as the water bowl, food, toys, and even humans in the home. Never try to pull fighting dogs apart; instead, spray the dogs with water from an outdoor hose or kitchen sink sprayer, or dump a bucket of water over the dogs' heads. Scream, whistle, stomp the ground—do anything you can to distract the dogs until they stop. Once you separate them, check for wounds and get prompt veterinary care for any dog who has been injured.

Physical Therapy

The benefits of physical therapy cannot be understated for hardworking dogs, dogs who have suffered traumatic injuries, obese dogs, and amputees. Even dogs who aren't ill or injured but who need to stay in top physical form to perform at high-level sports are taken to canine physical therapists or rehabilitation specialists.

Most canine physical therapists are veterinarians or veterinary technicians who have taken hours of advanced training in musculoskeletal development and injuries. Therapies they utilize might include cold or heat massage, exercises to retrain muscle memory or to rebuild damaged tissue, underwater or above-ground treadmill sessions, and specific water-based exercise. The therapist will do a comprehensive gait analysis and look for abnormalities in the dog's muscular or skeletal systems. Veterinarians will refer a client to a rehabilitation specialist or physical therapist, and owners can also go directly to a specialist.

One of my Labs had a weight problem due to an inability to exercise after major surgery, exacerbated by my own delusion that giving her a treat would make up for her inability to walk unaided for almost two years. Working with my vet, we tried everything to get the weight off Gracie—from prescription diets to home-cooked meals to adding more strenuous exercise to her life. Finally, we consulted a canine physical rehabilitation specialist.

The therapist showed me that arthritis had begun to affect not just how Gracie sat, walked, and jumped but that because of the disease, Gracie couldn't even put equal weight on all four paws. The therapist's recommendations included specific home exercises, underwater treadmill sessions twice a week, a different prescription diet, and a cold-turkey removal of all treats, even training treats, from Gracie's diet. For six months, we followed the regimen. I learned when and how to massage Gracie's sore and weak muscles, where to put the heat packs, and when to use ice. We taught her how to use her rear legs not just to walk but to jump, to gather herself up and lift off the floor, to finally soar like a Labrador Retriever.

Gracie's life changed. Instead of lying in her soft orthopedic pillow at the foot of our bed, she could do a standing 18-inch (45.5-cm) leap onto the bed. She was able to compete in rally and obedience. She became a therapy dog extraordinaire, with energy to visit senior citizens and children. Gracie finally seemed, well, happier. In the process, she lost almost 20 pounds (9 kg) and at this writing, is at her target weight, where's she been for more than a year. The prescription food is no longer necessary. She doesn't snore (well, no more than most Labs), and she doesn't pant after long walks. Gracie actually runs now, and there is no one happier with her progress than me.

TTouch

Related to physical therapy, another adjunct therapy is TTouch, or Tellington Touch, named for its founder, Linda Tellington-Jones. She developed her light touching techniques in the 1970s; these touches don't manipulate the animal's muscles but rather stimulate the nervous system by light sensory stimulation of the animal's skin. TTouch is said to calm hyperactive or aggressive pets and ease stiffness and pain in sore muscles. Each different stroke in the TTouch program has a different goal, such as relaxation, reduction of anxiety, or pain relief. Trained TTouch therapists can be located at the website www.lindatellington-jones.com.

EMERGENCY CARE

In addition to health and wellness knowledge, Labrador Retriever owners should have a

Because weather- and sports-related injuries are not uncommon in Labrador Retrievers, it's important to have a basic knowledge of first aid and emergency care.

foundation in emergency care for their dogs. Our breed is active, curious, and strong, qualities we dearly love, but they can also get our dogs into trouble. Weather-related illness and injury, eating the wrong food or household items, even stings and bites, cause untold amounts of suffering in animals. Kennel clubs, animal welfare organizations, and even the Red Cross all offer classes and seminars in basic first aid for pets.

Faced with an emergency, would you know what to do for or with your Labrador Retriever? While the following is only a basic guide, and you must get your dog to a veterinarian or emergency clinic immediately, there are steps you can take that could mitigate a disaster or avert death. The mantra of emergency care is this: If you force yourself to think, you will not panic. Keep a pet first-aid kit accessible; if you travel with your dog, have a second kit in your car. This should include vet wrap, clean sterile gauze, scissors, tweezers, styptic powder, antiseptic lotion or liquid, a muzzle, and an extra collar and short leash or looped kennel lead.

Bites

Dogs can and do get bitten by other dogs, by cats, and by wild animals. Whether the bite happens during rough play with the neighbor's dog, by the household cat rudely awakened by your Lab, or by any animal out-of-doors, assess the severity. Most bites are puncture wounds, and they can close and clot quickly; ripped bites might gush bright red blood. If bleeding is heavy, put firm pressure on the wound, cover it with sterile gauze, and wrap with self-clinging vet wrap. If the bite is a puncture wound, it will still need to be treated. If you can, clip the hair away from the site so that your vet will be able to find the wound; clean the puncture and take the dog to the vet. All wounds need veterinary care; some dogs might have internal injuries, and others might need antibiotics, especially for puncture wounds. The risk of infection from a bite is high, so you'll need to watch the wound for any signs of abscess development.

Bleeding

Bleeding that doesn't clot after a couple of minutes, that is dark red, or that spurts bright red blood is very serious. To control bleeding, apply a gauze pad, clean cloth, or even a sanitary napkin to the wound. If blood continues to seep, don't remove the first pad. Place a second cloth or pad on top of that one, and continue to apply pressure to the wound.

Dogs who have serious wounds are likely to become aggressive or disoriented, and will need to be restrained, muzzled, and leashed. Find someone to drive you and your dog to an emergency veterinarian, and monitor the dog for signs of shock, which can kill in just a few minutes. Continue to apply pressure to the dog's wound, and wrap him in a blanket or towel.

Labrador Retrievers sometimes bleed from scrapes to their ear flaps, and it might look much worse than it is because blood vessels are so close to the surface of the skin there. An absorbent pad will stop the bleeding, and then you can cover the dog's ear with a section of pantyhose. Don't cover the dog's eyes, nose, or mouth, and don't make jokes about his new temporary look. Rather, tell him how brave he is to wear pantyhose in public.

Bloat

Bloat is an emergency condition that is on the rise and is especially prevalent in larger dogs like Labrador Retrievers. The reasons that dogs suffer bloat aren't entirely clear, and several researchers are looking at different causes. Whatever the cause, air gets trapped in the stomach and, as that organ swells, it presses against other organs and blood vessels in the dog's abdomen. The stomach might twist—called volvulus or torsion—so that the building pressure can't be burped or flatulated away. A dog with bloat has a painful, distended

Normal Vital Signs

- A dog's normal temperature is between 99.5° and 102.5°F (38° and 39°C).
- A dog's normal heart rate is 80 to120 beats per minute.
- A dog normally takes 15 to 30 breaths per minute.

Ensure your Lab's safety by always keeping toxic items, such as harmful plants, out of his reach both indoors and outdoors.

stomach, behaves restlessly, and may try to vomit without success.

Your dog's life depends on your actions in the next 30 minutes. If you live far away from your vet, call her and ask for instructions. Immediately start driving the dog to a vet, any vet. The dog may go into shock and could die in just a few minutes. If his gums are pale and he becomes weak, keep him warm to combat the shock. Wrap him in a warm blanket and turn the car's heat on.

Emergency surgery can untwist the stomach, but almost 10 percent of dogs who suffer one episode of bloat will have a repeat. To reduce the chance, feed your dog several small meals throughout the day, and monitor him so that he doesn't gulp his food down all at once.

Poisoning

Because Labrador Retrievers are sneaky thieves and will snarf (our word for eating inappropriate items) anything they can fit in their snout, the risk of poison ingestion is high. Some things you can plan for as you pet-proof your home; basically, if you don't want "it" to end up in your dog's stomach, don't leave "it" lying out where the dog can see or smell your valuables, your shoes, the bread, cleaning supplies, even shower soap.

The great Sam, my first Lab, was renamed "that Gillette dog" by the vet after Sam gulped down a disposable razor. He'd jumped into the shower and emerged with a blue plastic razor dangling from his mouth. It all pretty much came out the same way it went in, mangled but almost whole. For days, I followed Sam and inspected all of his poop just to make sure that the plastic and the blade were intact. Another young Lab of mine managed to gnaw the end off of a puppy-proofed plastic teething toy. Again, hours were devoted to monitored poop time, and she was none the worse for her trip to the vet nor the multiple doses of petroleum jelly sandwiches we fed her (with vet supervision) to help the plastic slide right on out.

Not every item your Lab ingests will have such a good outcome. Prepare for poison accidents and be able to identify the toxin.

Disaster Preparedness

Disaster preparedness for your family should include plans for your Labrador Retriever. Family fire drills, tornado drills, wildfire escape routes, and hurricane preparedness should take into account the needs of your dog during and after a disaster. Pack enough food and water for your dog for at least three days, and put the items in a solid plastic container that you can grab and go, if necessary. If your area is prone to flooding, know how you will get your dog out of the area if you evacuate. In the event of a tornado, place crates in your storm shelter area. Put the dog in his crate during a drill so that he won't panic if a storm approaches and the family takes shelter. In the event of a hurricane, know your evacuation route and take your dog with you. Painful lessons from past hurricanes have at last led to legislation that requires shelters to take in family pets also.

Most poisons can be treated by forcing the dog to vomit, but only if he is alert. One or two teaspoons of hydrogen peroxide for every 10 pounds (4.5 kg) of body weight, squirted on the back of the dog's tongue, should cause him to vomit. When you take the dog to the vet, make sure that you take the bottle of poison along with any vomited material. Most poisons have specific antidotes, and the vet can begin treatment right away.

The National Animal Poison Control Center, a service of the American Society for the Prevention of Cruelty for Animals (ASPCA), maintains a comprehensive database of animal poisons and will give telephone consultations. Their telephone number is (800) 548-2423; there may be a charge for the service. Most pet first-aid books and pamphlets include a list of common plant and chemical poisons, along with recommended treatments.

Weather-Related Injuries

Weather-related injuries are not uncommon in Labrador Retrievers because the breed is exposed to elements that many other dogs won't encounter. Working field Retrievers are more vulnerable, but even family pets can suffer frostbite and heatstroke.

Frostbite

Pets with frostbite might limp, or their earflaps might hang awkwardly. Redness and blisters could appear hours or days later. Because most dogs with frostbite will also suffer hypothermia, veterinary care is urgent. If a toe or paw appears pale, gray, or blue beneath frozen skin, begin to dunk the area in lukewarm water. Warm harder-to-reach areas with a lukewarm, dripping wet towel held against the skin for about 20 minutes, and get your dog to the vet as soon as possible.

Heatstroke is more common than frostbite in Labrador Retrievers because, as summer descends, families take their Labs out and about and don't notice that their dog is getting overheated.

Heatstroke

Heatstroke is more common than frostbite in Labrador Retrievers because, as summer descends, families take their Labs out and about and don't notice that when their dog is getting overheated. Dogs don't sweat to regulate body temperature; rather, they pant. A dog with moderate heat illness will have a bright red tongue, and his gums will feel sticky. Encourage him to drink cold water, and park him in front of an air conditioner or fan. If his temperature goes above 106°F (41.1°C), he is in danger of heat shock. Go immediately to the vet; keep the car cool, and try to lower the dog's temperature with ice packs on his neck.

Never, ever leave your Labrador Retriever in the car while you go on errands. "But I leave the windows cracked," or "But I left the engine running and the air conditioner on" are excuses that have led to dog deaths. Engines sputter, air conditioners conk out. Last year in my area, a police officer left his K9 partner in the safety of his cruiser, with the engine running and air on, while he stopped for lunch. Twenty minutes later, he returned to the car to find a dead dog because his car engine had malfunctioned. Over the past ten years, more than 100 K9 dogs have died in this manner, along with untold numbers of family pets. In most states, it's against the law to leave a dog in the car, even when precautions have been taken for the dog's safety. Just don't do it.

CHAPTER 9

LABRADOR RETRIEVER TRAINING

What excites your Labrador Retriever? Is his favorite thing a particular toy, play retrieves in the backyard, or the promise of a belly rub at the end of a day? Does he drool when the refrigerator door opens? Any of these things—or a combination of all of them—are motivators, and you can use them to your advantage as you train your dog.

A young adult Lab begins to assert his independence and free spirit in a number of ways, which might be fun for the family but also could be destructive. Consistent training can prevent problems or redirect your dog's energy if his behavior devolves. Daily obedience exercises not only help establish the hierarchy within the dog's pack, but the training also teaches him that his owner is in charge, not the other way around. By adulthood, the Lab is a strong dog physically, and if he is not trained, he can become hard to control.

INTERMEDIATE OBEDIENCE TRAINING

Obedience training begun in puppyhood continues through the Labrador Retriever's adult years. Now that his growth plates have closed, he can take on more strenuous exercise, training, and fun. In order to enjoy all the activities and canine sports in which this breed excels, the dog must be trained to respond to his owner's commands. Whether competing in obedience or agility, hunt tests or dock diving, or whether the dog is a beloved pet that spends his time on walks with his family, these commands cross all venues from the backyard patio to the hunt line.

Before You Begin

Before you begin a training session, make sure both you and your dog are calm. If you come home to find that he has taken the toilet paper on a merry twisting roller-coaster run through the house, it's not the time to train him. Take some deep breaths and clean up the mess before you begin a session. Likewise, if your dog is diving after chipmunks in the backyard, have him sit and redirect his focus.

Want to Know More?

To review training the *sit* command, see Chapter 4: Training Your Labrador Retriever Puppy.

The heel is a position on your left side.

Whether you devote 5 minutes several times a day or 30 minutes all in one session to training, have a goal and make a plan. For example, in 5 minutes, you can teach your Lab "doggy pushups," and have him perform the *sit* then the *down* in rapid succession. This expends pent-up energy, and he'll be able to give you better attention. The next time you train your dog, work on teaching him the *down-stay*.

Randomize the lessons, and randomize the rewards. You don't have to keep popping a treat in your dog's mouth; he'll only learn that you give out food a lot. Instead, make him work for his dinner and his training treat. Practice the "nothing in life is free" principle, whether it's a special game, or breakfast, or that soup bone in the freezer. Every time you give something to your dog, expect him to do a trick or follow a command first. This also reinforces your position in the pack hierarchy.

THE *HEEL*

Many trainers use the word "heel" as a command that means, "Let's go this way." Heel is actually a position, and it means "I want you to sit here on my left side, with your ear lined up to my pants seam, and wait until I tell you what to do next." Now, your dog isn't going to understand all that at first, so you'll teach this in increments. He might be forging ahead of you, or he might be lagging behind you. He might even sit behind your legs as you begin to train this. The goal is to have your dog sit by your side and occasionally check in with you, and be attentive enough to hear or see the next command you give.

As one of the basic commands for most canine sports, your dog will need to understand the concept of heel. He will have to calmly walk to the line during a hunt test, or he will need to be in heel position as you walk the ring pattern in obedience and rally competitions. Later, when he understands the concept, you'll be able to say, "Max, heel," and he will walk by your side down the street, either on a leash or off.

Teaching the *Heel*

To teach the *heel*, your dog must understand that "heel" means "sit on my left side."

1. With a treat or other lure in your left hand, encourage your dog to sit to your left. Every time he does, say "yes" or "good" or any other word that you can remember, but make this word consistent. Also, the sound of your voice is important. Try to be upbeat; a deep, threatening tone or a high squeal will not sound pleasant to a dog. Keep your voice happy. At the same time that you say your particular marker word, give your dog a small treat.

2. Practice this often, and change out the treat or the toy. Perhaps one time you might say, "Good boy," and give him a bit of cooked hotdog; the next time, say, "Good boy," and engage him in a game of tag. Keep your dog guessing so that he'll never know what you're planning to do next. Make this fun, make it a game, and make it one he wants to play with you.

3. Every time your dog comes and sits to your left, whether you asked him to or not, give him a reward. This is the time to pair his action with your command word, which is "heel." Whenever your dog sits or stands next to your left leg, say "Good heel, Max." Let him begin to understand that the position and the word "heel"

are one and the same. This won't happen overnight. Despite their high level of intelligence, not all Labrador Retrievers learn at the same rate. One dog might begin to understand the concept after 30 minutes; another dog might still be learning after six weeks.

4. Once that concept is understood, though, you can begin to up the ante. Expect your dog to sit straight or to sit forward on both haunches and not rolled over on one hip. Do bunny hops: take a half-step forward and say "heel, sit," in rapid succession. Take your dog for a walk on leash, and occasionally tell him to heel. If he doesn't respond, you can give the leash a tug while you pat your left hip. In your upbeat voice say, "Silly dog, did you forget where heel

By the Numbers

Use the "20 times 20" rule when training any obedience command. Practice the command 20 times a day for 20 days before you expect your dog to truly understand the command. For example, have your Lab practice a *sit-stay* five times in one session, and do this four times each day. These are short spurts of training, not long, drawn-out, formal sessions. After 20 days of consistent work, your dog will know what behavior you want from him when you say, "Sit, stay." Always end with praise, and tell him that he's the most brilliant dog that ever lived.

The *stay* command asks your dog to remain in place until released.

be thinking, "What is the crazy woman gonna do next?"

6. When your dog can walk with you in a straight line for 10 paces, then 20, then down the street to the neighbor's house and back, it's time to increase the game expectations again. Inside an enclosure, whether it's your fenced yard, a vacant ball field, or a tennis court, allow your dog to be off lead and just start walking in big loops. When he runs up to your left side to check in, give him a treat, tell him he's beautiful, and keep walking. Your dog is now learning to come to heel when he has other options, like running to the fence edge and sniffing for squirrels. He'll become more consistent, though, and begin to stay by your side while you walk in a big circle around the yard. And you're going to give him a jackpot every time he stays with you.

position is?" then let him remember where he's supposed to be.

5. As your dog becomes proficient, and when he understands the *heel* command and what his reaction should be, then you can begin short walks on leash. Give your command to heel and take a few steps. When your dog can take a few steps in proper position, step away, throw up your hands, and have a party! Tell him that he is just the most brilliant Labrador Retriever in the whole world, and offer him a food reward. This type of random reward will leave him guessing; he'll

Training Tidbit

If your dog continues to break when you train the *down-stay*, apply gentle pressure to his shoulders when you give him the command. Tell him to *down*, then as you say the word "stay," put one hand on his shoulders and use the same amount of pressure as you would if you were about to brush or pet him; the gentle push down will help him understand *stay*. Never forcefully hold your dog down; rather, as soon as you feel his muscles relax, use your marker word ("yes, good, etc."), then release him and give him a treat.

7. Randomly, as you walk this loop, call your dog to heel. When he responds correctly, say your marker word with the command: "Good heel, Max!" Give him something really tasty, like a chicken nugget. Break away and play a fun game, throw a ball for him to fetch, or start a game of tag.

Your dog's skill at heeling will take a long time and many hours and miles of practice, but the more sessions you practice this command, the better he will become. Be patient and consistent, and most of all, make this fun for your Lab.

THE *STAY*

The *stay* command is the life-saver of obedience, and it will be one of the most important lessons you teach your Labrador Retriever. A dog who understands and obeys the *stay* won't rush the door when a neighbor rings the bell. A dog commanded to stay will not chase a ball out of the yard and into the street. The *stay* is also a basic exercise in competitive obedience and rally, agility, and field work because the dog must be able to stay in position while another dog works.

Teaching the *Stay*

When you tell your dog to stay, you want him to understand that it stay means "to wait right where you are until I tell you otherwise." Ultimately, your dog should keep eye contact with you and wait for the next command, whether that next command is a recall (come to me) or a go find (to pick out an item with your scent on it and bring it back to you).

1. Begin to teach the *stay* command close to a door.
2. With your dog on leash and either sitting or lying down, wave the palm of your left hand just beyond his muzzle and say, "Stay."
3. Open the door, and when he breaks his position, close the door and say in a calm voice, "Uh oh, nope," and put him back

where he was, then tell him again to stay.
4. Once you can open the door and he doesn't move, praise him, allow him to move around, give him a huge jackpot treat, and practice again. Get him used to hearing a release word, such as "okay," when you release him from the *stay*.

This command can be practiced all day long throughout the house and yard. When you pour kibble into his bowl, tell your dog to stay out of the kitchen until you place the bowl on the floor. When you get ready to take your dog for a ride in the car, command him to stay until you get the car door open. Again, as he starts to understand the *stay* command and the proper response, he'll start to really pay attention. Since you are practicing "nothing in life is free," your dog knows that he will not get that belly rub until he holds his position and waits for your release word.

Reinforce the behavior you want by rewarding you Lab with food.

The *down-stay* allows your dog to begin to exhibit more self-control as he becomes proficient with obedience commands.

THE *DOWN-STAY*

As your Lab begins to understand that the *stay* command means "don't move until I say otherwise," you can start to pair the *stay* with a position, either down or sit. The *down-stay* allows your dog to begin to exhibit more self-control as he becomes proficient with obedience commands. This command has practical applications, too. On a walk around the block, when you stop to talk to a neighbor, you can put your dog in a *down-stay*, and then step away from him to carry on a conversation. When you come home from a shopping trip, put your dog in a *down-stay* before you prop open the door to bring in the groceries. To control a Labrador

Retriever's excited jumping up on people, a *down-stay* command is a great tool.

Teaching the *Down-Stay*

To teach the *down-stay* command, your dog will first need to be reliable with the *stay*.

1. Lure your dog into a *down* as you did when he was a puppy, then say "Stay."
2. Step directly in front of him, wait a moment, then step back into heel position. If he didn't move, give him a treat and tell him that he's a brilliant dog.
3. Repeat this throughout the day in many different locations in the house.
4. Begin to require longer stretches: command the *down -stay* during all the commercials

that interrupt your favorite television show, or while dinner cooks, or while the laundry is folded. Randomize the appearance of the *down-stay*, also. Sit in your favorite chair, and put your dog in a *down-stay* either in front of you or to the side.

When you are sure that the dog understands the *down-stay* command, take the show on the road. During a walk, if a jogger approaches, command the *down-stay* until the jogger has passed. Do the same with other strangers: bicyclists, babies in strollers, motorcyclists, and delivery trucks. Get your dog used to following the command despite all the different sounds, smells, and locations. Put him in a *down-stay* while you clip his nails or while you clean his ears. When you finish the grooming chores, release him and play, and tell him how beautiful he is after his pedicure.

THE *SIT-STAY*

The *sit-stay* command has the same practical applications as the *down-stay*. Because you'll combine two different skills, the *sit* and the *stay*, make sure your dog understands both of these commands before you pair them together. He will learn not only that he has to sit right where he is told to sit, but he must remain sitting in that spot until he is told to do something else. He'll apply this knowledge in canine sports like agility, rally, and obedience.

Teaching the *Sit-Stay*

Train the *sit-stay* command much like you train the *down-stay*.

1. With your dog on leash sitting in heel position, wave your left palm in a sweep across his face, say, "Stay," and stand right in front of him, toe to toe.
2. Move back into heel, give him a treat, or say your marker word. Repeat this dozens of times in varied locations.

Training your Lab well will make him a more valued member of the family and community.

3. Once your dog can sit and stay with you nearby, begin to step farther away from him. You can go behind him, take two steps to the side, or step in front of him and go the length of the leash. Again, reward randomly with a treat, but always praise your Lab when he doesn't move. If he does move, correct him with a calm, "uh oh," and put him back where he was before he moved. When he's back in position, praise and treat.

If you have difficulty training the *sit-stay* at any point, then back up a step or two. If your Lab follows you when you move to the end of his leash, you've tried to train this too quickly.

Slow down, and just move a couple of steps away from him. Once he reliably will sit and stay, you can begin to require the behavior at other times. Before you clip his leash to his collar to go on a walk, have him sit and stay for a few moments. Before you put down his breakfast bowl, command a *sit-stay* and then release him to eat. Teach him to *sit-stay* before you throw his tennis ball.

Practice the *sit-stay* on a long line, and work up to the full length, whether the line is 10 feet (3 m) long or 30 feet (9 m) long. In a basement or other room where there are no distractions, work your Lab off leash. Start from a close distance, though, as you transition from on leash to off leash work. If your dog breaks position, you've gone too far too quickly. Clip him back to the leash, and when you are sure he understands the commands, you can begin off leash work again.

Your dog is probably a genius Labrador Retriever, but there will be many instances when he'll test you. My yellow Lab, Gracie, was proficient on the off-leash *sit-stay*. One day we were practicing in the yard when a cat rustled in the bushes suddenly. Gracie broke her position and was off, darting in and out of the shrubs. I had to do the infamous Labrador run to catch her, bring her back to her prior location, and command her to sit and stay again. This is a pretty typical situation. Our dogs are curious and strong-willed, so we must be more creative and stronger than they are.

THE *STAND*

The *stand* command is one of the easiest to teach, and it has practical applications. Veterinarians love clients who have taught their dogs to stand still for an examination. Vet technicians appreciate a calm dog who stands while blood is drawn. A groomer who has to work with a squealing, squirming dog won't be able to bathe and rinse him, but a dog who is calm and stands quietly in the tub will quickly become a welcomed client.

Teaching the *Stand*

This command is much easier to train when your Labrador Retriever is hungry.

1. Start with your dog sitting in heel position. Then, with your tasty treat in your right hand, move that hand to just in front of his mouth. He might try to scoot forward to grab the food. At first, reward every movement with a nibble, but because you want him to stand, don't tolerate those bunny hops for long.

2. If necessary, slip your left hand under his collar. Put your right hand (holding the treat) in front of his nose. If he scoots, hold him back. As soon as he pops up into a stand, release the treat and praise him for being so smart. Then, put him back in a sit

Multi-Dog Tip

Involve all the dogs in the household to your advantage when training, but train only one dog at a time. Put your other dogs in their crates and let them watch as you work with one dog first. Then, put that dog in his crate, bring out the next, and let him perform the commands. It won't take long for your dogs to clamor in a "Me first," or "Me next," manner. This game doesn't create jealousy or tension between dogs; instead, it helps to create drive and willingness to work.

and do it over, and over, and over again. This exercise can even be trained using his evening meal as his training treat.

3. Once your dog fully understands the notion that when your right hand is in front of nose, he should stand up, you should begin to randomize the treats. Instead of popping a piece of food into his mouth when he stands, say your marker word followed by praise. If your dog struggles during this phase, just be patient with him. He's learning, again, that nothing in life is free. He might throw a different behavior at you, like a belly flop, a fast down, or a twirl around your legs. Your dog is giving you effort as he begins to understand what you want, so never correct these indiscretions. Once he stands and is still, give him a treat.

The *stand* command can be road-tested at the pet supply store, at the veterinarian, and on your daily walks while he's on leash. Practice without distractions before you expect your dog to comply while there are other dogs and cats in the store or at the veterinary clinic. Use different length leashes, too. Clip a long line to his collar and go to the front yard, rather than the backyard. Command the *stand*, and walk a few paces away. Pause, then return to heel position next to your dog. Throw a party, grab a toy, and play with your dog when he follows your instructions. Let him know that when he complies, he gets extra hugs and treats and pats on his head.

PRACTICE OFTEN

All of these commands can be trained simultaneously. During one short session work, on the *sit-stay*; later in the day, practice the *stand* and leave your dog for a few moments. Later, while the evening news is on television, put him in a *down-stay* while you enjoy your dessert.

Correct and Praise

Every time your dog breaks from position, you must correct him, put him back in position, and then praise him. Every correction—whether you verbally scold with an "oh no, that's not right" comment, or whether you turn your back on your dog and refuse to look at him until he noses your hand—must be followed by praise. This teaches your dog that when he does something wrong, he might get in trouble, but you will still love him.

Correct and praise, over and over, hundreds of times in various settings, using all the commands you are training, to teach your dog that he won't get what he wants until he does what you've commanded. Don't begin to add distractions—another dog in the house, children at play in the yard, or the television volume turned up high—until your dog reliably follows a command.

Labrador Retrievers learn quickly, but they also learn to manipulate their owners. When your dog refuses to obey a command, turn your back or put him in his crate for a few minutes. Don't let him nose your hand. Don't play with your dog, pet him, or encourage bad behavior, and that bad behavior will begin to fade. Your dog is grown physically, but he will always retain that Labrador Retriever puppy mentality. Your job is to teach him when puppy playtime is appropriate, and when adult behavior is required.

CHAPTER 10

LABRADOR RETRIEVER PROBLEM BEHAVIORS

Most canine behaviors described as "destructive" or "problematic" by dog owners are normal actions or interactions that can be avoided, mitigated, and prevented. Labrador Retrievers are active dogs, with a high need for strenuous exercise, dogs who thrive on work. The Labrador Retriever who is denied daily activity becomes a dog who will dig, bark, chew, and annoy his owners. More Labrador Retrievers end up in shelters because of their owner's inability or unwillingness to properly train them, and they become pulling, out-of-control bundles of muscle.

A DOG'S NATURAL INSTINCTS

Dogs repeat behaviors that are intrinsically satisfying. They dig in the garden, they steal bread off the counter, they jump on visitors, and they pull hard on their end of the leash, the owner flailing along behind and trying to either keep up or stop them. Excessive barking results from boredom. Chewing the children's clothing becomes a management issue. Jumping up on people reflects a lack of consistent adherence to house rules. Most of these behaviors are normal, although

inappropriate for the time or place. These dogs can relearn proper house manners, and need to be retrained for their own safety.

The temperament of the Labrador Retriever is supposed to be stable, warm, loving, biddable, and willing. Some Labs fall within those guidelines, others are very mellow, and yet others are highly strung. Your dog's personality probably falls somewhere in the middle, but even those mellow dogs will find creative ways to challenge their owner's authority from time to time. Problem behaviors can get out of control in a hurry if the owner isn't proactive. Anticipate what your dog is likely to do in any given situation, and then take steps to prevent escalation.

SEEKING PROFESSIONAL HELP

There are two things to keep in mind if you are faced with a problem with your Lab. First, always look for a medical or physical cause of any behavioral issue, especially if the onset is sudden. For example, if your Lab starts to growl when you pet his back, he may be in pain and his growl is a warning that your touch hurts him. Second, *do not* try to fix a serious problem behavior, such as aggression, according to any television or Internet program. You need a professional, in-home canine behaviorist consultation before beginning a behavior modification program for aggression.

Various professionals and groups offer assistance, evaluation, management, and training advice. Depending on the dog's history and temperament, the extent of the problem, and the ability of the owner to help the dog, here are some resources:

• Dog trainers have a long history of success with training or retraining a dog with a problem behavior. Experience counts when dealing with a peculiar behavior.

By the Numbers

More Labrador Retrievers are surrendered to their breeders, shelters, and rescue groups because of behavior issues than for any other reason. A dog can develop a problem behavior at any age. Just because your dog is an adult and out of the destructive puppy stage doesn't guarantee that he will behave properly all the time. Patient training or retraining will teach a dog that he doesn't get what he wants by engaging in negative behavior, and that he will receive special treats, lots of belly rubs, and warm praise from his owner when he behaves. Behaviorists and trainers with experience in the problem should be called upon to provide helpful advice and behavior modification techniques.

Ask your veterinarian and friends for recommendations, or ask any trainer for a referral from previous clients.

• **Association of Pet Dog Trainers (APDT)** maintains a list of member trainers who take continuing-education courses. A searchable database is on their website at www.apdt.com.

• **Applied Animal Behaviorist** uses known animal behavior to mediate conflicts or problems that occur between dogs and their owners. A Certified Applied Animal Behaviorist (CAAB) has a master's or Ph.D.-level education, at least five years of experience in the field, and a record of professional accomplishment. Search for these professionals at www.animalbehavior.org.

• **American College of Veterinary Behaviorists (ACVB)** promotes education and training of veterinarians in animal behavior. Veterinarians with this certification serve a residency, present case studies, and sit for a proficiency exam. Vets with the ACVB designation can be identified at www.dacbv.org.

• **American Veterinary Society of Animal Behavior (AVSAB)** includes those veterinarians who treat behavioral problems in their patients. Members of the AVSAB advocate the use of behavior modification and medications if necessary. The website is www.avsabonline.org.

• **International Association of Animal Behavior Consultants (IAABC)** is an organization of behavior consultants. Members must complete many hours of continuing-education credits and certifications in training techniques, animal behavior, and case studies. A list of members is available at www.iaabc.org.

• **International Association of Canine Professionals (IACP)** is a professional

Because aggression is such a complex behavioral challenge, the need for assistance from a professional behavior consultant cannot be stressed enough.

membership group of so-called "super trainers"— the high-level trainers whom other trainers look to for help with problem cases. A list of members is available at www.canineprofessionals.com.

- **Society of Veterinary Behavior Technicians (SVBT)** is a professional membership group that provides and promotes continuing and advanced education for veterinary technicians who consult on training, management, and behavior modification. Most SVBT members work in conjunction with a veterinarian, and they are listed at www.svbt.org.

AGGRESSION

Aggression in a dog is cited as a main reason for surrender to an animal shelter. Aggression is a range of behaviors such as snarling, growling, snapping, biting, and attacking. Threats can escalate without warning. The victim may be another dog in the household, or he or she may be the dog's owner. Because aggression is such a complex behavioral challenge, and the consequences can be disastrous, the need for assistance from a behavior consultant cannot be stressed enough.

Labrador Retrievers who display aggression do not have the normal Lab temperament. It's helpful, though, to look at the different

If your dog barks excessively when left alone, he is likely bored and lonely.

types of aggression while you wait for your appointment with a canine behavior expert. Your dog may be reacting in an aggressive manner because he's afraid. This is his defense mechanism, and it is his way of saying he thinks he is in danger of being harmed. If a dog perceives that a raised arm is a signal that he is about to be hit, he may bite or growl to protect himself.

Other dogs display aggression because they are protecting their territory, their people, or their toys. They defend their food, or they will defend other members of their pack. Some lactating bitches will display aggression to protect their puppies. If a dog is displaying social aggression, he may be taking advantage of an opportunity to advance in the hierarchy within his pack. Pack standing often determines which dog is fed first, which dog gets petted first, or which dog gets to sleep on the bed versus the floor. A type of canine rivalry develops when pack dynamics becomes unstable; perhaps the alpha dog has become ill or has died, or a new dog in the household thinks he should be the most dominant.

A dog who is in pain might growl when his owner attempts to treat him or to move him to a more secure location or take him to a veterinarian for an examination. Dogs will bite out of pain, so it's wise to muzzle any dog that has been injured before transport to a veterinary clinic.

How to Manage Aggression

Because canine communication is complex, many people don't understand their dog's postures, growls, and barks. Dogs who display aggression should never be treated harshly, but will have to be confined while professional help is sought. Working with an aggressive dog can be dangerous, and the priority should be safety for all members of the house, human and canine alike. Avoid exposing him to stimuli or locations that have elicited aggression; for example, if your dog fights with other dogs in the house, keep them separated.

Behavior modification programs typically focus on reward-based methods. Good behavior is celebrated and rewarded with food, play, and attention. Dogs who don't care about rewards are difficult to work with, and behavior modification takes much longer to achieve, if it ever occurs. All behavior modification requires daily training sessions, and the owner who cannot commit the time, energy, and money to solving an aggression problem needs to consider whether or not she can keep an aggressive dog.

BARKING

Nuisance barking is a common Labrador Retriever behavior. Dogs bark at squirrels in the yard, and they bark when the leaves fall off the oak trees during autumn. Dogs bark at neighbors, and they bark at the neighbor's dogs. The noise causes tension in the house, between you and the homeowners next door, and between dogs separated by a fence. While barking is perfectly reasonable dog communication, continuous barking for long periods of time is a sign that trouble is brewing.

Dogs bark for many reasons, so the owner must try to determine the cause for excessive barking. With a breed that is extremely active, like the Labrador Retriever, barking is usually a sign that the dog is bored. He's frustrated, or feels isolated, or he is looking for attention. In other words, he needs a job, and he needs it *now*, and if he doesn't get the attention/play/work, he will let everybody know about his frustration.

How to Manage Excessive Barking

Excessive barking is one of the simplest problem behaviors to manage. Simultaneously, you'll want to both increase his play or activity time, and teach him when his barking is inappropriate. Also, if your dog barks at certain stimuli, then you can desensitize him to that stimulus.

Begin by teaching your dog the *quiet* command. If he barks at a skateboarder rolling down the street, allow one or two barks and then say "Quiet." Interrupt your dog's barking by shaking an empty can filled

Training Tidbit

To prevent your Lab from chewing the furniture or your favorite things, give him plenty of acceptable chew toys, like the ones Nylabone makes. Rotate different toys so that he has a different option to play with each day. Also, spray a bitter substance on the furniture so that, if he starts to chew, he'll get a mouthful of nasty taste. These products are safe, and they should be used liberally throughout the house. Dogs who routinely chew shoes or other clothing shouldn't have access to those items. Put your belongings in a closet and keep the door closed.

with a few pennies in his direction. Startle your dog with a shake, and as soon as he is quiet, tell him "Good quiet" and offer a pet or a treat. The noise should not be a punishment; it's just a method to redirect your dog's attention away from the skater. Also, ignore your dog when he barks; when he stops, reward him.

If your dog barks at visitors approaching the house, teach him that your friends and neighbors are associated with good things. With help from a friend, give your dog a special high-value treat if he is quiet while your friend walks past the house. Advance this training over several days, and as the person gets closer and closer, teach your dog to sit and remain quiet in order to get his treat. Eventually, your friend should be able to approach the house and give your dog a treat for being so brave and quiet.

Some dogs bark out of fear of certain noises, like firecrackers or thunderstorms. In some instances, you'll have to provide background music to redirect your dog's auditory system; in this way, some dogs can be desensitized to the noise. As gundogs, most Labrador Retrievers are not bothered by loud noises; if yours is, however, there may be an underlying medical condition at work, such as an ear infection.

Most excessive barking, especially with Labrador Retrievers, results from boredom. Give your dog more attention: Take him on more frequent walks to explore his surroundings, teach him tricks or retrieving games, take him to an obedience class and let him expend energy, or give him interactive toys to play with while you are away. Make sure he gets attention from you every day, whether it's an obedience training session, a ride in the car, grooming time, or just all-out play. A tired Labrador Retriever is a happy Labrador Retriever, and he will be less likely to bark for attention.

CHEWING

Labrador Retrievers chew. Chewing is one way a dog learns about his world. This is a "mouthy" breed, and a retriever will put his mouth on anything, and he'll chew on anything to figure out his environment and his role in that environment. Chewing behavior is an expression of his normal behavioral repertoire, but inappropriate or destructive chewing is pretty much a mismanagement problem. Intervention can be highly successful, but the owner must commit to teach the dog what is and what is not an acceptable chew toy.

Make sure your Lab has plenty of appropriate chew toys to keep him occupied.

Supervise destructive diggers while they're outdoors.

How to Manage Inappropriate Chewing

Keep valuables and personal belongings out of your dog's reach. If you don't want your Lab chewing on certain items, like the remote control, don't leave the remote control lying on a coffee table. Socks, shoes, books, magazines, eyeglasses, cell phones, children's toys, wallets, and underwear all seem to have Labrador Retriever magnet-like allure. Put everything away in a drawer or basket, plastic bin, or closed cupboard. Do not offer your dog an old shoe for a toy and then expect him to differentiate between the ancient sneaker and the brand-new leather loafer. Also, be realistic in your expectations. A dog is going to be a dog and chew up something he shouldn't. When that happens, interrupt the behavior and offer something more acceptable, like one of the safe chew toys Nylabone makes. Never scold a dog

for chewing, especially if you haven't caught him in the act.

Mitigate your dog's need for inappropriate or destructive chewing by giving him more opportunities for mental stimulation. Set up a mini agility course in the house or yard using large boxes for tunnels and pool "noodles" for jumps. Give him interactive toys that dispense kibble, or give him toys meant for determined, active chewers. Teach him to retrieve a thrown toy or a frozen bird wing, but do this on leash at first so your dog won't get the idea that he can munch on the item. Reel him back toward you, encouraging him all the way, and then throw the toy again.

If your Lab is determined to chew up the deck rails or fence posts or kitchen table chairs, spray them liberally with a bitter-tasting substance. Cover them in aluminum foil or double-sided tape. These tactics might deter some dogs until they grow up, mature, and don't feel the need to chew.

DIGGING

Digging is another normal dog behavior, part of their repertoire, but dogs dig for a variety of reasons. Some dogs are just trying to escape their enclosure because they are trying to protect themselves from a threat within the fence, and others are after the squirrel on the other side of the fence. Dogs dig for entertainment value or to get attention—they know from prior experience that digging often brings humans out of the house and into the yard. Digging becomes self-rewarding: A dog digs a hole, and suddenly there's a mound of black soil behind him, which he then digs at, and voilà, another mound appears! How fun is that? Labrador Retrievers who dig are engaging in grand fun, but you can manage this behavior rather than eliminate it entirely.

How to Manage Inappropriate Digging

If there is an area where you don't want your dog to dig, then don't allow him access. Roll chicken wire over the ground where he's not wanted, and bury the edges to prevent accidental injuries. Keep him on a long-line only if you are able to be outside and supervise his activities, but be ready to reel him back to your side if he starts to dig. Use a shaker can to distract him, and offer him something else to do. Also, give him an area in the yard where he's allowed to dig. Bury "hidden treasure" in loose soil or sand, and let him go after toys or bones there.

Dogs will dig to get out of the sun or rain, so if your Lab is digging to find protection from the weather, then you need to give him a better outdoor shelter, such as an insulated doghouse

that is raised off the ground. If his digging is along a fence line, then bury chain link fence sections or chicken wire, or place large rocks that he can't move, along the fence row. Don't try to fill the holes with water. Remember, Labrador Retrievers are water dogs, so you've just given your dog a mud hole to wallow in, and he'll continue to dig and think that his reward—in the form of another water hole—is forthcoming.

JUMPING UP

Dog greetings. Who doesn't love a puppy's soft kiss on a cheek, or a snuggle to the hand from a grizzled veteran's grey muzzle? Puppies learn early how to greet each other and older dogs. They sniff, they lick, and then they body slam. They run and jump at each other, roll each other, growl, and play bow. These are perfectly acceptable dog greetings, normal between members of the same species. In the wrong place or at the wrong time, or between a dog and a person, these greetings can be misinterpreted.

A Labrador Retriever who isn't taught how to greet his owner will jump up, his paws on the owner's chest, just for attention and to say, "Howdy! It's been a long time since I saw you!" Even if you have just left the house to get the mail, your Lab will express so much joy that you've returned, he can hardly contain his enthusiasm. He's not only greeting you, however. Jumping is an attention-seeking behavior, too. It's time,

Want to Know More?

For a refresher course on training basic obedience commands, see Chapter 4: Training Your Labrador Retriever Puppy.

A dog who jumps on people is a nuisance and potentially dangerous. Teach your Lab not to jump up unless invited to do so.

Labrador owner, to teach your dog that "four on the floor" is a much more rewarding game for him.

How to Manage Inappropriate Jumping

The obedience lessons of *sit* and *stay*, reinforced on a daily basis, can be used to teach an overly enthusiastic Lab that he cannot jump on people, ever. Your dog must be trained that kinder greetings will be rewarded with your praise and a treat. Also important is consistency. All members of the family, as well as visitors, must adhere to the training regimen, or else your dog will think that it's okay to jump on some people, but not others.

When your dog jumps up to greet you, turn your back and say, "Off." Once all four paws are on the ground, quietly praise him and offer a small treat. If your dog understands the *sit* command, then tell him to sit but only if all his paws are on the ground. Once he sits, give quiet praise and a small treat. Any overly loud praise right now will be an invitation to your dog to jump up again. Keep your voice soft, and only treat when he responds to the *off* and *sit* commands.

Some owners keep a secure container of treats at the front door, and every visitor comes in "pre-armed" with a reward for the dog who sits quietly and waits for the treat. Similarly, prior to family members returning from work or school, tell your dog to *sit* or *down-stay* before people start streaming in. When your dog behaves and doesn't jump up to greet his human pack members, each person should offer him a gentle pat, quiet praise, and a tasty tidbit.

Every single time that your dog responds to the commands, and every single time that he refrains from jumping, he must be rewarded. Don't ignore him when he does his job correctly, or he'll begin the attention-seeking behavior again. Your Lab soon will realize that he gets attention when he sits, and he doesn't get petted, praised, or fed if he's jumping up.

When you walk your dog up the street or take him to the pet supply store, insist that he sit and accept friendly pats from strangers. If he attempts to jump up on people at the store, remove him from the situation until he can curb his enthusiasm. Don't put your Lab in a position that he might not be able to handle emotionally. After all, his job is to be a friendly ambassador of the

Giving your Lab an outlet for his energy is one step in helping manage leash pulling.

breed, but he still has to be taught the job skills. On-the-job training might be fine for some dogs, but Labs needs in-home training before they're able to go out into polite society and behave.

LEASH PULLING

Polite behavior also extends to leash walking. Who hasn't seen an extraordinarily strong dog pulling his owner along while the owner tries to stop her dog? Or watched the owner dig in her heels and get tangled up in the leash while her dog charges on? This is a common problem because cute fuzzy black, yellow, and chocolate puppies grow quickly, and they become quite strong in a short amount of time. Even a puppy who has been taught proper leash manners will begin to pull because, as his world expands, there are so many exciting smells, sounds, and sights he must investigate.

Because Labrador Retrievers have been bred to work away from their handlers in the field, the breed is hard-wired to "get out there," so to speak. This independence is cheered in one setting but not in another, and the untrained Lab can't be faulted for not knowing the difference. Again, it's up to the owner to teach the dog when he can pull—during a tracking training session or test, for example—and when he cannot pull.

How to Manage Leash Pulling

To take control over a strong leash puller, there are behavioral, training, and equipment tools the owner can utilize. Is the dog pulling and straining at the end of his leash because he smells the garbage and wants to find the leftover pizza? Does he yank suddenly to give chase to passersby? Does he pull to hurry along and sniff, then stop and wait for his owner, then yank again?

It may take months before a strong, young, Lab stops leash pulling, and then, only after daily, consistent practice and training. The owner has at her disposal a number of training tools, including collars, halters, harnesses, clickers, and treats. A training tool imparts information to the dog. For example, properly taught, a dog will respond to a whistle because he's been taught that if he returns to his owner when he hears a series of short blasts, he'll get something really tasty. But a tool is only as good as the operator. If any training tool is misused, or if a treat is offered that the dog finds dull and uninteresting, then the tool and the information it gives the dog are useless.

Reducing and eliminating a dog's leash pulling will require patience from both the owner and the dog. Begin training in an enclosed area, armed with tasty treats. Let your dog wander to the end of his leash. If he looks back at you, even from 20 feet (6 m) away, say your marker word ("yes"), and offer him a treat. Praise him when he runs back to get his reward. Let him wander around, still on leash, and every time he checks back in with you, reward him with praise and a treat. Once he reliably stays closer to you—because by now he knows that he gets something incredible from his person—take the training to the street or the front yard, a place that has few distractions.

Again, let your dog go to the end of his leash. When he looks back at you, reward him. If he still pulls, let him go to the end of his leash and practice the "Be a tree" principle: When your dog strains, do not move. Plant your feet, and let him tug, but do not move. He'll figure out that he's not getting what he wants, and he'll look back at you and wonder, "What the heck?" As soon as he looks at you, or when he circles back to see what is impeding his progress, give him a treat. Take a step forward, and repeat the above scenario.

Labrador Retrievers are notoriously hard-headed when it comes to leash pulling, and this behavior will not be solved overnight. You may need to work on this training multiple times each day, for hundreds of

Multi-Dog Tip

If one or more of your Labrador Retrievers pull and strain on their leashes, walk each of them separately. This takes more time, but it's hard to train a dog not to pull when all of them are misbehaving. Take each on a short walk, and praise and treat for proper leash behavior. Separate walks also increase the bond between you and each individual dog—rather than jostling between the dogs for a position next to their owner, they will each get to experience one-on-one time with you. Once each dog is able to walk politely on leash, you can try to walk them together again, as long as they behave as a group.

Keeping your yard clean is the best way to prevent coprophagy.

days, before you and your dog can even take a walk around the block. That's okay. Give your Lab other outlets to expend energy, like running in butt-tuck circles around an enclosed field, before you try to teach him polite leash walking.

NIPPING

The adult Labrador Retriever who engages in other unacceptable behaviors, especially mouthing or nipping, has not been taught from puppyhood that he cannot put his teeth on skin. Nipping behaviors begin early in the Lab's life because he has used his mouth during play with his siblings. Puppies naturally want to mouth the hands that reach to pet them. This behavior is not typically an aggression issue, but your puppy or adult Lab does need to be taught that his teeth on human skin are a big no-no.

How to Manage Nipping

Redirect nipping with a more appropriate chew toy when you pet your dog. Offer the toy with one hand while you pet him with the other hand. Pet your dog only for short periods of time, because the longer your hand is on your dog, the more excited he's likely to become, and then he'll want to nip.

Your dog also must be taught that if he puts his teeth on your skin, he will lose all his privileges, and that includes attention from you. Every time your dog nips, holler "Ouch!" in a loud voice, then ignore him. You might need to leave the room or put him in his crate for a brief time-out. Many repetitions will be required before a nipping dog understands that his actions caused the reaction he didn't want from his owner, so be patient and consistent.

OTHER INAPPROPRIATE BEHAVIORS

The most disgusting problem behavior that Labrador Retrievers engage in is coprophagy — stool eating. The causes are poorly understood, and researchers, breeders, and Labrador Retriever owners disagree as to why their dogs take up such a nasty habit. Solving the dilemma will be up to the will and energy of the owner, as this behavior is rarely curbed until the dog is much older.

How to Manage Coprophagy

If you know that your neighbor's cat regularly defecates under a certain shrub along your walking path, then don't allow your dog access to that shrub. If your dog waits and anticipates that his canine housemate will eliminate at the same time in the same place in your backyard, then don't let the dogs out simultaneously to potty. You can try to interrupt the coprophagic dog's habit with use of a shaker can, or put a commercial product on the dog's food that causes stool to taste bitter. If you have a cat, and your dog anticipates the kitty crunchies, then keep the litter box enclosed.

I had occasion to board my Labs once, and on return, a kennel worker told me excitedly, "Do you know your dog eats the other dog's stool?" I told her that yes, I was aware of that disgusting habit. I then heard a litany of things to try: cayenne pepper sprinkled on stool,

products put in food to make the end result less tasty, etc.

To my surprise, the entire kennel staff eventually came to join in on the discussion.

"There is one thing I found that's foolproof and keeps all dogs from eating stool," I said. They all leaned toward me, waiting for my words of wisdom. "It's called a pooper scooper," I said. "Follow the dog and pick up after him every single time." Pretty simple, I thought, but they all shook their head and mumbled as they returned to their duties. But for many dogs, this is the only solution: Deny access.

The dog who continues to eat stool or other inappropriate substances on a regular basis (a related disorder called "pica") is at high risk for contracting diarrheal disorders such as coccidia, whipworms, and tapeworms. The Labrador Retriever owner has a duty to minimize her dog's health problems, and must keep a watchful eye on her dog to prevent this behavior.

CHAPTER 11

LABRADOR RETRIEVER SPORTS AND ACTIVITIES

A perfect blend of intelligence, strength, endurance, size, and enthusiasm, the Labrador Retriever has all the attributes necessary to participate in almost every canine sport and activity imaginable. Labs even excel at sports reserved for terriers: Don't try to tell my dogs they can't "go to ground" while they chase critters that tunnel through their territory.

From hunting, retrieving, and fishing to more complex tracking and obedience skills, the Labrador Retriever is the ultimate companion dog. He's as comfortable in the bow of a boat as he is in the backseat of the family car. The Lab pays it backward and forward. He works for his family or for the hunter, and just as willingly engages in dancing, camping, and therapy. Versatile, biddable, agile, there may be no other breed that can outperform the Labrador Retriever.

OUTDOOR ACTIVITIES WITH YOUR LAB

Labrador Retrievers are excellent camping companions. Their history as a rugged outdoorsman's dog developed in harsh environments secured the breed a spot beside the campfire. Today, families routinely include their Labs on camping trips. They're happy curled up next to sleeping bags inside a two-person tent, or they will snore away at the foot of a queen-sized bed in a recreational vehicle.

Camping and Hiking

Before taking your Lab with you to wander the great outdoors, be sure that he is vaccinated for any of the diseases endemic to the area in which you travel. Because diarrheal illnesses can be acquired from drinking contaminated water, pack enough fresh water from home for your dog to drink. Take his shot records with you in case of emergency, and pack a canine first aid kit along with other emergency items. Pitch your tent or open the RV and let your dog get accustomed to the surroundings before you expect him to settle quietly on a camping trip. Before embarking on a strenuous hike, let your Lab build up his stamina by taking short day trips.

Walking and Jogging

Walking and jogging are good stamina-building and energy-busting activities. Short walks will help your dog learn about his neighborhood and give him excellent opportunities for socialization and bonding time with you and the rest of family. Daily walks help build strong muscles and keep weight off. Longer walks will tire a dog who is bouncing off the walls with excitement.

Labs can learn to keep up with owners who jog, but just as a person can't sustain a 10-K (6-mile) run without building up mileage first, don't expect your Labrador Retriever to be able to run that far at first either. Also, puppies should not participate in long jogs or runs until their growth plates have closed. Try to run your dog on all different surfaces—from grass to leaves and dirt—before you take him to pound the pavement. Before walking or running your dog on a hot day, reach down and put your palm on the road; if it's too hot for your hand, then it's too hot for your dog's paws. Observe all local leash laws (and that includes picking up your dog's poop). Carry clean, fresh water, along with high-energy treats for long-distance walks or runs.

CANINE GOOD CITIZEN

Your Labrador Retriever will be welcome along city streets and in country stores, especially if he is a proven Canine Good Citizen® (CGC). This American Kennel Club (AKC) certification is a test of the dog's good nature, and shows off his basic obedience skills. The owner must have knowledge of canine health, safety, and quality-of -life issues, such as a need for exercise; she also signs a Responsible Dog Owners Pledge and agrees to take care of her dog both at home and in public.

The dog who passes the CGC test will be able to be attentive to his owner when a stranger walks by or stops to talk to the owner. The dog will sit calmly if the stranger reaches out to pat his head or rub his side, although the always-happy Labrador Retriever probably will never stop swishing his tail from side-to-side.

The CGC test evaluator will inspect the dog's coat and skin and make sure he is clean, alert

Want to Know More?

Before your Lab explores the great outdoors, make sure that he knows how to walk politely on the leash and will reliably come when you call him, in case he unexpectedly gets away from you. Along with making your outing more enjoyable, this helps to ensure your dog's safety. For a refresher on training these commands, see Chapter 4: Training Your Labrador Retriever Puppy.

to his surroundings, and isn't overweight. The dog owner supplies a comb or brush, and the evaluator will lightly brush the dog. She then inspects the dog's ears, and picks up each front paw. These tests show the willingness of the dog to be examined by a groomer or a veterinarian.

Because you've worked so hard and trained your Labrador to walk nicely on a loose lead, you can also show off that skill during the CGC test. The dog should be able to respond to the handler's commands; usually this portion of the test is a straight-line walk with some changes of direction, turns, stops, and starts. The dog doesn't have to respond immediately to his handler's requests, and the handler is allowed to give generous praise when her dog does recognize and react appropriately.

Several volunteer "pedestrians" will begin to mill about in the test area while the dog and handler walk through the crowd and along the edges. If the dog is able to handle being in the midst of his adoring fans without getting too excited, he should be able to pass this portion of the exam. After the crowd disperses, the dog gets to show off more advanced obedience training. The dog will respond to the *sit* and then *down* commands from his handler, and must stay in position when the handler moves up to 20 feet (6 m) away.

The recall portion of the exam demonstrates the dog's willingness to come to his handler from a distance. Usually, the handler walks off 10 feet (3 m) or paces, turns, and calls her dog. In typical Labrador Retriever fashion, he should react immediately and return eagerly.

Distraction training—whether around other dogs, strange sights, or unusual sounds—proves the dog's ability to be curious but not shy, interested but not overly enthusiastic. The dog should be able to walk along and encounter another dog and handler team, and show no more than a friendly interest in the other canine. Other distractions are introduced to the dog, such as a person in a wheelchair or using crutches, or another who opens an umbrella near the dog. His reaction should be mild at the most, and the handler is allowed to reassure him. A fearful or panicked reaction indicates the dog needs more training in unusual situations.

The final portion of the CGC test is supervised separation. The dog should be able to sit quietly and exhibit good manners when his owner leaves him with one of the evaluators, and then exits the room. When my Labrador Retriever, Sam, passed this section, every evaluator came up to me and praised his calm demeanor in my absence. One even paid the ultimate compliment: "I *love* your dog," she said. Apparently Sam had marked time during our separation by kissing every one of the testers.

CANINE SPORTS

Many organized programs and activities show off the Labrador Retriever's good nature and

The Labrador Retriever has all the attributes necessary to participate in almost every canine sport and activity imaginable.

intelligence, and some of these can be pursued with young puppies. Training for higher level sports usually begins with early, frequent, and short obedience training sessions. Ultimately, canine sports show the incredible bond between handler and dog, whether the pursuit is a novice obedience title or a fast-paced agility course. The dog and handler who together train and compete in sports have developed a silent communication that is unique to that team. Subtle cues such as a dropped shoulder, a finger flick, a waved hand, or even a look, become the language between the two.

Agility

Agility is perhaps the fastest paced canine sport, and it shows off the ability of the dog to perform complex tasks far away from his handler. Labrador Retrievers do well in agility, with their willingness to take jumps, tunnels, and teeters. A typical agility course includes a series of weave poles, several jumps, an off-the-ground dog walk, a teeter-totter, an A-frame, and a hoop or tire jump. Most agility equipment grew out of dogs' jobs in the field, in service, or at play: Retrievers regularly jump logs and fence lines and bob through trees. Military and protection dogs have always needed practical skills in climbing tall fortress-like walls and tracking suspects through pipes and other narrow openings.

While Lab puppies should not jump full heights until their growth plates are closed (to reduce the risk of orthopedic injuries), youngsters can be taught agility skills. A pool noodle placed on the ground teaches a puppy to walk over and then jump low heights without dragging his rear toes. Encourage your pup to tunnel under bedcovers or blankets, or through large boxes, to build fast drive through agility tunnels. An old tire swing lowered to an appropriate height for your dog can be used in

By the Numbers

More Labrador Retrievers earn companion sports titles in AKC competitions than any other breed—in part because there are just so darn many of our beloved dogs competing than other breeds, but also because Labs are easy to train. The AKC National Obedience Champion in 2008 and 2009 was a big black Lab named Tyler, who is owned, trained, and handled by Petra Ford of New Jersey.

place of a more expensive agility hoop jump.

Several organizations offer agility competition, and training schools are located throughout the country. Before selecting an agility instructor, sit in on beginner's classes, ask questions, and find out the instructor's qualifications. How many dogs has she taught and/or titled, and what breeds has she worked with? Talk to her students and get their opinions. Finally, go watch agility trials. They can be confusing and fast paced, so take someone who has experience, or plan to meet up with an agility training group at a trial.

Canine Freestyle

If you are at all like me, a typical Labrador Retriever owner, you may crank up your favorite music, whether Broadway show tunes or good old rock and roll, on the days you groom your dog's hair, wash his bed, and sweep out the hairballs. Then you sing, loud and out of tune, and your dog responds. My dogs jump and jostle and spin and whirl around— perhaps they are trying to get me to be quiet, but I think they just want to dance. So, we do. Gracie puts her front paws in my hands, and we curtsey round the coffee table. Story prefers to weave between my legs in figure eights or back and forth. Sam, bless his heart, puts his big black paws over his ears. Well, one can't please all one's Labs at the same time.

Canine musical freestyle grew out of instances like the one I just described, but the sport involves so much more than a broom and a boom box. Today's freestylers devise elaborate routines based on obedience and dressage movements set to music, and they wear sparkling costumes. Did somebody say "dress up, get up, and move to the music?" Both human and dog team members are allowed more creative demonstrations than in more rigid obedience sports. Canine musical freestyle puts emphasis on the handler's dance abilities and the dog's corresponding tricks.

Freestyle heeling is heelwork accompanied by music, and the dog and handler stay close to each other during the routine, tethered only by the dog's devotion and the trainer's technique. All canine music routines—whether in heelwork or musical freestyle—showcase the dog and handler's absolute joy as they work together.

Competition rules vary from one organization to the other, and even between countries, but are based on artistic and technical merit. For more information, contact the World Canine Freestyle Organization at www.worldcaninefreestyle.org; Musical Dog Sport Association at www.musicaldogsport.org; or Canine Freestyle Federation at www.canine-freestyle.org. Other regional, national, and international groups offer training and competition; those sites can be found on an Internet search.

Conformation

Conformation dog shows grew out of old-fashioned stock competitions in which a kennel's breeding stock was evaluated based on the progeny and its future potential. Today, conformation dogs are judged against the ideal Labrador Retriever, as illustrated by the breed standard. Judges put their hands on the dog to check bone structure, muscle development, weight, and overall condition. Keeping in mind that Labrador Retrievers were developed as sporting dogs to work in difficult field trials, judges watch the dogs' movement in the ring. Some dogs are beautiful, but might not have fluid movement; other dogs move well but don't have the true Labrador double coat. The judges pick those dogs and bitches they believe are most representative of the breed's required form and function. Points are awarded to the winning dog and the winning bitch

It's All About Time Spent Together

At the end of the day, after the competition is complete—whether at a rally trial, a National Retriever Championship Stake, or junior showmanship conformation competition, and regardless of the performance of the team—the Labrador Retriever handler still gets to take the best dog home: hers. The outcome might be an Obedience Trial Championship title, or the team might have earned one of those NQ—not quite—qualifying scores. The lovable Labrador Retriever still will curl up at her owner's feet, or on her owner's lap, and prove that he's the best dog for her, on that day or any day, regardless of the course time, or track followed, or the number of birds retrieved.

In a conformation show, a dog is evaluated on how closely he conforms to the breed standard.

based on the total number of Labradors in the competition, and after a certain number of points have been accumulated, dogs and bitches are named "Champions of Record."

This aspect of dog showing is a perfect family sport, and many of the top Labrador Retriever breeders, owners, and handlers began as juniors with the family Lab. Children ages eight and up can compete in the ring, but they don't show off the dog necessarily; rather, they are showing off their skills as a handler, and against other juniors their age. The Labrador Retrievers Club, Inc. (LRC) has a Junior Showmanship Incentive Program to get more youngsters involved in the sport. National and regional specialty shows—those with only Labrador Retrievers entered—usually waive entry fees for children and teenagers who enter junior showmanship classes.

Labrador Retriever owners who just want to dip their toes into the conformation show venue can begin with an evaluation of their dog without the stress of a ring environment. The LRC, Inc. offers a Conformation Certificate program open to all Labs, even those who are spayed or neutered. The judge evaluates the dog to see if he possesses the basic attributes of a Labrador Retriever, and then checks for any disqualifying faults. The dog or bitch should not be lame, deaf, or blind, and he or she should exhibit a majority of breed characteristics, such as a true double coat and otter tail. Conformation Certificate exams are conducted at the breed National Specialty and at some regional specialties. While the certificate isn't a title, per se, it's considered an accomplishment to have a Lab with all the true hallmarks of his breed.

Obedience Trials

Obedience trials and the related sport of rally obedience also trace their roots to the Labrador Retriever's early jobs. In the field, a dog must be able to work away from his handler and follow a downed bird, then find it and bring it back. The field dog has to be steady on the line and not bolt away when he's off leash. He must sit and honor another working dog, and not move when the dog next to him scampers to retrieve.

Similarly, an obedience-trained dog is able to understand his handler's commands, whether verbal or hand signals, and then perform the requested exercise.

The obedience exercises range from intricate heelwork patterns to a simple stand for a judge's examination. Labrador Retrievers excel at the scent-discrimination and retrieving exercises, and their strength is evident during all of the jumping tests—over high jumps, bar jumps, and broad jumps. The trained Lab will mark the direction his handler indicates, and he'll bring back to his handler the object he was sent to retrieve. The obedience competition might include some of these exercises, or all of them, depending on the class or level.

Rally obedience is similar to an automobile rally race: The dog and handler begin at point A, the start, and go to point B, the finish, but they execute turns, pivots, jumps, sits, and downs, as well as heelwork, all through the course. Winning teams are based both on time and on points lost due to dog or handler errors. Rally is an excellent sport for green or immature dogs, and for veteran dogs who can't jump the full heights required in obedience. People age 5 to 95 can easily compete, and handicapped handlers who require assistance or adaptations are encouraged to participate.

Obedience and rally competitions are hosted by several different organizations, including the AKC, the United Kennel Club (UKC), the Association of Pet Dog Trainers (APDT), and the Australian Shepherd Club of America (ASCA). Rules vary from group to group, but there is a lot of carry-over in most of the exercises. Labrador Retriever owners who want to give obedience and rally a try can find nearby trials. Take the family and watch, ask questions, and read the rules. Practice the exercises either by yourself or with a training group, and prepare to become hooked. Not only will you and your dog develop a more intense bond, but you'll likely meet people who will become mentors and friends for life, folks who share your common interest, and friends who are happy to help you train your dog.

Tracking

Tracking events have grown out of the dog's innate ability to search and find, whether sniffing out a lost wallet in tall grass or finding a frightened child or a victim of a natural disaster. Tracking tests demonstrate a dog's high level of scent capability. We know that Labrador Retrievers can smell a neighbor's steak on the grill another town away, so it's not surprising that Labs excel at tracking.

A vigorous outdoor activity, tracking Labs can earn multiple titles from various organizations, from the basic tracking dog (TD) to the complex variable surface track (VST). Depending on the level, a dog is required to follow a track upwards of 1,000 yards (914 m)

The author and her Lab, Story, finishing her rally Novice title.

Natural swimmers, Labs excel in water sports.

long that has been "aged" from 30 minutes to five hours. Dogs might follow a track through fields or urban areas, with multiple changes of direction, and find a designated, previously scented article at the end of the track.

Field Trials and Hunt Tests

The ultimate tests of the Labrador Retriever are field trials and hunt tests. Field trials trace back to the early days of the breed, when avid hunters developed a way to evaluate their hunting dogs in a competitive performance event. Initially, retrievers had to be able to mark a downed bird from about 100 yards (91 m) away; today, a dog is expected to mark multiple retrieves from 250 to 300 yards (229 to 274 m) away, and also find and retrieve downed birds that the dog did not watch as they fell (known as a "blind retrieve"). Competitive retrievers today are in excellent shape, physically and mentally. Labrador Retrievers are some of the best-trained, highly skilled, best-conditioned dogs in competitions, and they bring home most of the bragging rights.

Dogs as young as 6 months can be "brought out" in a Derby Stake; other major stakes or trials may be restricted by the dog's age or the handler's skill. Professional trainers, those who are paid to train and trial others' dogs, have field trials separate from those held for amateurs. Depending on the points accumulated by the dogs at the various field trial levels, they can be designated a Field Champion and/or Amateur Field Champion. There also are National Championship competitions for dogs at the highest levels of training, proficiency, and experience.

Hunt tests were developed in the 1980s by sportsmen and sportswomen who had decent retrieving dogs, but who did not have the time or resources to enter field trials. Hunt tests can be just as demanding as field trials, but are not as time consuming, and the dogs must be physically fit and trained to retrieve birds and ducks on land and in water. Depending on the level of the hunt test, the dog might be required to retrieve just one mark; master-level retrievers are expected to find and retrieve multiple marks and also make blind retrieves from land and water.

The LRC, Inc. sponsors a program called the Working Certificate for owners who want to test their dog's ability to retrieve, but who don't want to dive head-first into the competitions of hunting or retrieving tests. The program tests a dog to make sure he is not gun shy, and tests as well his level of willingness to enter and retrieve from water and on land. The Working Certificate is a true accomplishment for Labrador Retrievers, and tests are usually conducted in conjunction with national or regional specialties.

Water Sports: Dock Diving and Big Air Competition

If your Labrador Retriever is a water hog or mud puppy, then dock diving or the related Big Air competitions might be a venue for companionship and competition. Our natural swimmers do well in these water sports, where they show off either how far they can jump into water or how high they can leap before landing in a pool or pond. Dock diving and dock leaping shows and competitions are sponsored at local, regional, and national levels.

THERAPY WORK

A constant willingness on the part of the Labrador Retriever to be a steady companion, as well as his calm nature despite the daily grind, is what makes this breed a terrific ambassador and therapy dog. Whether a member of a library reading group for schoolchildren, or an animal-assisted therapy dog in a senior center, Labrador Retrievers play vital roles in settings as diverse as rehabilitation centers and shelters for victims of domestic violence.

Sam, my big guy, loved his visits to a local senior center, perhaps because he could always count on somebody dropping a cookie or part of their sandwich. He was most gentle, though, with the patients in the Alzheimer's Unit, where he'd lay his massive muzzle on a person's arm and just wait. Sometimes the client would talk to him, other times, not; but he always was ready to listen. Gracie, my yellow female, adores the younger crowd, and vice versa. At holiday parties for children who live in shelters, the youngsters who are afraid of dogs usually reach a timid hand to pet her soft ears. Others take hold of her leash and walk her around the room. For children and adults whose life events have turned upside down, sometimes just taking the end of a dog's leash gives them a sense of control that they had lacked.

Many local, national, and international organizations train, test, and certify therapy dogs. These dogs must pass tests similar to the CGC, and specific behavioral and veterinary health certificates have to be signed. Dogs must be kept up-to-date on vaccinations, and the dog and handler go on a series of supervised

Multi-Dog Tip

Before you try to walk or jog with more than one dog, make sure that each has acceptable leash manners, which includes no jumping and no pulling. Some multi-dog walkers use a coupler, a leash with two separate clips that attach to each dogs' collars. Others will hold a separate leash for each dog. Be sure you have good control over all the dogs, or you're liable to end up in the center of a tangle of leads while the dogs investigate different smells along the path visits with other therapy dog teams before final certification is granted.

TRAVELING WITH YOUR LAB

Whatever activities or sports you engage in with your Labrador Retriever, there are some basic petiquette travel rules to prepare for before taking to the road. You must always plan for emergencies, decide how you'll transport your dog, and make prior reservations with hotels along your route to be sure they accept pet guests.

Preparing for Your Trip

Before you load up the car for a trip, take your dog's safety into account. Like humans, dogs need a restraint system. In case of an accident, an unrestrained dog in a car becomes a missile, and a 60-pound dog can seriously injure other passengers and himself if he is not secured in a moving vehicle. Canine seat belt restraints attach to a dog's harness, and this system gives the dog more room to stretch out. However, the safest way to travel with a dog is to use a crate, either heavy wire or hard plastic, which is strapped or tied down inside the car. A comfortable crate pad and a long-lasting chew toy will keep your dog happy for the duration of the trip.

Pack plenty of your dog's food and bottles or jugs of water from home. Some dogs with sensitive stomachs will suffer gastrointestinal distress when they drink water from different locales. Keep waste disposal bags handy, and on a long drive, stop every couple of hours to let your dog stretch, have a drink and a treat, and potty. Bring along a copy of his shot records, especially his rabies vaccination number, along with microchip identification, and any medications he takes. Label the crate with his name and your contact information,

too. On a long drive, never leave your dog unattended in the car while the family stops to eat.

Air Travel

Air travel with a Labrador Retriever can be problematic and fraught with anxiety for both dog and owner. Unless a puppy is small enough to ride in the cabin with his owner, dogs must go as baggage in the belly of commercial flights. Air transport–approved crates, which are solid plastic or heavy steel-aluminum confines, must be used. Flights can be delayed and cancelled, adding to stress for pets and owners. Some airlines now refuse to transport dogs, and others restrict air travel to certain times of the year, when animals are not as likely to get too hot or too cold in the freight compartment.

For some, air transport is the only option, however. Depending on where you live, Pet Airways, an airline that services pets only, is an attractive alternative to commercial flights. Pet Airways, launched in 2009, serves cat and canine clients with first-class cabin service between select cities. Travel crates are provided, as are cabin attendants who keep a close eye on their passengers.

Lodging Requirements

Many hotels and motels allow pets to lodge with their responsible owners, but some have restrictions on size and number. Call ahead to make reservations, and ask about pet policies. Most dog-friendly hotels charge a deposit in case your Labrador Retriever decides to eat the hotel bed comforter. For that reason, it's wise to have a crate in the hotel room so that your dog is safe and free of temptations when you must leave him.

Never use a hotel room shower or tub to bathe your dog. Dog hair clogs drains, and no matter how dirty your dog is from the day's activities, it's considered bad manners to do so. Rather, find out if the hotel has an outdoor hose you can borrow or find a local groomer who can fit your dog into the schedule for a bath. Always pick up your dog's waste on hotel grounds and in all public common areas; inconsiderate owners cause problems for the next canine guest.

Boarding Kennels and Pet Sitters

Vacations or business trips don't have to include the family Lab, and there are options for frequent travelers. If you cannot take your dog along, ask your friends, family, and veterinarian for recommendations and referrals for pet sitters and boarding kennels. Your dog's age might help you decide between a kennel and home care while you are away. Older or infirm Labs may be more comfortable with an experienced pet sitter. Younger, healthy dogs who need plenty of exercise will be perfectly happy at a kennel.

Boarding Kennels

Boarding facilities range from the basic cage-and-a-concrete-run accommodation at some veterinary clinics and businesses, to elaborate, free-range, indoor and outdoor "doggy hotels" that offer fun and games. Some boarding facilities have ponds and pools, hiking trails, and fields where dogs can play and interact. Again, get references for the boarding facility, take your dog's food and medications, and make sure the employees can reach you at any time in case of a canine emergency or illness. Give the boarding facility the names of your veterinarian and an emergency contact; decide before you leave if you will grant your vet the authority to treat your dog in case he becomes ill or hurt. Most boarding facilities will ask for this prior authorization.

Pet Sitters

A dog sitter should visit several times a day to feed and exercise your Lab, and she should be able to give any medications your dog might need. Some sitters will come and stay at your house overnight, others will bring in the mail, water the plants, and turn on the lights in the evening, in addition to taking care of the dog. Before handing your house keys over to a pet sitter, get references and check to be sure the sitter is bonded and has insurance in case of an emergency or injury to her or to your dog.

Training Tidbit

Before taking off by car with your Labrador Retriever, get him used to either his car harness or crate prior to travel. Let him wear his harness around the house and on short trips; make sure it fits him well and doesn't rub his belly or armpits raw, but is secure enough that he can't wiggle out of the straps. Feed your dog in his crate to get him accustomed to crate travel, and give him a treat every time he willingly enters it. Make a game out of crate entries and exits: Have your Lab sit calmly before you let him in or out, and give him a treat for good behavior before you open the crate door.

PART III

SENIOR YEARS

CHAPTER 12

FINDING YOUR LABRADOR RETRIEVER SENIOR

Labrador Retrievers mellow and their muzzles begin to gray by age seven or eight, when the breed is considered a veteran by conformation standards. Most dogs, however, are still active well into old age and don't slow down until they reach "forced retirement" due to injury or illness. Senior Labs still compete in obedience, they continue to mark and retrieve shot birds, and their noses can still find the track to a glove or a treat.

Sam, my black Lab, had perfected patience as a puppy. He sat at the bay window for hours to watch a squirrel pick its way through the pine island. Then he'd jump, two huge paws on the sill, bark a frenzy that rattled the glass, and startle the squirrel into a freeze before it darted up the nearest tree. Sam would lie back down, content that he had battled back yet another rodent. This was his routine from eight weeks of age until old age. He never tired of his game, just like most Labs don't tire of their activities well into their elder years.

Like other Labrador Retrievers at that age, the bad habits of puppyhood, the hard driving body slams and runs and jumps of adolescence and adulthood, had changed for him. He still sat near the kitchen table and drooled while we ate, but he no longer forced his block head into our laps. If he got a treat or table scrap, he was happy. He didn't drag dirty underwear through the house as he did during his youth; rather, he'd pick up an odd sock and deliver it to the hamper or hand. If he heard the word "no," he stopped what he was doing to see which of the pack had just gotten into trouble. He matured into a graceful, content leader of the younger dogs in the house.

WHY ADOPTING A SENIOR LAB IS A GOOD IDEA

Old dogs settle into their role as gentle leader, occasional enforcer of house rules, and patient teacher of the younger dogs. An older Lab might allow a young puppy to climb over his back or suck on his ear flaps, whereas he won't tolerate that behavior from

Want to Know More?

For information on the needs of a senior dog, see Chapter 13: Care of Your Senior Labrador Retriever.

the adolescents or "middle-aged" adult dogs. A senior Lab sits patiently while a child reads to him, or waits patiently while his senior human pulls on her shoes and fumbles with collar and leash, readying them both for a walk. He's always ready for a car ride or a slow amble. The senior Labrador Retriever has left a trail of memories for his owner: paw prints in winter snow, muddy tracks through the house after spring rains, tipped water buckets on kitchen tile during the heat of the summer, and the crunch and crackle underfoot during walks in the fall.

Labrador Retrievers age gracefully and slowly. Although technically the breed is senior by age 7, many Labradors live to be 14 or even 16 years old. While some fanciers think it incomprehensible that our old dogs wind up in shelters or in Labrador Retriever rescue organization foster homes, for some owners, the decision is a difficult one.

Surrender of a senior Lab might be the end result of a job loss or home foreclosure. The dog might have veterinary issues that are well beyond the means of a family's financial abilities, or he may need more care and attention than his owners can provide. Families move, children are born or leave home, crises come along, and sometimes,

the dog's needs cannot be accommodated when a family's needs become overwhelming. Other dogs are dumped along roadsides or at a shelter's door when their health issues are identified; rather than taking care of the dog, those owners depend on Good Samaritans to rescue their pets.

HOW TO FIND YOUR SENIOR LAB

Shelters and rescue groups place special emphasis on veteran Labrador Retrievers. Many groups will provide a good, safe, and loving foster home in which the dog can live out his final days. For those special families that decide to adopt a veteran Lab, most rescue organizations will guarantee payment of veterinary bills, and some will help with lifetime nutritional needs.

Training Tidbit

A senior Labrador Retriever shouldn't require more than a few days to get used to his new routine before he's following commands. To help speed the process along, offer him soft string cheese as a training treat; his old teeth may not be able to handle crunchy kibble. If you need to leave your senior Lab alone soon after adoption, give him a safe and warm place to rest while he waits for your return. Always praise your elder statesman for being such a good boy while you were gone, and treat him to a short walk and quiet time with you.

Breed rescue organizations have strong presences on the Internet, and that is the best way to begin your search for a senior Lab. The LRC, Inc. has links to breed rescues throughout the country on its website (www.thelabradorclub.com).

Before taking on a senior Lab, ask the rescuer or foster home if they have a history on the dog, including health problems, prior training, and reasons the dog ended up in their care. If the dog's health history is not known, be prepared for unusual expenses and decide if you can emotionally and financially afford the costs of an unexpected illness. If the dog was an owner turn-in, try to find out why: did his previous owner die, or were there circumstances that prevented the owner from being able to care for him? Does he have temperament problems that cannot be trained?

Before you fall in love with a photograph of an older Labrador Retriever on a rescue group website, make sure he and your family are a good match; after all, a senior dog deserves a forever home and shouldn't be shuttled from one person to another. Try to meet the dog in person to ensure the best decision. Sometimes a dog is better left with his foster home rather than having to adjust to changes yet another time.

For more information on adopting a senior dog, check out The Senior Dogs Project, an organization that educates owners and potential adopters on the unique needs of senior dogs. The website is www.srdogs.com.

A senior Labrador Retriever will provide unconditional love, affection, and companionship.

SENIOR LABS AS FAMILY DOGS

These second-chance dogs seem to understand and appreciate the kindnesses of their new adoptive family. While a Lab puppy or adult needs near-constant attention and training, a senior dog has learned the basic commands. He might take longer to get up off his bed for a walk, and his steps might be shorter as he proceeds snail-like along a path, but he still is willing to go along. He won't strain against the leash like a puppy or young adult, and so he's unlikely to pull a child off her feet but can still tug that child's heartstrings. Families with

Most senior Labs can adapt to their new homes easily.

very young children benefit by adding an older Labrador Retriever rather than a puppy because a senior dog doesn't require the same chunks of time carved out of an already hectic schedule for training, exercising, and socializing.

A retired conformation dog is an excellent and reliable dog for a child who might want to begin in a junior showmanship program. Breeders sometimes have to thin their kennels and will mentor children and teenagers on breed standards, health, and wellness issues in the breed. A co-ownership agreement with a breeder for a veteran Labrador can sometimes be negotiated; some breeders might give or sell their older Lab outright to the right home. If you hang around dog shows, ask questions, and show a genuine interest in the breed, the right older Labrador Retriever might become available for your family.

If you adopt an older Labrador Retriever, he probably can still compete in select canine sports. Rally is an exciting and safe sport for almost all dogs, and unless the veteran Lab has extensive arthritis and cannot comfortably sit, he can train the rally doodling exercises. My dogs all got their obedience start in rally in their elder years, Sam at the age of nine and Gracie at the age of seven. Fellow trainers and competitors stand ringside and cheer loudly for the elder dogs who qualify and title in rally trials. There's no more satisfying way to give back to a dog who loves you unconditionally than to let him shine one more time in the ring, in the field, or on the track.

Adoption Fees

Adoption fees for most Labrador Retriever rescue groups can be expensive, but for people willing to adopt a senior dog, the fees can be considerably less. Many organizations and shelters will waive a part or all of the fee, especially if the senior Lab is adopted by a senior citizen. Rescue fundraisers help offset the adoption fees, which usually go for boarding and veterinary costs for dogs who have yet to find a forever home. In addition, senior citizens can qualify for reduced veterinary fees through some Labrador Retriever rescue groups. Veterinary assistance money is available from groups such as Labrador Life Line and LabMed, both of which help with catastrophic veterinary fees. For information, contact www.labradorlifeline.org or www.labmed.org

SENIOR LABS FOR SENIORS

Because the older Lab is gentler, he makes a wonderful therapy dog or companion for an older person. Some rescue organizations offer special "Seniors for Seniors" programs to encourage senior citizens to adopt senior dogs. In many cases, the adoption application or placement fees are waived.

Multi-Dog Tip

Don't allow a younger dog to assert himself at the expense of a senior dog. Older dogs are not inclined to upset an established hierarchy, but if younger pack members object to the addition of an older dog, keep him separated from the youngsters. Allow each dog in the household some one-on-one interaction time with him so they can warm up to each other's presence. Establish boundaries and enforce them, and continue to give the younger dogs the attention and training that they need.

SETTLING IN

After a brief period of acclimatization, the veteran Lab settles into his new pack within days. He makes friends quickly, and won't challenge younger dogs in the home for dominance. He won't demand attention, but he will soak up every "Good dog," gobbling the praise like he used to gobble his morning meal. Unlike a puppy, an older dog usually won't wake the family in the middle of the night for potty excursions. In other words, the senior Lab owner will get a good night's sleep almost every night.

Like a soft quilt on a sideboard, the elder Labrador Retriever is there if you need him for warmth or comfort. He can show spunk and vigor one moment, like Sam with his squirrels; the next minute he is serene, asleep, and probably snoring.

CHAPTER 13

CARE OF YOUR LABRADOR RETRIEVER SENIOR

Senior Labrador Retrievers are bundles of spunk and stoicism, grace and gentleness. By the time your Lab is seven or eight years old, he has begun to show some of the effects of those years, but he is not likely to slow down for at least another couple of years. For those reasons, senior Labs have health and wellness needs rather different from those of their younger cohorts, if only to prevent them from further harm or illness because of their active and willing nature.

Even though you might begin to see tufts of white hair poking around your Lab's feet, or find a few gray strands nestled in the black or chocolate hair on his withers, or notice his muzzle has started to lighten a few shades, don't think he is ready to hang up his leash just yet. But because Labs are incredibly stoic, you will need to watch for injuries or illnesses that your dog tries hard to hide.

WHEN DOES YOUR LAB BECOME A SENIOR?

If your Lab has been a hard-charging field dog, or if he's been the agility course star, or even if he's been the family pet that bounds up and down steps to follow the children, he will begin to slow down by around age 10. The signs are subtle, but noticeable. His big brown eyes may begin to cloud or take on a greenish tinge—but don't be fooled into thinking he cannot see that hamburger you just put on the counter. His sense of smell likely will not diminish, even as he ages. His hearing might become more selective than it was during puppyhood, but for good reason. A dog's ability to hear does lessen, and some can even become deaf, although that is rare in Labs. He might not hear your footfall late at night, but he still will hear your laughter, and he will feel your gentle touch.

Recognizing the Signs of Aging

Because dogs can't speak directly to us in our language, we have to watch them and understand what their body language and vocalizations are telling us. If your dog vocalizes more than usual— whimpers, howls, or growls—or if he's quieter than he

Want to Know More?

For a refresher on detailed grooming techniques, see Chapter 6: Labrador Retriever Grooming Needs.

typically would be, then he could be feeling the pain of old age. Similarly, if a normally placid dog becomes aggressive or displays apprehension, or stops wagging his tail when you approach, these could indicate a painful condition. If he's restless and keeps shifting his position on his bed, or if he seems less alert, you should have your dog checked by your veterinarian.

Trust your instincts regarding canine discomfort and pain. The senior Labrador Retriever does feel pain, especially in his back, along his hips, and in any joint where he's suffered a prior injury, as well as at the onset of arthritis. If your dog moves more slowly or is unwilling to move; if his body seems stiff; if his appetite wanes; if he bites, scratches, or seems to guard against touch to any region or limb; or if he pants or shivers; he could be feeling pain.

Effective treatments exist for pain relief, including medications, alternative therapies like chiropractic and acupuncture, and physical therapy. Massage therapy can soothe old and sore joints and muscles, and you can learn how and where to touch your dog so that he won't experience so much pain as he gets older.

The older Lab might begin to lose muscle mass, especially if he's been active in field sports or high-energy canine competitions. Just as with people, muscles can wither and atrophy when no longer used. If contact sports are too much for your senior, take him swimming for some low-impact activity. Swimming is the perfect sport for an aging athlete, and something he can continue to enjoy with his family as he ages.

FEEDING YOUR SENIOR

As your dog ages, consider slowly changing his diet from a hard kibble to a softer and more palatable food. A senior Lab will continue to enjoy his meals, albeit more slowly. If his eating habits change, if he refuses food or eats very slowly, or if he leaves food in the bowl, then he may be telling you that the kibble of his youth is too difficult on aging or sore teeth. This might be the time to prepare home-cooked meals for your senior. Make sure the meals are balanced and nutritious for a less active dog, and add supplements wisely.

Your veterinarian might suggest a prescription canned food if your older dog has underlying health conditions, like kidney disease or gastrointestinal issues. At this time in his life, your Lab may need to be fed smaller meals more often. Rather than twice a day, split up the food into three or four meals. If your dog develops laryngeal paralysis, one of the disorders common among older Labrador Retrievers, you will need to adjust his food. A soft gruel, fed either by hand or in a raised feeder, and offered to him four or more times per day, will be easier for him to eat.

By the Numbers

Veterinarians estimate that 30 percent of senior dogs have a hidden disease or disability; at least 60 percent of dogs 10 years old have some cognitive dysfunction; and a whopping 80 percent suffer from dental disease. Mitigate some of these numbers by brushing your dog's teeth on a regular basis. Keep his mind sharp and his body active with daily, slow walks. Take him to the vet at least twice a year for geriatric checkups.

As your dog ages, consider slowly changing his diet from a hard kibble to a softer and more palatable food.

Don't worry: Your senior will let you know if he's hungry or when he's satiated. He'll probably still beg for table scraps, and unless he has difficulty swallowing or chewing certain items, or unless he has a medical condition that forbids table scraps, it's okay to feed him some leftovers. Of course, that still depends on what you are eating. If your diet consists of pizza every day, it won't be good for your dog, and he'll begin to put on too much weight from eating the crust.

GROOMING YOUR SENIOR

In addition to the increase in gray hair on your dog's muzzle, feet, and along his withers, you may notice that his hair begins to thin. While this could be a sign of a medical condition, it's also a normal part of the aging process. Grooming sessions should continue, but instead of a bristle brush or undercoat rake, consider using a hand mitt instead. This tool is gentler on

the elderly Lab's skin, and your direct touch can help you find sensitive areas. If your dog flinches from your hand, he's telling you that you've hit a painful spot, and you can either avoid that area, or learn to massage his sore muscles. Also consider adding an inexpensive heat pack to your grooming supplies. Fill a tube sock with dried rice, tie off the top, and microwave the sock for about four minutes. Check the heat against your skin, first; this simple heat pack can be molded around your dog's painful joints, like his knees and hocks.

Your dog will probably be more comfortable during his grooming sessions if you have him lie on his side. You can whisper into his ear while your hand mitt comforts him, and you can stare right into those big beautiful eyes while you adjust a heat pack around his neck. Be slow and deliberate in your movements, and he will be less likely to startle.

As you groom your senior, don't neglect his teeth. Continue a twice-weekly cleaning with a finger brush or special canine dental toothbrush, but be sure to use doggy toothpaste. Human-grade toothpaste can be toxic to dogs. Pay special attention to his ears and his eyes; discharge from his eyes or ears, or a yeasty or moldy smell from his ears, warrant a trip to the vet. If your dog develops a body odor, this could indicate an underlying treatable medical condition.

SENIOR HEALTH CARE

Senior Labrador Retrievers should begin to have a twice yearly veterinary checkups starting at about age eight. Veterinarians can intervene early as old-age illnesses creep up on a dog. Sometimes, an owner might not even notice specific symptoms, or she might dismiss a sign as just part of the aging process. Geriatric dogs need more extensive checkups, and additional blood tests and physical exams can detect treatable illnesses. Some vets might suggest chest X-rays, urinalysis, and blood tests to check endocrine gland function, such as a thyroid panel.

Your veterinarian might ask about your pet's changing habits: Does he take longer to get up, or does he seem reluctant to sit? Does he drink more water than he used to? Is he sleeping more? Talk with your vet if your dog's coat and skin have changed, if his gait seems stilted or if he's lame, or if his overall posture seems different. Tell her about any body odors, especially bad breath, and if your dog seems to have trouble eating or swallowing. Changes in weight, either a gain or loss, might be significant. A health checkup will also include simple tests to check hearing and vision.

Urgent or emergency signs that your dog might display, which warrant an immediate veterinary appointment, include increased

Training Tidbit

Your old Labrador Retriever can learn new tricks, but his abilities and motivations might have changed over the years. If he has trouble sitting because of hip dysplasia, or if he can't stand for long periods of time, you can teach him other useful positions, like lying down for his weekly grooming session. Lure him into a down with a soft, smelly treat that he won't have trouble chewing. Let him choose which side he lies on, and never force him into a position. At this age and stage of his life, your dog should be allowed to decide how he's most comfortable for coat and teeth brushing, nail clipping, and ear cleaning.

water consumption, the inability to urinate, excess urination or household accidents, and disorientation or lack of focus. These symptoms could indicate a serious canine geriatric illness. Most senior Labrador Retrievers, however, just slow down and suffer the typical conditions that result from old age.

Senior Illnesses

The illnesses that strike senior dogs are similar to the disorders that senior humans face. These include joint, vision, heart, and endocrine gland dysfunctions. With proper management, however, these illnesses don't have to be debilitating. Your veterinarian is your best source of information for treatment, and she can help you keep your senior Labrador Retriever comfortable as he ages.

Arthritis

Arthritis is the most common illness seen in senior Labrador Retrievers. This disease, which affects the joints, may be unnoticeable to the owner, but it also could result in debilitating pain and loss of motion that affects your dog's quality of life.

Signs: Typical signs of arthritis include stiffness, limping, lameness, reluctance to climb steps, or reluctance to jump, even up onto a comfortable sofa. Arthritis can be caused by prior ruptured anterior cruciate ligaments and the resulting surgery; fractures; heritable or genetic diseases, such as elbow or hip dysplasia; cancer; degenerative joint disease, otherwise known as osteoarthritis; inflammatory joint diseases that result from Lyme disease; hormonal changes from thyroid disorders; and disc disease, such as a bulging or ruptured disc in the neck or back. Obesity is a major cause of arthritis in older dogs, because the extra weight causes pressure and grinding of bone-on-bone in the dog's aging joints.

Treatment: With Labrador Retrievers, the type of arthritis seen and treated most often results from inherited dysplasias. While no treatment will prevent the development of dysplasia, medical and surgical modalities can keep a dog with hip or elbow dysplasia active as he ages. Eventually, however, the arthritis that develops in a loose hip or elbow will force the dog to slow down. Medical management will be multifaceted.

Your dog's overall quality of life should be the most important factor you consider as he advances in age.

Glucosamine and chondroitin combination supplements have shown some effectiveness on canine arthritis. These supplements help prevent the formation of bone-on-bone contact, and research indicates they also help build new cartilage within a damaged joint. Other supplements, taken along with prescription medications, can help as well. Some medications prevent cartilage breakdown; others are for pain relief. Check with your vet before giving your dog over-the-counter medications: Buffered aspirin is an inexpensive anti-inflammatory for dogs, but given long-term it can cause gastrointestinal upsets and ulcers. Nonsteroidal anti-inflammatory medicines are strong and effective, but again, they all have side effects. Talk to your veterinarian to decide how to manage your Lab's arthritis so that he can live in less pain.

If your arthritic Lab is overweight, as are almost half of all pet dogs in the United States, those extra pounds must be shed. Weight management is a critical component in arthritis treatment. Even if surgery is indicated, or if the veterinary treatment includes supplements and pain medications, other treatments are less likely to be successful if your dog is overweight. Your vet may recommend a prescription weight management food, or she may refer both you and your dog to a canine rehabilitation specialist for nutrition advice. However approached, though, you control what your dog eats, so if your arthritic dog is overweight, do not give in to his soulful brown eyes when he begs at the dinner table or sits and stares longingly at the treat jar.

Exercise also will help an arthritic dog, but not joint-jarring workouts like agility practice. Slow leash walks, swimming, and underwater treadmill sessions will help maintain and even increase range of motion and will build

Multi-Dog Tip

Some dogs who begin to suffer canine cognitive disorder will welcome visits or play dates with younger dogs; interactions with other dogs help keep an elderly dog's mind and body active longer. Make sure that the younger, active canine visitor isn't aggressive or assertive toward your older dog. Encourage short games of fetch. Better still, take the dogs on a leash walk, and let the older dog teach the younger dog how to take life a step at a time and savor the smells along the path.

muscle mass around arthritic joints. Exercise should be individualized for your Lab and his specific needs, and it should be done on a daily basis. He may feel less pain before and after an exercise session if his muscles are warmed up first; use either a heat pack, or begin each daily walk with a 10-minute slow roam, then increase distance and speed. Always end a walk with a cool-down, too. Use the last 5 or 10 minutes of a walk to allow your dog time to amble and sniff.

Other Considerations: Some arthritic Labs like their same old sleeping arrangement, whether on the sofa or in their comfortable canine bed on the floor. However, many dogs do better with an orthopedic foam bed, which helps distribute their weight evenly and supports all their joints. Your dog's bed should be away from drafty doors or windows; instead, put it in a warm place in the house.

Other practical solutions for the arthritic dog include using a ramp. Placed near steps in and around your home, a ramp can help your dog get in and out of the house more easily. A ramp for the car will keep him from having to jump in and out to go on rides or to see his veterinarian. Some dogs don't like them, but coaxing with a soft treat will help even the reluctant canine to take a ramp rather than the steps.

Canine Cognitive Dysfunction (CCD)

Hopefully, your Lab will never develop arthritis or feel the associated pain and loss of mobility. He might, however, begin to show signs of other disorders as he ages, such as canine cognitive dysfunction (CCD).

Signs: If your dog begins to have housetraining accidents, stares off at imaginary objects, develops separation anxiety when you leave him alone, appears to become confused or doesn't recognize people or items in the home, wanders aimlessly, licks a paw in an obsessive manner, or pants or drools more than usual, he could be developing CCD.

This is typically a diagnosis of exclusion. Your veterinarian will rule out other reasons for your dog's distress, like vision and hearing loss, urinary tract infection, and pain from arthritis or other injuries. But there's no doubt that as dogs age, they, like many humans, may begin to suffer some form of dementia.

A recent study at a university veterinary school concluded that 32 percent of dogs over the age of 10 were afflicted with symptoms of CCD; 100 percent of dogs 16 years and older showed symptoms of CCD.

Treatment: Although most very old dogs will show some symptoms, the behavioral changes of CCD are not normal, and some can be managed medically. A prescription medicine that increases the amount of dopamine in the dog's brain and also helps prolong this neurotransmitter's activity has shown some effectiveness in treating cognitive

dysfunction. Dietary changes and supplements, including an increase in certain antioxidants, also help improve memory or orientation to surroundings.

If you enrich your aged dog's environment with new toys, teach him simple games like following your hand signals, and put your hands on him more often to groom or touch him, he will be better able to cope with the changes of old age.

Canine Congestive Heart Failure (CHF)

As my Sam aged, our vet was concerned that he was showing signs of heart failure. During one geriatric exam, he thought he heard the muffled flub of a heart murmur, and ordered more tests. The electrocardiogram seemed normal, but a radiograph showed a mildly dilated, or enlarged, heart. "Of course," I said, "Sam has a big heart." Sam was a big-all-over Labrador Retriever, and I had no doubt that his heart was larger than all the rest of ours combined.

Canine congestive heart failure (CHF) isn't uncommon in large dogs like Labrador Retrievers. The disease occurs when the heart is no longer able to pump blood to the lungs and throughout the body at the required pressure. Eventually, fluids congest the tissues surrounding the heart. Dilated cardiomyopathy, a progressive enlargement of one of the heart chambers, is more likely to happen in large and giant breeds. Labrador Retrievers also have an increased risk of developing tricuspid valve disorders, and some veterinary research facilities are searching for the gene or genes responsible for this disease.

Signs: Regardless of the type of CHF, common signs include sleepiness, cough, decreased appetite, exercise intolerance, and accumulation of fluid in the abdomen.

Certain behavioral changes in seniors may be signs of a medical disorder, so have your dog examined by your vet if you notice anything unusual.

A veterinarian might diagnose CHF using an electrocardiogram, echocardiogram, radiographs, and blood chemistry tests, in addition to a hands-on examination and careful evaluation of the heart's sounds.

Treatment: Medications can manage some of the symptoms of CHF. Some increase the dog's urine output; others dilate the dog's blood vessels so the heart doesn't have to work as hard. Cough medicine might be indicated. Most dogs with CHF should go on a sodium-restricted diet. The prognosis depends on the cause and type of CHF, and while symptoms can only be managed, many elderly dogs live another year or more with cautious veterinary and home care.

Cataracts

Happily, Sam did not have CHF. His heart was large, but it wasn't enlarged, not more than usual for my big black Lab. His eyes began to take on a bluish-gray tint, though, which led us to be concerned about cataract formation. He didn't have vision loss, as confirmed by our veterinarian. He had developed a condition called nuclear sclerosis, which happens to most elderly dogs. This is a normal change to a dog's eyes, and treatment isn't necessary. For other dogs, however, cataract formation is an inevitable problem of aging.

Treatment: Canine cataracts are a breakdown of the lens fibers in the dog's eye(s), which allows extra water to move into the lens. The resulting loss of transparency leads to vision loss. Quite often, the dog will have a milky white color in the lens of the eye. Some cataracts result from metabolic disorders, trauma to the eye, infection, toxicity, or congenital diseases. These forms of cataracts are different from late-onset disease, but the treatment for all cataracts is surgical removal.

If your elderly Lab is not a good candidate for cataract surgery, he can still maintain a good quality of life, even if the disease progresses to old-age blindness. Continue to play with him, but change out his former toys to special adaptive balls that beep or whistle, so that he can still fetch. Don't move the household furniture around so that he won't bump into chairs or tables; instead, keep his environment as stable as possible. Your touch will comfort him if he seems confused by his surroundings. His other senses likely will still work fine, so use those to your advantage if your dog becomes blind. Make his food smell more delicious by heating it slightly or adding water to make a gravy, and encourage him to scent out his bowl location. If he is asleep, don't wake him unnecessarily; if you do need him to move from his snoozing spot, clap loudly or stomp lightly on the floor to make him aware of your presence.

Cushing's Disease

Your elderly Labrador Retriever may begin to suffer from metabolic diseases, especially Cushing's disease. This condition develops from chronically elevated steroids that are naturally produced in concert by the dog's pituitary and adrenal glands. The disease can be a result of a tumor on either the pituitary gland, located at the base of the dog's brain, or because of a tumor formation on the adrenal, a tiny gland that sits atop each kidney. Regardless of the cause, the symptoms are similar.

Signs: Dogs with Cushing's begin to drink much more water, and then naturally have to potty more frequently. A dog who has been housetrained for much of his life might have accidents because his bladder fills more quickly. His appetite might increase also. If your dog starts to beg continuously, or if he steals food from other dogs in the house, or raids the garbage, these behavioral changes may be symptomatic of Cushing's.

Your dog may begin to look like a Labrador Retriever-sized pig if he has Cushing's. Fat begins to shift around in the body to the abdomen, and along with the shift, the muscles begin to waste and weaken around the abdominal area. He might begin to shed hair more rapidly than normal, and his skin may begin to appear thinner. While it's sometimes hard to know if this sudden hair loss is a symptom of disease or a typical Labrador shed, hair loss is the main reason dog owners take their pets for a veterinary exam.

Treatment: Depending upon the type of tumor causing your dog's Cushing's disease, he may be treated medically or surgically. Most Cushing's-related tumors, sadly, are inoperable

Senior Dental Health

Despite your best efforts to keep your canine's canines in top condition, his teeth could more easily chip or crack as he ages, and dental disease might be evident. If your Lab develops bad breath, make sure a veterinarian takes a look at his teeth and gums. Dental abscesses or plaque may not only cause infections and organ damage in a senior dog, but may prevent him from comfortably eating his crunchy kibble.

because they are caused by pituitary tumors and resulting abnormalities. The location of the pituitary gland doesn't lend itself to surgical intervention. There are standard medication protocols to treat the disease, however, and some are quite effective at managing the symptoms and disease course. The various drugs do have side effects, however, and some dogs relapse despite aggressive medication maintenance.

Thyroid Disease

Thyroid disease is another common metabolic disease in senior dogs.

Signs: Because some of the symptoms of thyroid disease are similar to those seen in dogs with Cushing's, such as hair loss and skin problems, your veterinarian should be consulted. Hypothyroidism, which occurs as thyroid hormones are diminished, can cause weight gain, lethargy, dry hair or excessive shedding, anemia, and in some dogs, a slowed heart rate and snarkiness or even aggression.

Treatment: Treatment for canine hypothyroidism is relatively inexpensive and consists of daily thyroid hormone supplementation. Sometimes the dosage must be adjusted before the proper amount can be determined. Once a dog begins synthetic thyroid supplementation, he will need to remain on the drug for the rest of his life, but the treatment is highly successful, and most symptoms resolve fairly quickly.

TRAINING YOUR SENIOR

Despite your elderly Labrador Retriever's infirmities, and even because of them, you can and should teach him to learn new tricks. This type of activity can help your dog maintain mobility and in some cases can even prevent loss of muscle mass. Keeping your dog's mind active and alert will help him have a better quality of life, and all you'll need is an abundance of patience, some soft and tasty treats, and a positive attitude toward training.

Activities for Fun and Fitness

With canine old age comes the usual changes in habits and abilities. Training, whether for fun or to make certain activities easier for your senior, can help keep both his mind and body healthy.

Learning New Tricks

Who says old dogs can't learn new tricks? Here's an easy one to start with. If your dog needs to go potty more often, teach him to ring a bell that hangs from a doorknob to let you know about his need to go outside.

At first, use your marker word ("yes") and give your Lab several treats for just looking at the bell. If he noses the bell, give him a jackpot of treats; choose treats that are soft and easy for him to chew, like cut-up turkey hotdog bites. The next time he noses the bell, open the door. Thereafter, every time he noses the bell and you open the door, give him a treat. He will begin to associate the bell sound with an open door. Next, work on encouraging your dog to go outside. Continue to chain one behavior with the next. When your dog noses the bell, open the door, then begin to add the word "potty" and help him go outside if he needs a hand. Tell your dog what a brilliant genius he is when he finally understands the relationship between the bell and his potty duties; at that time, you should begin to fade the use of treats and let your praise and love become his rewards for ringing the bell.

If your dog begins to lose some auditory skills, and you haven't already taught him hand signals, this is a perfect lesson to train now. Ask him to respond to the obedience commands he already understands, and begin to pair them with a hand or finger signal. For example, hold your arm up and palm forward as you say, "Down." For each attempt, praise and treat him. For the sit signal, hold your right arm outstretched to your side; for the come or recall, bring your outstretched arm toward your body. Every time your dog reacts to a signal, encourage him and reward him for the effort.

Outdoor Fun

Elderly Labrador Retrievers should not continue joint-jarring sports like agility or obedience, but other fun activities can be learned at this age. Tracking is an excellent canine sport for an older dog, and many senior Labs excel at following a track. The dog uses his scenting abilities, and follows a track that has been set and aged by the tracklayer. The reward at the end of the track, other than a nice day out with his owner or handler, is the "find," usually a leather article like an old wallet. The only equipment necessary to begin tracking is a harness and a long line, made of either leather or cotton web.

Teach your dog the sport with short training sessions at first. Scatter bits of hot dog in a circle, and then add a second circle of treats a few yards (meters) away. As you encourage him to search for and find this succession of treats, you can begin to add distance and place different articles on the track. Let your dog use his natural scenting abilities to find each treat or item you leave. Once your senior begins to follow turns on the track you've laid and can find the treats and articles, you're ready for a certification test. Seek out other canine trackers in your area, and enlist their help as you teach your Lab to track. Most obedience training clubs have someone in their ranks who will help you.

Whatever activity you are engaged in, whether it is obedience training or dog sports, never use harsh methods to correct your senior Lab; instead, use praise and positive rewards like soft treats, soothing words, and a gentle pat on his head. Your Labrador Retriever has loved you well all the days of his long life; he deserves at least that from the person to whom he has devoted his lifetime in service and companionship.

Keeping your senior Lab's mind alert and his body active will help him have a better quality of life.

CHAPTER 14

END-OF-LIFE ISSUES

Woodstock: Car accident. Luke: Spinal disc disease and paralysis. Lucy: Bloat. Schroeder, my foster puppy: Parvo and distemper. Libby the Lab: Degenerative joint disease.

These are the dogs who my family was honored to raise, play with, care for, and be tended by over dozens of years. They are also the animals that needed help when end-of-life questions arose. Just as each pet was remarkable regardless of his or her age, so, too, were their deaths special.

Decisions about end-of-life care for a Labrador Retriever are made around dinner tables and in hushed bedrooms daily. This breed—these big, goofy, lovable, and loving dogs—is the most popular in the world. Each time one of our chocolates or our yellows or our blacks face crippling diagnoses, I imagine the world stops turning for that dog's family. A collective sigh might be issued by all of us who love this breed, and the symbolic ocean of tears would raise sea levels.

Perhaps the decisions we make for our dog, whether prolonged treatment for a disease, canine hospice care, or euthanasia, wouldn't be so painful if the relationship hadn't been

as deep over so many years. As much as we enjoy their companionship during the healthy, strong, vital years, don't our Labs deserve our strength and compassion during their tender, elder age?

WHEN IS IT TIME?

Our Sam. He seemed comfortable; the powerful canine antianxiety medication he was taking kept him from pacing, choking, and gulping mouthfuls of air. I wanted a cure for the canine laryngeal paralysis that didn't allow Sam to completely close his windpipe so that when he drank water, it dribbled down his larynx and caused him to choke. I wanted another day, another month with my big guy, another moment when he would lay his block head next to mine and

Want to Know More?

If and when you're ready to add a new dog to your family, see Chapter 2: Finding and Prepping for Your Labrador Retriever Puppy, or Chapter 5: Finding Your Adult Labrador Retriever, for some pointers.

his pant would seem to whisper, "You can do this," if I was immobilized by my own injury or illness.

What Labrador Retriever owner has not experienced moments like these? Who among us has not felt strength from our dog, been comforted by him, laughed at his antics or hollered at his pesky habits, and then been thankful that his life and yours seemed entwined?

However the decision is made, whether because of catastrophic injury or debilitating illness that would require protracted treatment with no guarantee of success, or perhaps because you know your dog is asking for relief from his suffering, the decision to euthanize is never easy.

Hospice Care

Hospice care for pets, as it is for human patients, provides palliative care and pain relief for the animal that suffers from a terminal illness for which a cure is not possible. Pain medications, dietary changes, and comforting human interaction all combine to make your pet's final days more pleasant for him in his home and surrounded by his family. Pet hospice is a choice, a philosophy that death is a dignified, sacred part of life. The goal of hospice is a peaceful end-of-life experience.

Making the decision that your beloved dog is ready to go is the most difficult and painful part of responsible pet ownership, but perhaps the most important.

By the Numbers

The average life span for Labrador Retrievers is 10 to12 years, although some can live to 13 or 14.

Hospice care for your Lab may be an option if you have a trusted veterinarian who can advise you on pain management, alternative treatments, and teach you how to administer fluids and oxygen if your dog requires those. However, it may be necessary for your vet to be available 24 hours a day in case your dog's pain cannot be controlled or if he begins to seize. Also, someone will need to be with your dog every hour, willing and able to provide constant care. Hospice care is an active commitment to your dog, and there is never a guarantee that he won't require euthanasia despite the caregiver's skill and devotion. Hospice providers and veterinarians will not prolong the suffering of any pet in pain or with a poor quality of life.

Quality-of-Life Issues

What determines your dog's quality of life? Perhaps he has given you some clues: Is he irritable and restless? Does he avoid participating in his favorite activities, ignore his food, or drink water excessively? Do other animals in the house show aggression toward him because he is now the weakest pack member? Does he look for places to hide or to sleep? Is he in constant pain, and does he gasp for breath? Is he incontinent and unhappy with his inability to control his bladder or bowels? Has that thick yellow, black, or chocolate otter tail stopped swishing or banging or sweeping back and forth?

We have taken on the role of pet owner, and loved our Lab for many years. We have made decisions on his behalf for his entire life—his food and nutritional needs, his training and socialization, his activities and sports, his veterinary visits and wellness protocols, his grooming needs—and he deserves our best decisions prior to and during his death. This is the most difficult and painful part of responsible pet ownership, but perhaps the most important.

MAKING THE DECISION

Sam's muzzle had whitened. His flanks rose up and down in a smooth rhythm, thanks to the medications. He seemed in that blissful sleep that old dogs occupy, a complete, total, "I am not getting up but if you need me I'll keep an eye open" type of slumber. But his larynx was paralyzed. Sam would choke to death without constant monitoring. I leaned over and kissed the top of his flat head just between his ears,

cried wet specks onto his shiny, jet-sleek coat, told him that I loved him, and assured him that we'd get through this last time together.

Euthanasia is a painful decision, but a peaceful process. The veterinarian places a needle into a vein in either a front or rear leg, and then injects a drug that relaxes your pet. The next medication she injects, a rapid-acting concentration of anesthetic drug, works within a few seconds. The animal's heart stops beating, his muscles may relax or contract, and he might pass urine or stool. Involuntary muscle contractions may cause the animal to jerk, or move a leg, or gasp, but these

Remembering Your Pet

Although the grieving process is very personal, many people find it is eased by channeling their sorrow in positive ways. Consider framing your Lab's CGC certificate or puppy kindergarten diploma. Make a scrapbook that includes photographs, ribbons, and condolence cards from friends and family. Save his collars and leashes for your next Lab because you know that a new puppy or adopted dog will benefit from all the equipment, experience, and memories that you gathered during your cherished pet's lifetime. You may also choose to honor his memory by donating time or money to organizations that help animals, such as a local animal shelter or rescue group, or an organization that backs disaster relief for animals, or perhaps you may choose to work as a volunteer for an organization that provides pet grief counseling.

contractions are post-death. The veterinarian gently closes the dog's eyes.

Many people cannot handle the euthanasia process and therefore are not in the room at the time of their dog's death. Others hold their dog until long after he has passed. There are no wrong feelings as you decide whether or not to be present. Your dog will not be alone if you cannot sit with him through this final procedure because the vet and techs will comfort him with soothing words and pats. The veterinarian will give you an opportunity, either prior to or after euthanasia, to say good bye to your dog.

COPING WITH THE LOSS OF YOUR PET

Whether or not you accompany your dog and are present at the time of euthanasia, the grief you feel might be overwhelming at times. It's natural to feel sorrow, because the bond with your dog had been so strong. The stages of grief might be felt all at once, or randomly and in no particular order. First, a dog owner is likely to react with denial that her dog has died or that death is imminent. Denial might begin when she learns the seriousness of the dog's illness.

Anger might be directed at your veterinarian, or at friends and family. People coping with death, or those who are uncomfortable talking about the death of a pet, sometimes say or do hurtful things. A pet owner facing the loss of her beloved animal most likely will feel guilty that she could not afford further treatment, or that she didn't recognize her dog's illness sooner, or perhaps she feels like she failed her pet. These are normal feelings for someone grieving.

Depression often accompanies these feelings of grief, and manifests in tears, mood swings, exhaustion or sleepiness, and a lack of motivation or interest in other tasks. If depression becomes all-encompassing, a bereaved pet owner might need grief counseling. Grief can be resolved, and the loss of a beloved Labrador Retriever can be accepted. Because grieving is a personal process, it may take some pet owners longer to come to terms with these feelings. Guilt and anger, depression and denial, resolve and acceptance can wax and wane. If painful feelings resurface, they are typically less intense than originally. Dozens of books, websites, and telephone hotlines exist to help pet owners and their families as they grieve the loss of their dog. For more information, and for links to pet bereavement resources, check out these websites:

- Association for Pet Loss and Bereavement, wwwaplb.org
- American Veterinary Medical Association, www.avma.org

Multi-Dog Tip

Your remaining dogs may be depressed, sullen, unwilling to play, or even aggressive as they come to terms with the loss of their pack leader. They might obsessively visit his favorite places in the yard or decide to sleep in his crate or bed. You may want to back off intense training during this period of mourning, but continue to exercise your dogs with walks and bursts of play, which will help all of you—humans and dogs alike—work through your grief.

- American Society for the Prevention of Cruelty to Animals, www.aspca.org

In time, grief will be replaced by fond memories of your pet. You'll laugh when you remember his puppyhood, cringe when you think about all the inappropriate items he ate from the counter, wonder how you ever got him to adulthood, and take joy in his composure during his elder years.

Explaining Pet Loss to Children

Your Lab's death might be hard for the children to understand, or they may be more matter-of-fact than you anticipated. Most experts feel that very young children should not be present during euthanasia. But regardless of a child's age, he or she should have an opportunity to say goodbye to their dog. Sometimes the veterinarian will help a child understand what has happened, but parents need to be able to provide support and answer their child's questions. Some children feel a range of emotions, and others may hide their sadness. Encourage your child to talk about the pet, draw pictures, look at photographs, and share memories.

Helping Other Pets Deal With Loss

Other animals in the home may show grief in unexpected ways. During the evening prior to the death of one of our pet dogs, all the other animals in our home—cats and dogs— each jumped on the bed, licked the old dog's muzzle, then jumped away. Surviving pack members might display odd behaviors, and even show signs of depression, such as a lack of appetite or a lack of interest in favorite activities. For those animals, it's helpful to maintain the regular household schedule. Routine is important, and so are the daily walks, training sessions, and time to lie on the sofa and breathe each other's air.

MEMORIALS

The economics of a broken heart at the loss of a Labrador Retriever can help others in need. To honor a special dog, consider making a donation in his name to any of the rescue groups, shelters, and veterinary funds that daily work to improve the lives of our Labradors. Sam honored us throughout his life, so his death benefited the AKC Canine Health Foundation, which grants funds to veterinarians who research and treat a range of disorders that affect Labrador Retrievers. His death will help another Lab's life.

Other animals in the home may show grief at the loss of their pack mate, so give them extra attention and patience at this time.

50 FUN FACTS EVERY LABRADOR RETRIEVER OWNER SHOULD KNOW

1. Labs drool.

2. Labs beg for food, and as they do, they drool.

3. Labs work for food, praise, and toy rewards equally well.

4. Labs gain excess weight easily, so don't give in to the begging.

5. Labs are born weighing between 12 and 20 ounces, and top out at 70 to 80 pounds, depending on their bloodlines.

6. The average life span for Labrador Retrievers is 10 to 12 years, although some can live to 13 or 14.

7. Labs come in three colors: black, yellow, and chocolate.

8. Yellow Labs can be as pale as cream or as dark as fox red in coloration.

9. Some early breeders culled their yellow and chocolate puppies, erroneously thinking the dogs weren't as adept as black Labs in the field.

10. Labs were bred to retrieve downed birds for both sportsmen and ornithologists.

11. The breed originated in Newfoundland, not the neighboring island of Labrador.

12. The breed was refined by sportsmen/breeders in Scotland and England.

13. By 1908, more Labs were entered in field trials in the United Kingdom than any other breed.

14. The first Labrador Retriever Club originated in Great Britain in 1916, formed by sportsmen to test the Lab's retrieving abilities.

15. The first United States Labrador Retriever Club was formed in 1931 in New York.

16. The American Kennel Club registered the first Labs in 1933.

17. The Lab has been the most popular breed in England and the United States since 1991.

18. In the United States, more than 100,000 Labs are registered each year.

19. The popularity of the breed leads to shelters and rescue groups that are overwhelmed with Labs and Lab-mix dogs.

20. There should be no difference in size, temperament, or working ability between the three colors of Labs.

21. Labs have a double coat for protection and insulation.

22. Labs shed. Color-coordinated furniture and clothing are helpful, as are brooms and vacuum cleaners.

23. Depending on the bloodline, a Lab can be full-grown at 9 months; others don't mature physically until they are 2 or 3 years old.

24. Labs don't mature emotionally until well into adulthood, so they retain that puppy mentality until they are 3 to 4 years old, some even longer.

25. Their inherent retrieving ability allows Labs to pick up items as small as a pen and as large as a backpack.

26. Labrador Retrievers are trained as guide dogs for the visually impaired and as seizure detection dogs for epilepsy patients.

27. Labs are popular therapy dogs, and they work around the world in animal-assisted therapy programs.

28. Labs as young as 12 weeks can be trained to scent out gunpowder or powdered cocaine, making them excellent partners for military or law-enforcement officers.

29. More Labs are registered with kennel clubs around the world than any other breed, making them the most popular dog in the world.

30. There are no "silver" Labs; dogs with that coat color are incorrect and not representative of the standard.

31. Lab puppies chew on anything and everything.

32. A "mouthy" breed, Labs should be discouraged from chewing on hands or other human body parts.

33. Labs need tons of exercise. A tired Lab is a happy Lab.

34. Labrador Retrievers are thieves; they'll steal everything from a box of tissues to the remote control.

35. Labrador Retrievers steal their owners' hearts.

36. Labs are easy to groom: brush the coat and teeth, clip nails, clean ears, and you're done.

37. Labs have few inherited disorders compared to other breeds.

38. Hip dysplasia is the most common joint disease among Labs.

39. A hard worker in the field and ring, Labs do suffer from knee ligament tears and ruptures because of their activities.

40. Pet Labs should be spayed or neutered between 6 months and 2 years of age.

41. More Labs earn American Kennel Club companion and performance titles than any other breed in competition.

42. The 2008 and 2009 American Kennel Club National Obedience Champion was a black Lab named Tyler.

43. More than 100 rescue groups in the United States devote time and resources to the welfare of homeless and abandoned Labrador Retrievers.

44. Labs adore their human companions, but if ignored they will bark or dig for attention.

45. Labs learn early, and can begin housetraining as soon as they arrive in their forever home.

46. Despite their cuddly appearance, Labs are strong leash pullers unless trained properly.

47. A gun dog, the Lab is not likely to be afraid of loud noises like thunderstorms or fireworks.

48. A strong swimmer, Labs excel at dock diving events and competitions.

49. Labrador Retrievers are considered "senior" dogs by age eight.

50. Most Labs 10 years and older will suffer from degenerative joint disorders, such as disc disease and elbow and hip dysplasia.

RESOURCES

ASSOCIATIONS AND ORGANIZATIONS

Breed Clubs

American Kennel Club (AKC)
5580 Centerview Drive
Raleigh, NC 27606
Telephone: (919) 233-9767
Fax: (919) 233-3627
E-mail: info@akc.org
www.akc.org

Canadian Kennel Club (CKC)
89 Skyway Avenue, Suite 100
Etobicoke, Ontario M9W 6R4
Canada
Telephone: (416) 675-5511
Fax: (416) 675-6506
E-mail: information@ckc.ca
www.ckc.ca

Chocolate Labrador
Owners Club
United Kingdom
www.chocolate-labradors.org.uk

Federation Cynologique Internationale (FCI)
Secretariat General de la FCI
Place Albert 1er, 13
B–6530 Thuin
Belqique
www.fci.be

Labrador Retriever Club
United Kingdom
www.thelabradorretrieverclub.co.uk

National Gundog Association
United Kingdom
www.gundog.org

National Labrador Retriever Club, Inc. (NLRC) (USA)
United States
www.labradorretrievers.org

National Shoot to Retrieve Association
226 North Mill Street, #2
Plainfield, IN 46168
Telephone: (317) 839-4059
E-mail: nstrfta@ameritech.net
www.nstra.org

North American Gun Dog Association (NAGDA)
13850 C.R. 31
Stratton, CO 80836
Telephone: (719) 348-5451
Fax: (719) 348-5999
E-mail: NAGDA@plains.net
www.nagdog.com

North American Hunting Retriever Association (NAHRA
P.O. Box 5159
Fredericksburg, VA 22403
Telephone: (540) 899-7620
Fax: (540) 899-7691
E-mail: nahra@nahra.org
www.nahra.org

North American Versatile Hunting Dog Association (NAVHDA)
Box 520
Arlington Heights, IL 60006
Telephone: (847) 253-6488
Fax: (847) 255-5987
E-mail: navoffice@aol.com
www.navhda.org

The Kennel Club
1 Clarges Street
London W1J 8AB
England
Telephone: 0870 606 6750
Fax: 0207 518 1058
www.the-kennel-club.org.uk

The Labrador Retriever Club, Inc. (USA)
United States
www.thelabradorclub.com

United Kennel Club (UKC)
100 E. Kilgore Road
Kalamazoo, MI 49002-5584
Telephone: (269) 343-9020
Fax: (269) 343-7037
E-mail: pbickell@ukcdogs.com
www.ukcdogs.com

Pet Sitters

National Association of Professional Pet Sitters
15000 Commerce Parkway, Suite C
Mt. Laurel, NJ 08054
Telephone: (856) 439-0324
Fax: (856) 439-0525
E-mail: napps@ahint.com
www.petsitters.org

Pet Sitters International
201 East King Street
King, NC 27021-9161
Telephone: (336) 983-9222
Fax: (336) 983-5266
E-mail: info@petsit.com
www.petsit.com

Rescue Organizations and Animal Welfare Groups

American Humane Association (AHA)
63 Inverness Drive East
Englewood, CO 80112
Telephone: (303) 792-9900
Fax: 792-5333
www.americanhumane.org

American Society for the Prevention of Cruelty to Animals (ASPCA)
424 E. 92nd Street
New York, NY 10128-6804
Telephone: (212) 876-7700
www.aspca.org

Royal Society for the Prevention of Cruelty to Animals (RSPCA)
RSPCA Enquiries Service
Wilberforce Way, Southwater, Horsham, West Sussex RH13 9RS
United Kingdom
Telephone: 0870 3335 999
Fax: 0870 7530 284
www.rspca.org.uk

Sports
International Agility Link (IAL)
www.agilityclick.com/~ial

North American Flyball Association
1400 West Devon Ave., #512
Chicago, IL 60660
www.flyball.org

The World Canine Freestyle Organization, Inc.
P.O. Box 350122
Brooklyn, NY 11235
Telephone: (718) 332-8336
Fax: (718) 646-2686
E-mail: WCFODOGS@aol.com
www.worldcaninefreestyle.org

Therapy
Delta Society
875 124th Ave, NE, Suite 101
Bellevue, WA 98005
Telephone: (425) 679-5500
Fax: (425) 679-5539
E-mail: info@DeltaSociety.org
www.deltasociety.org

Therapy Dogs, Inc.
P.O. Box 20227
Cheyenne, WY 82003
Telephone: (877) 843-7364
Fax: (307) 638-2079
E-mail: therapydogsinc@qwestoffice.net
www.therapydogs.com

Therapy Dogs International (TDI)
88 Bartley Road
Flanders, NJ 07836
Telephone: (973) 252-9800
Fax: (973) 252-7171
E-mail: tdi@gti.net
www.tdi-dog.org

Training

Association of Pet Dog Trainers (APDT)
150 Executive Center Drive, Box 35
Greenville, SC 29615
Telephone: (800) PET-DOGS
Fax: (864) 331-0767
E-mail: information@apdt.com
www.apdt.com

International Association of Animal Behavior Consultants (IAABC)
565 Callery Road
Cranberry Township, PA 16066
E-mail: info@iaabc.org
www.iaabc.org

National Association of Dog Obedience Instructors (NADOI)
PMB 369
729 Grapevine Hwy.
Hurst, TX 76054-2085
www.nadoi.org

Veterinary and Health Resources

Academy of Veterinary Homeopathy (AVH)
P.O. Box 9280
Wilmington, DE 19809
Telephone: (866) 652-1590
Fax: (866) 652-1590
www.theavh.org

American Academy of Veterinary Acupuncture (AAVA)
P.O. Box 1058
Glastonbury, CT 06033
Telephone: (860) 632-9911
Fax: (860) 659-8772
www.aava.org

American Animal Hospital Association (AAHA)
12575 W. Bayaud Ave.
Lakewood, CO 80228
Telephone: (303) 986-2800
Fax: (303) 986-1700
E-mail: info@aahanet.org
www.aahanet.org/index.cfm

American College of Veterinary Internal Medicine (ACVIM)
1997 Wadsworth Blvd., Suite A
Lakewood, CO 80214-5293
Telephone: (800) 245-9081
Fax: (303) 231-0880
E-mail: ACVIM@ACVIM.org
www.acvim.org

American College of Veterinary Ophthalmologists (ACVO)
P.O. Box 1311
Meridian, ID 83860
Telephone: (208) 466-7624
Fax: (208) 466-7693
E-mail: office09@acvo.com
www.acvo.com

American Holistic Veterinary Medical Association (AHVMA)
2218 Old Emmorton Road
Bel Air, MD 21015
Telephone: (410) 569-0795
Fax: (410) 569-2346
E-mail: office@ahvma.org
www.ahvma.org

American Veterinary Medical Association (AVMA)
1931 North Meacham Road, Suite 100
Schaumburg, IL 60173-4360
Telephone: (847) 925-8070
Fax: (847) 925-1329
E-mail: avmainfo@avma.org
www.avma.org

ASPCA Animal Poison Control Center
Telephone: (888) 426-4435
www.aspca.org

British Veterinary Association (BVA)
7 Mansfield Street
London W1G 9NQ
England
Telephone: 0207 636 6541
Fax: 0207 908 6349
E-mail: bvahq@bva.co.uk
www.bva.co.uk

Canine Eye Registration Foundation (CERF)
VMDB/CERF
1717 Philo Rd.
P.O. Box 3007
Urbana, IL 61803-3007
Telephone: (217) 693-4800
Fax: (217) 693-4801
E-mail: CERF@vmbd.org
www.vmdb.org

Orthopedic Foundation for Animals (OFA)
2300 NE Nifong Blvd.
Columbus, MO 65201-3856
Telephone: (573) 442-0418
Fax: (573) 875-5073
E-mail: ofa@offa.org
www.offa.org

US Food and Drug Administration Center for Veterinary Medicine (CVM)
7519 Standish Place
HFV-12
Rockville, MD 20855-0001
Telephone: (240) 276-9300 or (888) INFO-FDA
http://www.fda.gov/cvm

PUBLICATIONS

Books

Anderson, Teoti. *The Super Simple Guide to Housetraining.* Neptune City: TFH Publications, 2004.

Anne, Jonna, with Mary Straus. *The Healthy Dog Cookbook: 50 Nutritious and Delicious Recipes Your Dog Will Love.* UK: Ivy Press Limited, 2008.

Dainty, Suellen. *50 Games to Play With Your Dog.* UK: Ivy Press Limited, 2007.

Morgan, Diane. *Good Dogkeeping.* Neptune City: TFH Publications, 2005.

Morgan, Diane. *The Labrador Retriever.* Neptune City: TFH Publications, 2005.

Moustaki, Nikki. *Labrador Retrievers.* Neptune City: TFH Publications, 2005.

Magazines

AKC Family Dog
American Kennel Club
260 Madison Avenue
New York, NY 10016
Telephone: (800) 490-5675
E-mail: familydog@akc.org
www.akc.org/pubs/familydog

AKC Gazette
American Kennel Club
260 Madison Avenue
New York, NY 10016
Telephone: (800) 533-7323
E-mail: gazette@akc.org
www.akc.org/pubs/gazette

Dog & Kennel
Pet Publishing, Inc.
7-L Dundas Circle
Greensboro, NC 27407
Telephone: (336) 292-4272
Fax: (336) 292-4272
E-mail: info@petpublishing.com
www.dogandkennel.com

Dogs Monthly
Ascot House
High Street, Ascot,
Berkshire SL5 7JG
United Kingdom
Telephone: 0870 730 8433
Fax: 0870 730 8431
E-mail: admin@rtc-associates.
freeserve.co.uk
www.corsini.co.uk/dogsmonthly

Websites

All Labs
www.alllabs.com

LabradorNet
www.labradornet.com/labradors.
html

Nylabone
www.nylabone.com

TFH Publications, Inc.
www.tfh.com

INDEX

PHOTO CREDITS

Isabelle Francais, 14, 24, 42, 43, 44, 47, 49, 59, 64, 67, 74, 77, 81, 83, 92, 96, 105, 107, 112, 113, 116, 138, 140, 145, 150, 152, 155, 167, 178, 195, 197

Linda Rehkopf, 179

Shutterstock:
RCPPHOTO, 3; cen, 6, 17, 134, 148; Tina Rencelj, 8, 88 (top), 162, 190, 204; Howard Jones, 9; Kirk Geister, 10; Waldemar Dabrowski, 11; Uschi Hering, 12; Linn Currie, 13; Justin Paget, 16, 137, 153, 168; Milos Jokic, 18 (top); Kirk Geisler, 18 (bottom); Kato Inowe, 19, 63; pixshots, 20, 40, 69; Waldemar Dabrowski, 22, 32, 76, 78; Tomislav Stajduhar, 25, 90; artcphotos, 28, 35; sonya etchison, 30; Pawel Cebo, 31; Dennis Sabo, 33; Utekhina Anna, 34; tonobalaguerf, 36; ivan pavlisko, 38; Bonita R. Chesier, 39; Jan de Wild, 51; Dan Snyder, 52; April Turner, 54;Geir Olav Lyngfjell, 55; Denise Campione, 56; IKO, 57; Viorel Sima, 58; Maksim Nikalayenka, 60; Waldemar Dabrowski, 61; KR Crowley, 65; Joy Brown, 71; Stephen Inglis, 72; Sharon Moris, 80; Vukoslavovic, 85; Art_man, 87; Richard A. McGuirk, 88 (bottom); Shutterstock, 89, 109, 118,154, 158; L Higgins, 94; Alexander Ishchenko; Kevin, Chen, 100; Marek Pawluczuk, 101; Cameron Cross, 103, 185; Wendy Kaveney Photography, 110; Vlad Ageshin, 114; Kelly Richardson, 119; Kinetic Imagery, 121; Linda Z Ryan, 123; JaBa, 124; Egorius, 127; HANA, 128, 131; Brooke Whatnall, 133; Elena Ray, 141; Cindy Lee, 143; KR Crowley, 147; Martin Valigursky, 161; Hefr, 165; Vinicius Tupinamba, 170; Eric Lam, 171; George Lee, 172, 175; Gorilla, 180; Bull's-Eye Arts, 184 (top), 203; Hannamariah, 184 (bottom), 200; ansem, 186; Dee Hunter, 189, 192; RCPPHOTO, 206; Lina Z Ryan, 209

Cover: Petspicture (Shutterstock)

VETERINARY ADVISOR

Wayne Hunthausen, DVM, consulting veterinary editor and pet behavior consultant, is the director of Animal Behavior Consultations in the Kansas City area and currently serves on the Practitioner Board for *Veterinary Medicine* and the Behavior Advisory Board for *Veterinary Forum*.

BREEDER ADVISOR

Marian Gardner and husband **Lawrence Gardner**, of Dewberries Labradors in Robertsdale, AL, have been involved with Labrador Retrievers for 12 years, both in AKC conformation and pet therapy. When breeding their Labrador Retrievers their emphasis has always been on health, personality, and the Labrador Retriever AKC standard. Most recently they have teamed up with an area field trainer and are offering "started dogs" from their breeding stock.

Marian's background in clinical psychology has proven valuable in the assessment of puppies and potential families to ensure a proper "fit" between puppy personality and family dynamics. With this medically related training, Marian focus on the health of the Labradors as well as their personality, believing all dogs should have a job, whether in the conformation/agility/rally rings, the field hunting or competing, therapy/service settings or curled up next to your feet offering companionship and devotion. With a thorough placement contract, Marian and Lawrence maintain that all puppies they bring into this world are their lifetime responsibility, and they will take back, with no questions asked, any placements that do not work either for the owner or the Labrador. This includes any situations found to be in any way detrimental to the health and well-being of the Lab.

Marian plans to add this book to her "must read" list for new Lab owners.

DEDICATION

To Chris and Leigh Anne, with thanks and love, for the gift of my first Labrador Retriever, Sam. To Graylin's Carbon Copy Editor CD RN, a.k.a. Sam.

ACKNOWLEDGEMENTS

The freedom to own, train, handle, and travel with my Labrador Retrievers is not free or easy, and I thank my husband, Chris Rehkopf, Jr., and my daughter, Leigh Anne Rehkopf, for their help and support as I threw myself into this hobby called "the fancy." Their unselfish willingness to feed, walk, and play with the dogs gave me the time to work on this book. They both helped me with technical issues (re computer challenges). For all the times I paced the house and yard and stared into space, and they recognized it was the mind of a writer at work, I can only say, "Thank you both." I could not have written this book without their complicity and understanding.

Numerous canine writing colleagues and friends offered encouragement and suggestions along the way; my mentor in this field, Debra M. Eldredge, DVM, was always available as I researched and wrote the text. Marion Gardner of Dewberries Labradors graciously reviewed the manuscript and gave valuable comments; dozens of Labrador retriever owners around the country generously shared their experiences with their dogs.

My editor at TFH Publications, Heather Russell-Revesz, made this project painless; the copy editor, Mary Grangeia, always covered my back.

Thanks to my good friend and my dogs' long-time veterinarian E. Scott Friedrichs, DVM, and the vets and staff at Sprayberry Animal Hospital in Marietta, Georgia, for answers to endless canine health questions over the years, and for expert and compassionate care of all my family's animals. To my training buddies at Ironclad K9 Academy in Woodstock, Georgia, and instructors Pam Long and Vail Hanna, thank you for the gifts of your knowledge and patience with this newbie and her dog so many years ago.

Special thanks to my Labrador Retrievers, who remind me daily that it's fun to play in the dirt.

ABOUT THE AUTHOR

Labrador Retriever owner/trainer/handler **Linda Rehkopf** is a journalist specializing in canine care, health, and training topics. Her work has appeared in many local and national magazines, newspapers, and websites and has been nominated for a number of awards from the canine writing community. She writes a regular column for novice dog trainers for Front and Finish magazine and serves on that publication's Editorial Advisory Committee. Linda competes with her Labrador Retrievers in obedience and rally competitions, trains in agility and tracking, and with her dogs she is an active member of Happy Tails Animal-Assisted Therapy Group in the metro Atlanta area. She lives with her husband, Chris, and their Labs in Marietta, Georgia.

Author photo: Leigh Anne Rehkopf

NATURAL with added VITAMINS
Nutri Dent ®MD
Promotes Optimal Dental Health!

Visit nylabone.com
Join Club NYLA
for coupons &
product
information

360° Design
Cleaning Action!™

Dog's Love'em!™

AVAILABLE IN MULTIPLE SIZES AND FLAVORS.

Nylabone®

Trusted For Over 40 Years

MADE IN THE USA

Our Mission with Nutri Dent® is to promote optimal dental health for dogs through a trusted, natural, delicious chew that provides effective cleaning action...GUARANTEED to make your dog go wild with anticipation and happiness!!!

Nylabone Products • P.O. Box 427, Neptune, NJ 07754-0427 • 1-800-631-2188 • Fax: 732-988-5466
www.nylabone.com • info@nylabone.com • For more information contact your sales representative or contact us at sales@tfh.com   A275